MW00800897

So, You're Thinking About Owning, Operating or Investing in a Restaurant...

So, You're Thinking About Owning, Operating or Investing in a Restaurant...

How to Get into the Restaurant Business with Eyes Wide Open

From the editors and publishers of
Restaurant Startup & Growth magazine and RestaurantOwner.com

ART INSTITUTE LIBRARY

FIRST EDITION, DECEMBER 2015
Copyright © 2015 by RS&G, LLC
P.O. Box 14236
Parkville, Missouri 64152-9811
All rights reserved. No part of this publication may be reproduced, used on the Internet, or transmitted in any form by any means, electronic, photocopied, or otherwise, without prior permission from the publisher.
Published in the United States by RS&G, LLC, d.b.a. *Restaurant Startup & Growth*® magazine

Disclaimer of Liability

The information presented in this book has been compiled from sources and documents believed to be reliable and represent the best judgment of RS&G, LLC. The accuracy of the information presented, however, is not guaranteed, nor is any responsibility assumed or implied by RS&G, LLC for any damage or loss resulting from inaccuracies or omissions.

Laws may vary greatly by city, county or state. This book is not intended to provide legal advice or establish standards of reasonable behavior. Operators are urged to use the advice and guidance of legal counsel.

ISBN-13: 978-0692549551
ISBN-10: 0692549552
Printed in the United States
Book cover and design by Doreen Hann

ART INSTITUTE LIBRARY

Table of Contents

A restaurant is not a **thing**. It is not a **structure**. It is not a group of **people**. It is not a **recipe, concept** or a **brand**. It is a **process** that brings product and people together to create a **pleasant experience** for your guests, and profits for the owners.

~ Restaurant Startup &
Growth magazine/
RestaurantOwner.com

About the Editors

Joe Erickson

Joe is vice-president of RestaurantOwner.com and a frequent contributor to *Restaurant Startup & Growth* magazine. In his 30 years in the restaurant industry, he has created and developed several successful foodservice concepts as a manager, owner, and consultant. In the early 1980s, he was an early adapter to using computer technology in the restaurant business, and he collaborated with programmers to create software for restaurant accounting and inventory control. Joe is an expert in restaurant business processes and systems, and developed RestaurantOwner.com's "How to Prepare a Winning Restaurant Business Plan", which has helped hundreds of new restaurateurs plan their startup.

Jim Laube

Jim is founder and publisher of RestaurantOwner.com, an extensive management educational resource for independent restaurant operators. Trained as a certified public accountant, he has a diverse 30-year career in the restaurant business as a server, bartender, manager, controller and chief financial officer for a regional restaurant chain. Jim has advised hundreds of independent restaurants in the U.S. and Canada on profit enhancement, financial controls and business management. He has conducted over 700 presentations and training programs to thousands of restaurant and foodservice professionals in the U.S., Canada and Europe.

Barry K. Shuster, MBA, JD, MSB, CHE

Barry is founding editor of *Restaurant Startup & Growth* magazine, and interim chair of the Department of Hospitality and Tourism Administration at North Carolina Central University School of Business, where he is also professor of hospitality law and ethics, and hospitality financial management. He is an American Hotel & Lodging Association certified hospitality educator, with previous faculty appointments at East Carolina University School of Hospitality Leadership and Fayetteville State University School of Business and Economics MBA-Healthcare Administration program. Barry served on the board of directors of the International Foodservice Editorial Council from 2011-2014.

Chris Tripoli

Chris has 40 years of service in the hospitality industry as a designer, developer, owner and operator. He has developed award winning restaurants and provided assistance to many airport, park, theatres and retail center developers. Chris consults on operational, development, and growth related matters with a variety of chains (franchisors and franchisees) and independent operators. Chris teaches courses in starting and growing restaurants at University of Houston's Small Business Development Center. He also provides one-day seminars on restaurant operations and growth strategies throughout the United States and Mexico.

So, You're Thinking About Owning, Operating or Investing in a Restaurant...

9

Gary S. Worden

Gary S. Worden is founder, publisher and managing partner of *Restaurant Startup & Growth* magazine. A publishing executive for more than three decades, Gary founded *Restaurant Startup & Growth* after diversifying his company, Specialized Publications Company, Inc., into the restaurant business in 2001. He and his wife, Cristina, are co-owners of a successful upscale concept in Kansas City, MO.

Foreword

So You Want to Open a Restaurant?

The aim of this book is to help you gain a clear sense of the process and thought it takes as you consider your option of going into the restaurant business.

The more that you read, the more things you will know. The more that you learn, the more places you'll go.

— Dr. Seuss

According to the National Restaurant Association nearly 50 percent of all adults have worked in the restaurant industry at least once during their life, and over 25 percent of adults worked their first job in a restaurant. Cooking and food shows on television help fuel popular interest in food and drink.

It is no wonder why each year tens of thousands of people open restaurants. If you are reading this book, chances are you've considered joining their ranks.

Before you read another word, however, we have to point out an obvious but often overlooked fact: A restaurant is a business. Moreover, it is a business with a multitude of facets and proverbial "moving parts" that are not always apparent if you've not previously owned or managed a restaurant.

A restaurant is a service business, a retail business, a hospitality business and a manufacturing plant all rolled into one, and managing it is a very demanding occupation. You need an accountant's eye for numbers and a nurse's patience when dealing with the public. You have to effectively lead people from a variety of backgrounds and cultures. Staff turnover tends to be high in most hospitality businesses, resulting in a constant cycle of hiring and training.

And yet it is very possible to be happy and successful as a restaurateur, particularly if you like continuous challenges. Like marriage and parenting, restaurant ownership can bring daily frustrations and soaring delights. That said, if only desire, good intentions, and smarts were enough to succeed at any of these, then there would be no divorce nor shuttered eateries.

This guide is compiled and edited by the staff of *Restaurant Startup & Growth*, the official magazine of RestaurantOwner.com. The publishers, editors and contributors have first-hand experience in the business as owners, managers, consultants and advisors. Over the past decade, they have amassed an in-depth library of articles, webinars, videos and tools and hands on experience to help those who want to open a restaurant, be successful and profitable.

Our goal is to help you appreciate and understand what is involved in launching a restaurant and what to expect in the doing. Whether you are

> Profit in business comes from repeat customers, customers that boast about your project or service, and that bring friends with them.
>
> ~ W. Edwards Deming

So, You're Thinking About Owning, Operating or Investing in a Restaurant...

11

considering a "from scratch" launch, purchasing an existing restaurant or entering into a franchise agreement, we believe the following chapters will help you take your first steps with open eyes. If after reading the information you decide that the restaurant business really isn't for you at this time, we will be just as happy knowing you thoughtfully deferred your plans until you are ready to embark on the journey.

And if you decide to commit to this great business, all of us at *Restaurant Startup & Growth* and RestaurantOwner.com look forward to helping you on the way to build personal wealth, create jobs in your community and produce pleasant dining experiences for your guests and realize one of life's greatest, most satisfying accomplishments.

Are You Cut Out for the Restaurant Business?

Chapter 1

There is plenty of opportunity to enjoy profitable business ownership for smart independent operators who apply sound restaurant business practices and can provide guests a unique and memorable experience. The big question: Should you be one of them?

> *It is in your moments of decision that your destiny is shaped.*
> — *Tony Robbins, life coach and self-help author.*

Even if you have been successful in other endeavors, jobs and careers, opening or taking over ownership of a restaurant presents unique challenges unlike those in any other occupation or profession. Success in the restaurant business isn't just a matter of smarts or business savvy, but of being prepared for these challenges. In fact, some really accomplished and educated people have failed at the restaurant business. And others, with humble backgrounds and little formal education, have enjoyed resounding success.

Welcome to the Big Time

Particularly if your dream to own a restaurant is modest — perhaps you want to own a café in a small town — you might lose sight of the fact that you are becoming part of one of the largest industries in the country in terms of sales and number of employees.

The National Restaurant Association compiles extensive data on industry trends nationally and state-by-state. On a typical day Americans spend $1.8 billion in the more than 980,000 commercial foodservice establishments, including independent restaurants. And there is room for a lot more growth as the population continues to expand and consumers continue to increase their spending on away-from-home meals, a category estimated to comprise 47% of all food dollars.

While the major restaurant chains are often held up as the model to which all restaurateurs aspire to amass wealth, it is important to bear in mind that a significant portion of the restaurant industry is composed of single unit and small multi-unit operations. Recent statistics by The NDP Group, a market research company, indicates that independent restaurants represents 27 percent of restaurant industry guest traffic. According to recent statistics from foodservice research organization CHD Expert, independent restaurants make up over 90% of the full-service

The 10 Commandments for Opening a Restaurant

1. Work in the industry first. Cook, clean and manage some personnel. Hands-on experience working with staff and serving the public will tell you if you are in the right business.

2. Define your concept. Don't try to do too much. You can add and modify a little as you go to stay fresh, but don't confuse the guest with too much at the opening.

3. Do your homework. Travel, review other restaurants, and speak to other restaurateurs for input on your concept. Develop a mission statement and define how you are going to measure its success.

4. Carefully select your site. Use an expert to assist with market analysis. Select a real estate consultant who specializes in retail (check references). More than just demographics and traffic count around a site, you also want to know spending patterns and area growth as well.

5. Develop financial projections and a budget. Don't forget the little things. Allow for contingency and operating capital.

restaurant market, whereas in the quick-service restaurant market — which has higher per-unit guest traffic than the full-service market — it drops to 43%.

Millions of people eat out every day, so there is plenty of demand for good restaurants. Yet, there is also plenty of competition. Industry sources point out that 20,000 to 30,000 new restaurant business licenses are issued every year.

A big advantage veteran restaurant owners have when they open a new restaurant is that they've done it before. While experienced independent restaurateurs have a slightly different set of challenges than do first-time restaurateurs, there are certain principles, tactics, techniques that are common to all successful restaurant operations. The major chain restaurants have succeeded not necessarily because they have secret formulas or superior products, but because they have applied these core business tenets consistently, effectively, and, in many cases, with scientific rigor.

There is plenty of opportunity to enjoy profitable business ownership for smart independent operators who apply sound restaurant business practices and can provide consistently a unique and satisfying experience for guests. The big question to ask: Should I be one of them?

There Might be 50 Ways to Leave Your Lover, but Only Three Ways to Enter the Restaurant Business

Almost every restaurant, even the ubiquitous McDonald's enterprise, started with a single unit. Entrepreneurs tend to be creative and want to bring their vision to life. Certainly, many successful concepts began in the imaginings of their owners. Nevertheless, there are only three basics ways to be an owner in this this business, and each can be an avenue to success. Your choice will depend on which one seems to be a good choice for your personality, resources and tolerance for risk.

Build a concept from scratch. Entrepreneurs with restaurant experience (i.e., they've worked in the business as cooks, managers, servers, etc.) and especially those with a creative flair, often want the challenge and freedom to create their own restaurant from the ground up. It is both challenging and fun to craft a unique dining experience for others. Any restaurateur will tell you that the startup phase is a hectic but interesting and fun part of the business. That's why there seem to be so many serial startup restaurateurs. They like all the tasks that go into giving life to their vision. The process makes for a very fulfilling experience — one that many restaurateurs consider the most rewarding part of owning a restaurant.

Typically, this path entails the most risk. It also presents the danger of embracing a concept evolved from the owner's likes and dislikes, without adequate evaluation of its viability. This is why it is so important to research the market, study the competition and choose your location wisely. (We address these processes in Chapter 4).

Mind you, don't ignore your instincts. Providing a unique experience for your customers is what the independent business is all about and new approaches that delight guests often become the biggest stars in the industry. If you like using both sides of your brain — the creative and analytical — this is a good business for you. The keys to success with a start-from-scratch concept comprises having a clear vision, researching relentlessly the best ways to get guests in seats, and then executing your well-considered plan. This is not a one-time effort, however. It is an iterative process, which you will be refining over and over during the life of your business. The trick in the opening stages of the business is to 'get it right' as much as possible from the start so that you don't run out of money before your run out of ideas. As we will discuss throughout this guide, "getting it right" often means developing systems that allow you, at least one day each week, to work *on* the business, not just *in* the business.

Becoming a franchisee. When you enter an agreement to become a franchisee, you are essentially purchasing the right to use a proven business system, and benefit from the managerial know-how as well as ongoing guidance and support from the franchisor. Again, the key word is *systems*. In the case of a franchise, you trust the franchisor to have figured out the financial, marketing and operational details. Metaphorically, buying a franchise should be like acquiring a well-designed and -tested airplane with a detailed operating manual. Your challenge is to learn to fly it.

Starting out with a turnkey business system can greatly reduce the risks attendant to developing a new concept from scratch. For one thing, with a franchise you can find out how successful the concept has performed in among existing franchise holders.

You can talk and visit with franchisee owners who are in the day-to-day operations and can get their perspective on how it's going. When developing a concept from scratch there is no such operating history or track record to evaluate. There are also extensive regulations, both federal and local, requiring the franchisor to give you details on success or failure rates of a particular franchise program. This allows you to be better informed on what your success factor might be when you operate within a *system*.

Having already constructed and opened similar restaurants, franchise owners have a generally easier time estimating upfront and ongoing startup costs. In addition, there is usually a shorter development period, which means a new restaurant can get open and, hopefully, begin operating profitably relatively quickly. That means your investment has the opportunity to begin paying you back more quickly as well. Instant consumer name recognition can also be a big plus. One of the key components of consumer brand recognition is an immediate understanding by customers of what they can expect in the way of food and service. This is an important ingredient in building sales and awareness.

Another advantage of the franchise arrangement is that once you learn how to successfully operate one unit, you are in a better position to expand to additional outlets because of the standardized procedures and systems that particular franchise offers. Operations are 'by the book' and that's why franchise and chain operations are generally more profitable than indepen-

6. Supervise the pre-opening. Be involved in layout and construction. Check and double-check your schedule. Openings require proper planning, realistic timetables and diligent follow-through.

7. Train and develop your staff. You only get one chance to open. Allow managers time to put systems in place and train staff. Have two or three dry run test parties before opening.

8. Select your purveyors. Visit and compare your bakery, produce, meat and grocery companies. Team up with companies based on service and quality, not just price.

9. Stay the course. Maintain the integrity of your concept. Be consistent.

10. Never fear failure. You need to take a risk to reap a reward. Believe in what you are doing.

dents. There are relatively large privately held companies that are nothing more than multi-unit franchisees, often over large geographic territories. They have the ability to 'clone' themselves and take advantage of their higher position on the learning curve.

Of course, there are downsides too: Franchisees pay for these advantages with an upfront franchise fee of tens of thousands of dollars (or even more) plus ongoing royalties and advertising fees that typically run 6 percent to 8 percent of gross sales.

You definitely want a lawyer in your corner who understands how these arrangements work and has the ability to sort through the franchise agreement, which can run hundreds of pages and is among the most mind-numbing legal documents imaginable.

While this book does primarily focuses on restaurant ownership via starting an independent concept or purchasing an established restaurant business from a previous owner, there is a section on franchise opportunities and a list of names and addresses of major franchising companies.

The benefits of becoming a franchisee include the guidance you receive from the franchisor, and the advantages of operating a restaurant under a known national brand. There are also franchisee opportunities with lesser-known concepts, which can involve more business risk but cost less to get on board.

Getting in on the ground floor of what could become a franchise leader presents a lot of opportunity for expansion as the concept grows. Later in this book you'll find a more detailed review of some of the attributes of a successful franchise and the questions to ask before signing up.

Purchase an existing restaurant. With hundreds of thousands of independently owned restaurants in the United States, there are always plenty of restaurants for sale. Purchasing an on-going concept has some distinct advantages with details on past operating history, a shorter opening time with less red tape for licenses, permits, and less startup costs than what's demanded by a new development. In addition, a functioning restaurant has an existing and established customer base and there may be the possibility of obtaining owner financing of its acquisition.

There may be potential disadvantages too: higher repair and maintenance costs than those for a new facility, overcoming a poor reputation of past management and a lack of documented systems and procedures to maintain consistency and quality after the previous owner leaves.

All one needs to do is watch the plethora of restaurant reality shows currently on cable TV to understand the issues that may be involved in purchasing and operating an existing restaurant.

As in buying any business, a thorough examination of the existing restaurant prior to the sale is essential. Again, at minimum, a prospective buyer will want an experienced attorney and CPA on their due diligence team. An in-depth discussion of important business, legal and tax issues in purchasing an existing restaurant can be found in Chapter 10.

Tax Liability When Stepping Into the Shoes of a Previous Owner

People acquiring a restaurant business should be aware that most states impose successor liability on the buyer of a business for the unpaid sales tax liabilities of the business, even when the purchase is of the assets of a business versus the business entity directly. Accordingly, a buyer of a restaurant or the bulk of its assets should always require the seller to obtain a tax clearance certificate from the state revenue department showing that the seller does not have any unpaid sales taxes.

Real Restaurateurs, *Real People*
Stories about people who realized their restaurant dreams

No Problem

*I*t's not often that a new restaurant opens and an operator can report "Nope, no problems at all" after two or three months in business. But that's the case with Kit's Kornbread Sandwich and Pie Bar, which opened in Carrollton, Texas, a Dallas suburb, in February 2013.

"The big exterior sign hadn't arrived yet, but we just opened the doors on a Sunday afternoon and people started coming in," says manager Randall Allen. This is Kit's Kornbread's second location, but with the original store more than three hours away in Jefferson Texas, there wasn't much opportunity for cross-promotion to send the crowd to the new location.

Kit is Kit Williams who grew up near Carrollton, but opened the Jefferson location more than a decade earlier. Her extended family in Carrolton wanted her closer to home — or maybe they just wanted her cornbread to be closer — so they were always on the look-out for a great location.

She checked out several recommendations over the years before everything came together in Carrollton. An improving economy was certainly a factor in making the decision to invest in a second location.

The unusual concept for sandwiches made with cornbread is based on a recipe that Kit developed as a child. While most cornbread crumbles easily, Kit's holds together well enough to accommodate the multiple layers of a hand-held sandwich. Kit's offers three flavors of cornbread — original, Jalapeno and broccoli. Jalapeno is the best seller in both locations.

The easy and successful opening was based on that one factor that contributes to any restaurant's success — location, location, location. The new location is in the front end of a shopping center dominated by a grocery store. Now that the exterior sign is up, the restaurant is quite visible to traffic moving to and from a well-populated residential area, not far from an elementary school and middle school. The setting had once housed a spacious coffee shop, but for nearly two years the building had been sitting empty. However, it was in remarkably good shape. Other than needing a bit of touch up paint here and there, the dining room was walk-in ready.

So, You're Thinking About Owning, Operating or Investing in a Restaurant...

17

"We loved the rustic decor with the murals of horses," says Allen. "It works in Texas and it works with our cornbread sandwich concept."

The kitchen, however, was another story. All new equipment was needed, including a hood and heat shield. Fundamental to Kit's Kornbread is an oven that will accommodate up to 16 pans of cornbread at a time. Williams chose a double-stacked Vulcan SG Series Convection Oven.

In addition to cornbread, Kit's is renowned for homemade pies. A lovely woman named Miss Sarah comes in very early a couple mornings a week and does everything from scratch. And one reason she comes in so early is because she needs that oven before the cornbread starts baking.

The arrangement works out pretty well until the lunch rush begins. The baking table and sandwich prep table share space. It gets pretty crowded and hectic, and like most restaurant operators, Allen wishes the kitchen was a little bigger.

A week or two before the very soft opening, long before the big exterior sign had been installed, Allen hit the streets, walking to neighboring businesses with $1 off coupons and menus for Kit's Kornbread. He also placed a few coupon ads in local magazines, but his big success was based on something he didn't even have in his marketing plan.

One of the early guests at Kit's Kornbread was so impressed she 'tweeted' several images and good comments. A local radio station picked up on the tweet and called for an interview. From there, a local newspaper picked up the story and the rest is history. The customers just keep coming for their Kornbread fix.

Recipe for a Winning Restaurant

To the question: "How much of creating a winning concept is skill, and how much is luck?" The honest answer, of course, is, "There's no way of knowing." Yet some folks seem to have an uncanny knack of getting the concept right consistently.

One of the beautiful things about baseball is that every once in a while you come into a situation where you want to, and where you have to, reach down and prove something.
— *Nolan Ryan, former Major League Baseball pitcher and a previous chief executive officer of the Texas Rangers baseball team.*

How many boys and girls have daydreamed of stepping up to home plate with the bases loaded, their team three runs down in the bottom of the ninth, and then blasting one over the fence? Whether you played baseball or softball, from tee-league to the major leagues, it's an age-old fantasy.

Like baseball, restaurants are embedded in our culture. We watch a professional player bring fans to their feet with a great catch in deep center field, and we can imagine ourselves doing the same. We enjoy a meal at a great restaurant on a busy night, and wonder if we could offer the same kind of experience.

For many of us, our bats and gloves are collecting dust in the attic, but we like to feel our glory days are far from over. In the restaurant business, the closest thing to hitting a winning homer is nailing a winning concept.

You always hope that your creativity, timing, and sense of the market are dead-on when you swing that big bat called opening a new restaurant. As a clever journalist once pointed out about baseball legend Hank Aaron, "He was the luckiest player in the world. It seemed that every time he stepped up to the plate, a home run was hit." Well, the restaurant business has its Hank Aarons, too.

For casual and fine dining, among the best examples of an independently owned restaurant company that has developed many "winners" (more than 20 different concepts) in 35 years is the Chicago-based Lettuce Entertain You Enterprises. Its chairman, Richard Melman, can boast of an unmatched, extremely successful formula for research, development, and attention to the details within whatever market segment his new concept competes.

So, You're Thinking About Owning, Operating or Investing in a Restaurant...

19

Houston's restaurants, a 47-unit high-volume independently owned upper-casual national chain is another great example of success coming from consistently following the development principles highlighted within this book. Additional examples of well-known concepts that have found success time and time again by following their winning development principles include The Cheesecake Factory, P.F. Chang's, and McCormick & Schmick's seafood restaurants.

Whether you are opening a one-of-a-kind restaurant or trying to grow your existing restaurant into a chain, there are winning principles that can help shape your restaurant and improve its chances of succeeding. A well-defined concept stands a much better chance of long-term success than some vague notion one might have about making one's first million selling burgers and beer to the neighbors.

Nevertheless, there are many sources of inspiration for new restaurants, as you can imagine. Some start with having a promising space in a good location. Some start with a box of family recipes. Some start because someone thinks it would be nice to own a great place to hang out with friends. Some of these succeed, and some fail, and not because the inspiration was faulty, but because the owners did not have a well-defined plan.

To start, it is wise to set specific goals and decide on the ways you will measure your restaurant's success. Polling many successful operators, we have determined four distinctive characteristics that constitute a winning concept:

Longevity. This is the art of being able to maintain success over time while adjusting to meet the changing demands and the buying habits of customers. To open a restaurant successfully and become profitable is one thing, but to maintain that success over a long period of time is "winning."

Consistency. To truly develop a successful concept requires putting in place systems and procedures to ensure consistency of your operation. A well-executed Wednesday dinner shift means little to Thursday's lunch patrons. Winning-concept operators know that restaurants are a zero-sum game. Each day must be as successful as the one before. Each plate must be presented the same way and staff must be well-trained, continually supported and supervised. That is why they live by the credo, "Anything worth doing is worth doing right, again and again!"

Market appeal. All restaurants want to be busy, but winning concepts seem to have a broad appeal and well-developed "points of difference" that enable them to dominate their market niche. To be the first place the customer thinks of going when choosing to dine out is the goal of the winning concept.

Expandability. When Johnny Carrabba and Damion Mandola opened their second casual Italian restaurant (Carrabba's Italian Grill), it was suc-

> An entrepreneur tends to bite off a little more than he can chew hoping he'll quickly learn how to chew it.
> ~ Roy Ash

cessful because of the broad customer appeal, consistency of its quality and service, and operating systems and management procedures established in the partners' first unit. Little did the two men know that they were setting the foundation for what has become a fast-growing chain with units from coast-to-coast. Barry Katz thought that the family's 26-year-old deli-casual theme restaurant in Austin, Texas (part of the Katz's deli family) had growth potential. After developing the systems and procedures to maintain consistency, he opened his second successful 24-hour restaurant in the Montrose area of Houston, Texas. Most winning concepts grow.

Planning to Succeed

A winning concept is usually complemented early on by a well-constructed business plan. Developing such a blueprint is not just a good first step if you hope to beat the odds, but it also can be quite useful for securing a lease, and extremely important — essential, actually — when trying to obtain funding from a bank or investors.

Successful restaurant business plans provide more than the required cost estimates and annual financial projections. As important, they tell a story of concept development, individuality, commitment to service, proper management principles and notably how the concept will "win" against the competition within a crowded market segment. There are numerous variables to consider when planning a restaurant; some of them are strictly operational, some strictly design, and some a mixture of the two. The difference in winning is in the details. Developing a winning concept involves answering a lot of questions:

• **In which segment of the market will my restaurant compete?**

• **How will I create noticeable points of difference?** Will it be in the display kitchen?

• **Should I offer entertainment; to-go delivery or curbside pickup program; private banquet facilities;** or a combination of the above?

It used to be that good food, good service and a clean facility were sufficient elements for success. Today, these comprise the bare minimum. To "win" — i.e. be financially successful — you must realize that it takes a total favorable guest experience. The quality of your food and its presentation are certainly important, but how well the overall concept is communicated to the guest will determine the extent of the facility's success.

Let's assume you have developed your concept and menu (which we will discuss in more detail later in this guide). Then let's assume you have answered the next fundamental question, "How many patrons will I need to serve, how often, and at what price to satisfy overhead and make a profit?" Winning concept creators also consider a few more questions, such as:

Pace Yourself

Burnout certainly is the No. 1 threat to people opening their own restaurants. Because of their added energy at the start, they tend to throw themselves into their work utterly and entirely and that can lead to a fast decline in both physical health and stress management. Taking those breaks, hiring more staff and managers, and/or relying on your business partner can help give you some time away.

So, You're Thinking About Owning, Operating or Investing in a Restaurant...

21

What should be the size of my restaurant? The answer depends to some extent on your answer to the preceding question. For the sake of discussion, a restaurant can be understood in two parts: the back-of-house component, and the front-of-house component. The former includes the cook line, the food preparation areas, refrigerated and dry storage areas, office and the dishwashing area. The latter typically include the interior and exterior dining areas, bar area, waiting area, to-go area, restrooms, and private dining areas. The speed of food and drink delivery, the restaurant's casual or formal atmosphere, and number of patrons to be accommodated will all factor into the amount of space you will need for your restaurant. The goal is to maximize the number of patrons one can serve in a satisfying way, out of the smallest, most efficient back-of-house possible.

Will it have a bar? Not all restaurants that serve alcohol have a bar. You have to decide what is right for you. Are you primarily a bar or a restaurant? What percentage of your sales do you anticipate will come from alcoholic beverages? Will a noisy bar crowd affect the way you do business? Will there be smoking areas designated? What effect will smoking in the bar have on the the dining areas? (Assuming that smoking in restaurants is even permitted in your state or municipality.) Beer, wine and mixed drinks can be a significant source of revenue for operators; however, it might not make sense to offer bar service, depending upon the restaurant's concept. Alcohol sales are highly regulated and have significant inventory control issues, which add to the complexity of running a restaurant.

How much parking will be required? Different governing jurisdictions require certain minimum number of parking spaces based on restaurant and bar square footage. Your municipality's rules might require more spaces than you want to provide. Parking availability is important to most patrons. You need to have ample parking for the size of your business. If patrons have to walk a long distance from their cars to your restaurant's front door, that could be a barrier to building repeat patronage. This is particularly true if you depend on older patrons or families with kids. Also consider that while an ordinance may require 8 or 10 spaces per 1,000 square feet, your concept might need as many as 20 spaces per 1,000 square feet in order to accommodate the number of customers your restaurant needs to succeed.

Where should my restaurant be located? Where space and utilities are affordable, and patrons are plentiful. Typically, these things tend to be mutually exclusive. You'll have to strike a balance. Good concepts in the wrong places usually fail. To determine the right location requires knowing the target audience you intend to attract. Understanding potential customers and their shopping habits will help identify trade areas with the sustaining characteristics and demographics you require. For example, you might be impressed with a suburban location where the restaurants seem to be packed every Friday and Saturday night. Consider that restaurants might struggle with attracting patronage the rest of the week. You need to consider the market carefully in terms of dining trends, price sensitivity and competition.

How much will it cost to build my restaurant? A good way to determine this is to find out what average per-square-foot construction costs are in your area and multiply that by the number of square feet in your project. Then add in all your FFE (furnishings, fixtures, and equipment). If you intend to use design and construction professionals, make sure that they specialize in restaurants and add their costs in as well. Design professionals may bill in any number of ways — a percentage of construction cost, a fixed fee, hourly, etc.

Building a capital budget is normally completed in three steps:

1. Developing an initial estimate with pre-bid costs.
2. Updating the estimate once bids for construction, equipment, etc., are available.
3. Revising the estimate before paying approved expenditures.

Winning restaurant operators know that the best way to succeed at opening is to have had an accurate budget that includes contingencies and working capital. Things may happen during development that can increase costs and delay the opening timetable. Without a contingency fund, you may be financially defeated before your concept opens. And even after opening, capital expenditures continue.

Are you planning to put money back into your concept to keep it fresh? Some beginning operators might forget that it's the dining public that ultimately decides who succeeds. Paying attention to the public's needs and expectations stands to benefit you. Serve them well and they will reward you. The closer you listen to your customers, the smarter restaurateur you become. Planning to provide annual guest intercepts or focus groups is an ideal way to learn how you may keep your concept winning. Holding staff meetings to review ways to continually improve the operation's efficiency and employing "mystery" customers to check the key elements of quality, service and cleanliness are both tools to consider as well.

Winning concepts have operators who reinvest in their businesses. Seasoned operators plan for remodeling every three to five years. Since this is such a competitive market, they make sure to evolve their menus seasonally, update marketing strategies annually and continually improve on service execution. Your long-term planning should include ideas and a budget for incremental improvement of the dining and kitchen areas to satisfy your guests. These, for example, might include adding deck ovens to keep up with orders if it turns out pizza dominates your sales. Or you might decide that adding white tablecloths is a necessary expense to differentiate your restaurant as an upscale concept. Or, to be in the position to bid on the lease for the space next to your restaurant if it becomes available, and you believe you

> You can't run a business or anything else on a theory.
>
> ~ Harold S. Geneen

So, You're Thinking About Owning, Operating or Investing in a Restaurant...

23

are in the position to expand your dining area. Always look forward to take advantage of opportunities as they arise.

Do you have an expandable concept? Perhaps you have had grand success with the first unit. Does the concept lend itself to being replicated in the neighboring town? Is expansion of your concept even a goal? If it is, you need to start thinking about the next unit while you are still developing the first. You will need a facility, menu and system that will be easily copied in another space.

That said, you should not expand a moment before you are ready. A poorly executed expansion can drag down a successful first unit by diverting your money and resources over a long period.

Dressed for Success

Certain winning concepts are immediately identifiable. Everything about them seems to work well. The service is impeccable, the atmosphere is inviting, the food is both well-prepared and well-presented.

More often than not, this is the result of a well-defined and precisely executed effort to consistently provide a successful "experience." Some chain establishments fit into this category. They become recognizable by their food type, specific design requirements, and style of service. Whatever you think about the food at a successful chain unit, invariably the parts all fit together and the staff is trained to make them work in concert.

Countless hours of time and energy have been spent in developing and maintaining that brand. These concepts have been so closely studied and scrutinized that a unit in one place is virtually identical to another 3,000 miles away. For winning concepts, consistency in design, menu and execution of daily operations make for a successful guest experience and that is what creates customer loyalty. A satisfied guest is meaningless to a winning concept because it's the LOYAL GUEST, in capital letters, who frequents your restaurant, tells others about it, and helps form the basis for your growth. Creating and maintaining customer loyalty becomes the daily mission of every winning concept and requires personal contact by a sincere manager and well-trained staff.

We have all eaten at a local one-of-a-kind restaurant that had the right combination of great food, good prices, warm atmosphere, and disciplined service. We want them to remain unspoiled and unchanged. They defy categorization, and may be site-specific. They are idiosyncratic and they are quite successful, in their unique way.

Interestingly, the myth and lore of established chains often trace their roots to such a concept. In them lies the essential kernel of the winning concept. Be cautious and know that expanding a concept stands a chance of diluting the authenticity of both the original and the copy. It takes a discerning entrepreneur to abstract those underlying principles that translate from unit to unit without diminishment in order to create a winning concept that is expandable.

So what is it that separates the successes from the failures? How can you correctly expand? One important consideration is to maintain your "trade dress." Operators planning to expand their concept should be able to define and recognize trade dress — including in their own restaurants. Trade dress constitutes the collective materials that affect the look and feel of a proprietary concept. It is one's brand in actual, open-for-business form. If you operate a successful restaurant you may do well to carefully examine what you've done right, which often means what your guests like most about dining in your restaurant. Those things that establish the place's look and feel may translate forward into the next successful venture as trade dress, which is often the most valuable (and protectable) intellectual property of a restaurant. Common elements of trade dress are signage, finishes, furnishings, seating and lighting.

Do you want a fast or slow message? Every commercial space communicates a message to its occupants, oftentimes, subliminally. Fast-food concepts may use hard, durable, and relatively inexpensive finishes. The reason for this is its strength and low maintenance, which is an important way of controlling cost. Bright lights, bright colors, small tables and high noise levels (due to the hard surfaces) translate into getting the customer in and out quickly.

By contrast, slow food is usually served in a venue with lower light levels in quieter, more comfortable settings, with larger tables. It involves softer surfaces, such as carpeting, tablecloths, padded furniture, or drapes. However, creating such an elegant atmosphere comes at a price: in this case, higher initial construction and acquisition costs and higher maintenance costs. Ultimately, maintenance and durability of a space translates into how much you have to charge for a meal.

Clientele expect higher levels of finish as the cost of their meal increases. Can you imagine sitting in a fast-food restaurant drinking a $50 bottle of wine? Atmosphere is important to all winning concepts. As the "hipness" factor of an establishment increases, operators may well choose a concrete floor, but they'll probably be spicing things up with fine art, fancy lighting, and a polished and well-groomed staff. One successful operator told us he once hired supermodels to hang out at his bar to establish his concept as a "see-and-be-seen" scene.

The clean versus noisy box. Cost, durability and atmosphere are all considerations when choosing materials, but don't ignore noise levels. Stained concrete might be inexpensive, but it is also a highly reflective surface and perpetuates noise. Tile, terrazzo and stone, while more costly than concrete and equally noisy, can help create visual interest in the flooring. Carpeting can range considerably in price and requires greater care, but really helps cut down noise. Carpet tiles are becoming increas-

> About the time we can make the ends meet, somebody moves the ends.
>
> ~ Herbert Hoover

So, You're Thinking About Owning, Operating or Investing in a Restaurant...

25

ingly more available, which helps if you need to replace a particularly badly stained or worn area. Using combinations of these may be appropriate; as long as you make sure the transitions are well thought out. Differences in material thickness can create tripping hazards or unravel carpet edges. Each covering has a different design and operating value.

Walls offer some noise reduction capacity. Hard surfaces such as glass reflect sound, but drapes absorb it. Wall coverings absorb some sound and nonparallel walls help break up the sound waves. Ceiling tiles are also an effective tool for reducing unwanted noise and work even better than carpeting. Used together they can quiet things considerably.

Seating. Tables, chairs and booths typically constitute the majority of elements within a restaurant's public space. Some fast-food and fast-casual concepts may work well with inexpensive plastic chairs for the entire space. Others must have custom tables and chairs each costing hundreds of dollars or more. Whichever you choose, keep in mind there are going to be a lot of them. Getting the right mix of deuces, four tops, and larger is important for a successful space plan. It doesn't do you much good to base your pro forma income statement on a 100-seat concept with 25 four-tops; if your business is mostly couples camping. You need to be able to seat the tables and the chairs. They should be comfortable, durable, easy to maintain, and easy to procure.

Lighting and color. Lighting is one of the most important elements available to control spatial perception. Getting the right amount where it's needed can have a huge effect on how one experiences a space. Imagine a darkened stage with a spotlight. Without the spotlight nothing is seen. In design, it is useful to think of light in terms of general illumination, spotlighting and sparkle. General illumination creates ambience. Some winning concepts use spotting highlights to feature and create drama. (You can a pin-spot a bowl of salsa so tightly that it's the only thing lit on the table. It's very dramatic.)

While lighting design can become very involved and complex, remember that a scheme that enhances your concept should ideally be easy to maintain as well. If you've got a dozen or more lamping conditions (which is not that unusual) it can be quite a chore keeping track of all the spare bulbs, where to get them, where to store them, how to replace them. Try to strike a balance between effect and ease of use. Schemes that go overboard with different lamping might be too hard and costly to maintain.

Color is the twin sister of light. Color can add clarity or ambiguity to space. Warm colors advance, and cool colors recede. Unless you are gifted in its use and manipulation, it is best to leave color application in the hands of professionals. Color can be tricky. It can take on all sorts of characteristics once applied. Color is affected markedly by light and other colors. It is highly situational. A red wall can turn an adjacent white wall pink with its reflected light. In the hands of a professional it can be a powerful tool; in the hands of a dilettante, a disaster. As all materials have natural color, it is often a better idea to let color express itself through those materials. Winning concepts create a successful bond with their customer base by paying attention to all of these little things. Your guests respond with all their senses; what they see, hear, feel, smell and taste determines what they will say.

Trade dress represents the entire look and feel of the dining experience. It is that which is proprietary and repeatable. It is a way of doing business. It is the food, the menu, the presentation style, noise levels, comfort levels, the lighting, and the style of service.

A People Business

For independent restaurant concepts to be sustainable and grow, they must employ a people management program that is committed to continual improvement. A successful program includes ongoing training including workshops by purveyors to assist with product knowledge and service tips. Engaging the staff in pre-shift discussions regarding their steps of service, menu descriptions, and other operating issues help them to maintain their focus and improve service. Providing a work environment that encourages staff to grow professionally, become cross-trained into other positions, and assist management allows them to win at what they are doing. Developing a winning concept requires a team effort and the involvement of all staff members.

By investing the necessary time and dollars to select the right team members, involving them further in the daily operations, and providing them ongoing product and service training, operators have increased staff retention and maintained proper labor cost. Putting the right team members in the right positions and providing them with involved motivated management forms the very foundation of a winning restaurant concept.

The key elements that go into developing a winning concept all have a way of fitting together in order to provide a unique guest experience. For any restaurant to become a winning concept in the eyes of its customers, it must endure the two greatest challenges facing every business — time and change — while maintaining consistency on product quality, service, and design — the elements that engaged your guests in the first place. Although accomplishing all that is no easy task, it is what makes hitting that winning run so gratifying.

In the end, all business operations can be reduced to three words: **people, product and profits.** Unless you've got a good team, you can't do much with the other two.

~ Lee Iacocca

Lessons from Ray Kroc

You may be wondering what you could possibly learn from the man who created the McDonald's empire. What could you possibly have in common with a corporate giant that, in 2015, reported more than 14,000 restaurants in the United States and more than 21,000 in international locations?

From an operational standpoint, you may not have a lot in common with McDonald's, however, Mr. Kroc's ingenious approach and guiding principles are not only relevant but include gems of wisdom every restaurant owner should know. His leadership and business sense helped make McDonald's the biggest restaurant chain of all time and made more people (his franchisees) into millionaires than any one organization in history. Just how Ray Kroc was able build such a massive and extremely profitable business operation in a relatively short time span certainly deserves of some attention.

Going to Work "on" the Business

When Ray Kroc secured the master franchising rights to McDonald's, he didn't go to work "in" a McDonald's restaurant, he went to work "on" the business of McDonald's. To Kroc, the first McDonald's restaurant was just a model or prototype that could be reproduced again and again in cities and towns all over the country.

Instead of personally rolling up his sleeves to run the joint, he instead began analyzing every operational function of the original McDonald's, from purchasing to prep to the cooking and cleaning. Without changing the essence of the concept, he made refinements and proceeded to develop a comprehensive set of standards and procedures, essentially a system for running a hamburger stand "the McDonald's way."

When Mr. Kroc had completed his first objective of building a complete "set of instructions" for operating a McDonald's restaurant, he then he moved on to the next phase of his plan. He was now able to show franchisees exactly how to run a McDonald's restaurant.

Ray Kroc told his franchisees that following the McDonald's system would enable them to give their customers the same food and service as the original McDonald's and thereby provide them with the best opportunity for becoming successful business owners. We now know that it worked, almost without exception.

The Problem with Working "In" the Business

By contrast, many independent restaurant owners never stop working "in" the restaurant. They start out by doing the work of the manager, chef or ma"tre d, which, of course, may be the only option in a new restaurant. But five years later, they may still be doing the same thing. Thus, they continue to function, not as an owner, but as another employee.

Recognize the implications in the way you approach your business and how you function in it. If you're spending most of your time and energy running the restaurant, chances are your business isn't achieving its potential for success. And chances are you're not having much of a life outside of the restaurant, either. Why? Because you're not focused on the things an owner of a business, any business, should be doing.

The problem is that most people who open their own restaurants have always worked in one (no that's not a typo). There's a big difference between working in a restaurant as a cook, chef or manager and building a successful business. It's critical to accept the fact that a restaurant is not just a restaurant, it's also a business. And the knowledge, understanding and skills it takes to manage a successful business are very different from the knowledge and skills required to run a restaurant.

You've heard it before: The place to start looking for answers is in a well-thought-out business plan. This plan is not necessarily for potential investors (although much of the thought and research that goes into it can be used later for that purpose), it is to help you decide if opening a restaurant is something you really want to do and are prepared to do.

It's true that with enough capital anyone can open a restaurant, but that's not really the point. Anyone can throw money down the drain. We assume you want the word "profitable" in the list of adjectives that describe your business. There's an old saw that says the restaurant business is about making the customer happy while the business of a restaurant is about making the owner happy. A business plan, the development of which we discuss in detail in Chapter 6, helps you create a blueprint to accomplish both.

If you work just for money, you'll never make it, but if you love what you're doing and you always put the customer first, success will be yours.

~ Ray Kroc

So, You're Thinking About Owning, Operating or Investing in a Restaurant...

29

Building a Menu

The average guest spends only about three to four minutes with the menu, so it is important that your "carte du jour" makes a good first impression and directs the reader to the item you want purchased. This is true, whether you've been in business for a day or for a decade, but it is especially critical for the startup.

If we knew what it was we were doing, it would not be called research, would it?
— Albert Einstein

Every restaurant has a physical menu, whether it is six pages long or a simple sheet, a light board above the order counter or a slate at the entrance with the daily specials. This list of your restaurant's fare, however displayed, can be your most effective salesperson or greatest impediment to success. Your guests might well conclude how much they want to spend in your restaurant, and even whether they will return, based on their few minutes spent reading it.

The menu also helps define the cuisine and price points of your business. It serves as a product catalogue, billboard, and mission statement, and drives everything about your concept. It reflects your kitchen and staffing, your food and labor costs, your vendors, the size of your restaurant's footprint, and your market appeal, competitiveness, your refinement, attitude and taste. It describes both the food you offer to guests and the manner in which you present it.

The science of menu development goes beyond the scope of this book, and you are well-advised to hire a consultant for this process to get started. In this chapter, however, we will cover some of the basic menu concepts so you will have a better appreciation what is entailed, and how important it is to get it right from the start.

Service Style

Before you can even think about creating your menu, you need to define your style of service, of which there are five basic types listed below. This drives your menu on several levels. The style determines the type of cuisine and the level of culinary skill required in the kitchen. Do you need an accomplished chef or a cook? It also drives your target food costs; you won't last very long as a fast-food concept selling $20 hamburgers, unless those hamburgers are extraordinary. It also drives your range of menu items. A family-style restaurant needs to cater to a variety of tastes, ranging from those of toddlers to seniors.

Fast-food operations. Known in the business as Quick Service Restaurants, or QSRs, these establishments emphasize convenience and speed of service. Guests don't necessarily patronize them for the quality of food, but for dining ease. They provide calories for a reasonable price quickly. As category's name suggests, speed is this group's core competency, and keeping food and labor costs low is critical. To that point, other than trays, all containers and cutlery are disposable and diners clean up after themselves. QSRs can range from small-scale street vendors to the largest and most financially successful chain operations such as McDonald's or KFC.

Fast-casual restaurants. These restaurants differ from QSRs in that they do not offer drive-through service windows or street service, but typically do not have anything more than limited table service. The primary mode of dining is eat-in, although they often have significant take-out service. The quality of food and prices tend to be higher than those of a conventional fast food restaurant, but may be lower than casual dining.

Casual dining. This is a sit-down concept with moderately priced foods. Among the features that distinguish it from fast casual are slower table turns and more emphasis on alcohol sales as a revenue stream. Often restaurants of this type have a bar with limited wine lists and a large beer menu. As with quick-service and fast-casual concepts, keeping food and labor costs low is critical. Nevertheless, given the slow turn of tables, getting guests to order alcohol, appetizers and desserts is often necessary to boost sales.

Family style. A number of large chains such as Applebee's and IHOP dominate this niche, and offer large menus with comfort items that appeal to a wide range of tastes. Independent restaurants that tend to do well in this niche are ethnic in concept, such as Chinese and Mexican. Many of these concepts have significant bar service; but invariably these operations sequester the bar patrons from the main dining room to be appealing to multi-generational parties. Full table service is common with these concepts; however, buffet and salad-bar service works as well, with limited table services (e.g. refreshing drinks, bussing, etc.)

Fine dining and upscale casual. There used to be a clearer distinction between these niches. Today, true fine-dining rooms, with white tablecloths and elegant settings, are on the wane. On the other hand, lively and relaxed settings offering fine cuisine, wine and service are growing in popularity. As a result, the difference between the two types is getting a bit fuzzy.

This combined category generally features a highly trained staff, formal place settings, and decor that is sophisticated, unique and showcases kitchen talent. Fine-dining locations are almost always small businesses and, generally, with only one or two locations. It is impossible to maintain the cachet and quality that drives guests to such establishments when their concept grows beyond that. That said, some of the longest-running restaurants in the country, with 35-plus years in business, fall under this category as they become local landmarks, such as Commander's Palace in New Orleans, or the Four Seasons in New York.

Each of these five basic styles of restaurant service has many variations. While the chains depend on regimentation to ensure their guests get exactly what's expected, one of the attractions of owning an independent restaurant business is that you aren't confined to any strict concept and can let individuality shine.

The service style variations include brasseries and bistros, which reflect a French model known for hearty meals in unpretentious settings. Buffets and cafeterias offer a wide variety of self-service, ready-cooked foods at a fixed price. Cafes are informal locations with hot-meals, made to order foods and often serve breakfast. Coffeehouses have now also become casual restaurants offering limited selection of pastries and sandwiches in a relaxed setting.

Put Your Vision on Paper

No researcher starts the process without ideas. You've prepared meals, eaten in other restaurants, and know what you do and do not like. Start the menu development process by putting your vision on paper. This is the time to be creative and fearless. However, before the process is over, you will have analyzed and modified your choices to end up with a menu that is tempered by financial, marketing, and operational considerations.

That said, there are two caveats to bear in mind as you let your creative juices flow. First, you should not feel you have to offer everything to everybody. We know that when you stroll down the aisles of a typical supermarket or watch television for more than a few minutes, you are slammed with the seemingly infinite choices of food available to the U.S. consumer. That's why it's tempting to offer a supermarket of choices on your menu.

Slow down! The number of items on the menu is critical to cost and quality control. Vary it enough to interest the guest, but limit choices to maintain control.

Some operators make the mistake of trying to be all things to all people. On any given menu, 50 percent of the offerings typically attract 70 percent to 80 percent of the orders. Theoretically, that means you might be able to dump half your items and still maintain 80 percent of your sales. Now in practice, some of those less popular items are necessary to carry your concept, please your spouse, and/or cater to smaller, but important customer

Business, more than any other occupation, is a continual dealing with the future; it is a continual calculation, an instinctive exercise in foresight.

~ Henry R. Luce

So, You're Thinking About Owning, Operating or Investing in a Restaurant...

33

groups (e.g. children, vegetarians, folks on low-fat diets). The important thing is to understand the trade-offs, and have a strategic reason for every item on your menu, not just to take up space.

Establish early what you believe you can do well, and what you want to be known for. And then do it. Size of the menu will depend upon the concept, market and operational capabilities, as well as quality and profit goals. A general rule of thumb: the more items on the menu, the higher the food cost. If you feel the need for an extensive menu, then make sure it's designed with a limited inventory so that the same ingredients are used in several items.

This brings us to the next caveat. Some operators make the mistake of thinking everyone will fall in love with their favorite foods. They want to bring their grandmother's Italian recipes to local restaurant scene. A nice gesture, but can such a menu can be sourced properly by vendors and executed night after night, let alone attract enough guests to make it profitable? Will grandma's recipes translate to the hip, urban restaurant you would like to operate? Who is your competition? Consider the people whom you envision as your guests.

With that said, a great way to organize a menu is to create categories. As it sounds, categorization is simply the process of subdividing the menu into smaller, more specific categories, such as appetizers, soups, salads, and entrees by type — beef, seafood, vegetarian and so on. Done well, a properly categorized menu creates a perception of variety. It also can help certain diners find what they want sooner. As you have probably noticed, men generally do not take as long as do women to decide what they want to order. Women tend to read menus, while men tend to scan. Categorization makes either reading style more efficient at bringing items to the guest's attention.

And since categorization can shorten the time it takes for your guests to make an order decision, it could significantly influence your profitability by saving enough time to have an extra 'turn' of tables. Some consultants recommend a "postcard style" approach, as the quickest format to read. Essentially, you break up the menu in postcard-sized spaces, for each category. Instead of being overwhelmed by a running list of menu items, the guest can compartmentalize the decision by turning his or her attention to each "postcard."

Categorization also provides a way to merchandize particular items you want to sell. With desktop publishing software and affordable instant printing, you can reinvent your menus on a regular basis to promote certain items, driven by inventory levels and profitability.

It is critical that you identify all categories on the menu. Place a minimum of three to four categories, with a maximum of six items within a category. Any less and you lose variety/value in the category (and on the menu) — any more and the guests have too much to read and consider. Place high-profit categories in the prime merchandising areas on the menu — the top right-hand portion of the column or postcard. This is the first place our eyes are drawn to when looking at a page.

Marketing and Operational Concerns

A good recipe for home cooking doesn't always work out when you attempt to replicate it in a restaurant. Those not experienced in the restaurant business find out quickly that a recipe intended to yield four, six or even 10 servings might not be practical when feeding dozens or even hundreds of guests every day.

You also need to be able to turn around orders in the kitchen consistently and quickly. While your friends and family rarely mind waiting an extra half-hour or so for your home recipes or variations in one dish's presentation, your restaurant guests will not forgive slow service or variations in the final product. If your pasta primavera is phenomenal on one visit and lackluster on another, you will lose repeat guests.

Your first dose of reality will come when contemplating how to execute your menu. Every restaurateur in the process of developing a new menu will need to make a variety of decisions regarding the balance between preparing foods from scratch and using different pre-made menu products. Most food items, once they've been caught, harvested or slaughtered, become subject to some degree of processing, and that in turn will influence its convenience, cost and quality.

In this business, 'scratch' and 'pre-made' are common terms. As implied, scratch items begin with raw ingredients that have undergone little or no processing. Pre-made items tend to be prepared, in some cases to the point of being ready for heat-and-serve.

Rarely do you find restaurants who food items are either all scratch or all pre-made. Other than some quick-service operations that use all pre-made items to ensure rapid production and predictable food costs, most concepts use both, and adjust the mix over time. Figuring out the right balance of customer acceptance, kitchen staff and equipment capabilities, storage space, menu pricing and food costs all play a part in whatever combination you use.

Pre-prepped, prepared or precooked items have been around for hundreds of years and are used by the restaurant industry because they save time, money and are accepted by customers. There are many options available to restaurateurs because the variety and quality of pre-made items at all levels have improved dramatically during the last 40 years. For example, the variety of pre-made chicken products alone offers a glimpse of the staggering choices you have.

You can buy a whole chicken, a chicken breast or legs, chicken with or without skin and bones, portioned chicken, cooked chicken, marinated chicken. At the same time, the quality of pre-made items has kept pace with the variety of products. For example, rapid freezing techniques, advanced yeast performance, and packaging innovations in the bakery industry have made frozen dough welcome in both sandwich shops and French-style restaurants.

Economics and labor issues often drive the scratch-vs-pre-prepared decisions. For example, if you need a special piece of equipment for just one or two menu items, you might be wise to go with pre-made, if available. Using

> In the business world, the rearview mirror is always clearer than the windshield.
>
> ~ Warren Buffett

So, You're Thinking About Owning, Operating or Investing in a Restaurant...

35

The Origin of 'In the Weeds'

There is little dispute that the phrase "in the weeds" is restaurant slang for a situation when the wait staff gets behind in servicing their customers or tables. The origin of the phrase is not precisely known; however, some authorities claim it dates back to the U.S. Prohibition, when servers would hide cases of liquor behind the restaurant "in the weeds" to evade law enforcement. Other sources indicate that it refers to Prohibition-era servers heading behind the restaurant to take a shot of liquor hidden "in the weeds" to steel their nerves during difficult shifts. Others cite that the term simply means what it suggests, that is, servers getting so behind on their shift that they become "lost in the weeds."

prepared foods can reduce storage requirements. For example, in the case of a Caesar salad dressing, the spoilage rate and refrigeration requirements of its ingredients may make a pre-made dressing attractive. They can be kept in dry storage until opened and they are usually accepted by the industry and the guests. Moreover, adding additional ingredients to a shelf stable dressing before serving can make it a signature item.

Food preparation, such as slicing meat, requires labor and some steps that involve physical risk. Knife injuries can interrupt service and increase workers' compensation claims. Many restaurants, including large chains, are removing slicing equipment from their kitchens altogether. In the greater business scheme, they have found it less expensive to purchase precut meats and cheeses.

Today, almost any level of food preparation is available. Variations of premade items include:

Prepared but raw. This category includes individual ingredients that arrive cleaned, sized, stabilized, and/or blanched, but pretty much left in their raw state. While some of the preparation steps are already completed, you combine the ingredients in your own recipes to create, essentially, from-scratch menu offerings. Examples include washed lettuce, chopped vegetables, de-veined raw shrimp, prepared 14-ounce strip steaks, and sliced fruits.

Pre-mixed, flavored, and/or ready-to-cook. This category includes prepared foods that may be raw, partially cooked, or fully cooked, blanched, or combined with one or more ingredients. In any case, they are not ready to serve; rather, they require combination with other ingredients, cooking, and/or other additional preparation. Examples are partially or fully cooked chicken breasts, pre-breaded chicken, frozen dough, spice packets, flavor-injected products, marinated items, soup and sauce mixes, and ready-to-bake desserts. Also in this category are bar items, such as daiquiri or margarita mixes.

Fully prepared and heat-and-serve. These include ready to serve items such as salad dressings, fully cooked desserts, prepared meats with gravy, boil-in-bag items, fully cooked breads, and deli meats. These products offer maximum convenience and are ready to use by themselves, for assembling a menu item, or combining with other prepared or scratch items.

Making scratch-vs-pre-made decisions can be a little confusing. Half the proverbial battle is learning what's available and where you can get it. Once you educate yourself on the products and suppliers, you can begin figuring out how pre-made items might be an appropriate fit for your kitchen. Restaurant trade shows are a great way to learn what's new in pre-made menu items.

Local and national distributors are also a great source of information. You have to be proactive with your suppliers when you're searching for ways to make your menu better and your preparation more efficient. There's no way a distributor salesperson can read your mind, so it's up to you to pose the question. "Hey, we're thinking about a pre-made dessert item, but I want one that uses Dulce de Leche topping — do you know of anything like that out there?" The distributor representative who wants your business will begin the search immediately.

Now Sharpen Your Pencil

Dreams of five star ratings are lovely, but the numbers that really matter to most of us can be found on the bottom line. Simply put, we need to make money. Success and failure in the restaurant business is often measured in pennies. So, once you have a sense of what kind of cuisine you want to offer, your next assignment is to determine your target food cost.

The first step is to cost out your entire food list for all recipes, including prep items, condiments, cooking oil, etc. To accomplish this, you'll need a listing of each ingredient that you plan to use in each of your menu items. Remember that while this exercise is important during the planning stage, it is critical once your restaurant becomes operational. In the planning phase estimating costs is made easier and more accurate by calling local distributors for inventory pricing information.

On that note, establishing strong relationships with your local distributor and suppliers is a critical step in making your restaurant a success. Picking the right vendors ensures your access to reliable service, consistent supply lines, better delivery, the newest products and even the best values. Good distributor representatives also have tremendous restaurant industry knowledge and are often a source of ideas for improving your business.

You will want to create a 'menu costing sheet' similar to the one illustrated below. By using wholesale price listings, you can build a form cost of each ingredient you plan to use. Add the total cost of all ingredients used to arrive at the menu item cost. Complete this exercise for each offering. Starting early with this type of costing system develops an important discipline that will help in many planning and operations areas.

Menu Item: 12" Deluxe Pizza				
Item Description: New York style crust with pizza sauce, pepperoni, Italian sausage, bell peppers, onion, and cheeses.				
Recipe Unit	Quantity	Ingredient	Unit Cost	Extension
EA	1	Pizza dough, 6 oz. ball	0.31	0.31
OZ-fl	4	Pizza sauce	0.06	0.24
OZ-wt	0.5	Cheese, grated Parmesan	0.19	0.09
OZ-wt	6	Cheese, mozzarella/provolone blend	0.25	1.48
OZ-wt	2	Italian sausage	0.13	0.25
OZ-wt	1.5	Pepperoni slices	0.18	0.27
OZ-wt	1.5	Peppers, roasted bell	0.08	0.11
OZ-wt	1.5	Onions, yellow	0.05	0.08
EA	1	Plate cost (Q-cost)	0.10	0.10
			Total Cost	2.94
			Menu Price	11.95
			Gross Profit	9.01
			Food Cost %	24.60%

In the example above, note the cost for a 12-inch Deluxe Pizza is $2.94, or 24.6 percent of the selling price; and that this particular pizza has a profit contribution of $9.01. It is essential to know the expected food cost percentage for every item on your menu and the profit contribution in dollars. Of course, once you open, periodically update your menu cost calculations based on the actual purchase price for ingredients.

Ideal food cost (oftentimes called 'theoretical cost') is the cost expected for a given sales mix over a period of time, assuming proper portioning and normal waste and yields. It is impossible to know the ideal food cost unless you first know the portion cost for each ingredient of every menu item. Even then, as costs for ingredients change, so will ideal costs.

A Few Words About... Always Learning

Just because we've always done something a certain way doesn't make it right or best. One thing we've learned about the restaurant business is whenever you think you've got it figured out, someone will show you something new or different that tests your conventional thinking. Maybe that's why some of us should be in this business. It keeps us humble and open to new ideas.

Paulie's Pizzeria
Ideal Cost Worksheet
For the Week Ending 3/15/2009

Enter # sold from POS sales mix report

Restaurant owner.com

MENU ITEM DESCRIPTION	Menu Item Cost	POS # Sold	EXTENSION	TOTALS
Food Items				
12" Deluxe	$ 2.94	252.0	$ 740.88	
16" Deluxe	$ 3.94	108.0	$ 425.52	
12" Pepperoni	$ 2.14	366.0	$ 783.24	
16" Pepperoni	$ 2.99	186.0	$ 556.14	
12" Cheese	$ 2.04	90.0	$ 183.60	
16" Cheese	$ 2.88	54.0	$ 155.52	
Meatball Sub	$ 2.25	126.0	$ 283.50	
Breadsticks	$ 0.32	258.0	$ 82.56	
Med Wings	$ 1.80	498.0	$ 896.40	
Large Wings	$ 2.40	150.0	$ 360.00	
2 Ltr Soft Drinks	$ 0.83	432.0	$ 358.56	$ 4,825.92

Enter the menu cost from the menu cost card.

ACTUAL / IDEAL COMPARISON	$ Amount	% of Sales
Food Sales for Period	$ 18,046.92	100.0%
Ideal Cost	$ 4,825.92	26.7%
Actual Cost	$ 5,497.38	30.5%
Variance $ / %	$ (671.46)	-3.7%

Enter the total food sales for the period (week, month)

Enter actual food cost from the daily invoice log.

The 'ideal cost worksheet' example above is a simple tool for estimating your sample menus and estimating sales for each particular area. Simply list the cost of each menu item and the number of items you think you'll sell in a week. Then multiply those sales by 52 weeks to arrive at your expected annual sales. Do the same with the cost factors.

This example indicates that the expected (ideal) cost for the week ending 3.14 for this restaurant was $4,825. The sales for that same period were $18,046, resulting in an expected food cost percentage of 26.7 percent.

The next step is estimating the sales mix (the number of each menu item sold for a specified period) you expect and what the ideal cost would be. If one period you sell a greater percentage of high-cost menu items and the next period you sell more low-cost items, then the ideal cost for each period will differ; for that reason, ideal cost is an ever-changing target.

Your cash register or POS (point-of-sale) system should be able to be programmed to track individual sales for each of your menu items. The sales mix report is a basic feature found in most restaurant registers; it is critical that the system you lease or purchase has the capability to tell you the quantity and sales total of each menu item sold. Most registers provide this report for daily sales, and many can be programmed to maintain cumulative totals for the week or month. Make sure that information is used in your restaurant startup.

Menu Engineering

Menu engineering is the art and science of how and where to place items on the menu since that placement can dramatically affect your bottom line. Imagine you're a salesperson who boards an elevator with an important customer. He turns to you and says, "I'm thinking of purchasing products from your entire line, but I want you to sell me before we get off this elevator. Tell me what makes your products special, why your pricing is reasonable, which products are best suited for me, and how you quantify the quality of your service."

That's a lot of information to analyze and present in a few minutes. You're sizing up the customer's needs. You're running numbers in your head to determine the profitability of each product and the optimal pricing. And you want to use language that entices a sale. Well, your restaurant's menu shares a lot in common with that salesperson's time-squeezed task.

Since the average guest spends only about three to four minutes with the menu, it is important that your menu make a good first impression and directs him to the item you want purchased.

If you consider your menu simply a decorative price list, you're grossly underestimating its value. A menu is your most powerful merchandising tool. Everything that makes your restaurant special and profitable flows from the pages of your menu — your atmosphere, concept, pricing and cost-control strategy, and service ethic. Couple an effective menu with a well-trained service staff that interacts effectively with guests and you've got a winning combination.

The techniques used in menu engineering are not overly complex, but the results can make for an eye-opening experience. Many restaurateurs have simply ignored this tool, and ,quite frankly, are missing out on enhancing sales easily as a result. Menu engineering is a discipline, which is probably best led by a consultant, until the operator understands how to employ it. Once applied consistently in the restaurant, though, menu engineering can reap immediate increases in sales and, more importantly, profitability.

It is impossible to fully teach all the techniques and illustrate every restaurant scenario of menu engineering in the space of a single chapter. But using a simple illustration, we'll show you how it can be applied.

In some ways, a discussion of menu engineering is premature for someone who is still in the planning stages of his or her restaurant. You will not have the opportunity to apply menu engineering until your doors are open and you begin to sell product. Still, you need to envision the process now to understand how your choice of menu influences your sales and income. It also gets you thinking about where some of the items you have considered offering your guests might fall in terms of contribution to your bottom line.

One of the first steps in menu engineering is analyzing the mix and gross profit of each item. The chart and graph below provide simple but effective illustrations of this process, and how illuminating the exercise can be.

For simplicity, we examine a single category on a menu — burgers — during a given period, let's say a month. It is imperative that you keep careful track of item sales and food costs. We could devote an entire chapter to tracking this information, but for now let's just accept that tracking is important, and provides you with a powerful and invaluable analytical tool.

In this burger scenario, our data tells us what percentage of sales were attributed to each burger type (i.e., the "mix") and, second, our gross profit on the sale of each item (i.e., "gross profit contribution"). Turn your attention to the chart "Burgers by the Numbers" (below). Here, we see that your most popular item in this category was the Texas burger, and the least popular was the Big D burger. You can see that the average popularity for all items in the burger category was 9.09 percent and average gross profit was $5.60.

Burgers by the Numbers

Category by Mix and Gross Profit Contribution

Type	Sales Mix	Gross Profit
Texas	23.38%	$5.30
Cajun	9.94%	$5.20
Mushroom	6.31%	$5.50
Gorgonzola	4.42%	$5.40
Bacon Cheddar	18.14%	$6.10
Patty Melt	6.09%	$6.00
Black Jack	15.82%	$7.20
Stadium	8.62%	$6.90
Roma	3.67%	$6.30
Big D	3.60%	$7.70
Average	9.09%	$5.60

The story doesn't unfold until you plot the information on the graph "The Burger Landscape" (below) using a desktop computer spreadsheet program:

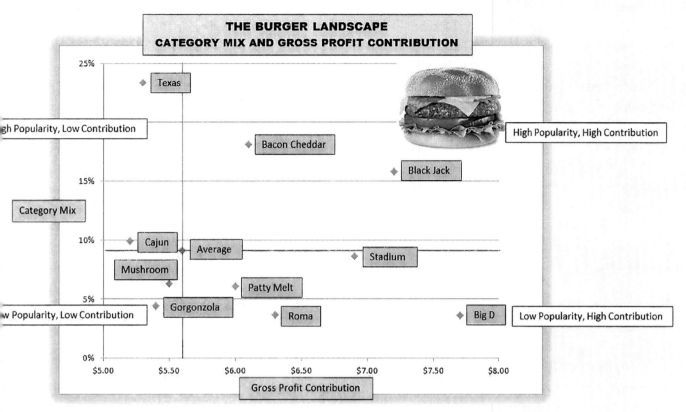

Here we can see our burger landscape in more detail, and where all the items fall in relationship to the "average," both in terms of popularity and profitability. As noted, the Texas burger is the most popular item, but is below average in profitability. Wouldn't it be great if we could sell as many or nearly as many of them and increase the profitability? The Bacon Cheddar and Black Jack exceed the average in popularity and profitability. Still, you would love to boost their sales, without having to increase their cost or cut their prices to improve their value to the top line of your profit and loss statement.

Now that we see "the trees for the forest," do we detect any "dead wood" in this category? Well, you're not selling many of the huge Big D burgers, but you might need to keep this on the menu to please big eaters, and to make the other burgers look like a good value. Remember that menu engineering is an art, and like all artistic endeavors, it requires experience and judgment to make the best calls.

The Mushroom and Gorgonzola burgers are below average in popularity and profitability. Meanwhile, the Roma burger uses a kind of tomato — Roma — that is not used in any other item on the menu, and that boosts the inventory cost of this burger. Plus, tomatoes are a relatively perishable item, which could contribute to wasted inventory costs. You need to search your soul to determine whether these low performers deserve "real estate" on your menu.

The Menu Matrix

A menu matrix will place each of your products into one of four categories based on their sales volume and contribution to profits. You will be able to see graphically which items have higher-than-average sales and profitability (often referred to as "Stars"), which items have higher-than-average sales but have lower-than-average profitability and vice versa, and which items do not sell well and have lower-than-average profitability (often referred to as "Dawgs").

The menu matrix gives you a visual representation of the landscape of your current menu, and helps you decide which items to feature more prominently on the menu, which items need to be made more profitable, and which items require some soul searching to justify their continued existence on your menu. The four categories described are:

Stars. Both popular and profitable, these items are your best opportunity to build a stronger, more profitable restaurant. For a start-up restaurant, these items will have a higher-than-average profit potential.

Puzzles. Products that make a higher-than-average profit, but lower-than-average sales, these items may be wrong for your restaurant, may be too high-priced, or may need to be marketed or named differently. In a start-up restaurant, these will be an unknown quantity, so this is where you will want to promote.

Continued on page 43…

A reverse consideration is is how to transform average or good performers into your "Superstars." You boost the popularity of an item by increasing its perceived value. Sometimes, but not always, this means lowering the price, or just giving it a sexier name. You can also give it better placement on the menu (more about this later). As always, you increase the profitability of an item by either reducing its cost, or increasing its price. Or, ideally, both.

Pricing is perhaps the most complex aspect of menu engineering. Here's one caveat: Always change prices in small increments, unless it is clear that the item is grossly undervalued or overvalued (this situation should not arise if you allow for sufficient profit margin from the get-go).

Menu Categories by Performance

Keeping in mind the preceding burger illustration, you will find four basic categories into which every menu item will fall. If you are a brand-new startup restaurateur, you may be developing a menu from scratch, and you might have to use a certain amount of "gut instinct" and "what if" scenarios. Soon you will have enough experience and data to make educated decisions about menu changes using menu-engineering techniques.

The first category includes menu items that have a high gross profit contribution and high product mix. These items have maximum menu power, and depending upon your offerings overall, should command the best real estate on the menu. The more we can influence the mix toward these items, the more profitable the operation will be. The Bacon Cheddar burger in our earlier analysis arguably falls in this category.

These items should receive the best placement on the menu and the most sales emphasis by your servers. Be careful about making significant changes to these items, in presentation or price, based on the "if it ain't broke, don't fix it" rule. If possible, try to find ways to reduce your cost of these items to increase your profit margin.

The second category includes menu items that sell well (high in product mix) but have less-than-average gross profit contribution. These items are often loss leaders, but necessary. The Texas burger is an example. Typically, these items are very price-sensitive; thus, you might find that even small price increases could reduce the sales volume. Again, finding ways to reduce the cost of these items could push them closer to "star" status.

Third, we have menu items that have greater-than-average gross profit, but lower-than-average popularity. Sometimes, these items act as "image makers" and provide a largely psychological benefit to the guest. Typically, these are the more expensive items on the menu. Yet having too many of these items can produce a negative effect on the rest of the menu and should be candidates for elimination, repackaging, re-pricing or replacement. Think of the Big D burger, which is so large you eat it with a knife and fork, but few people order it.

In cases like the slow-moving Big D, you might want to lower its price incrementally to gauge its price sensitivity. If at some point you can build significant sales volume and maintain a healthy profit margin, you might find yourself with a winner.

In any situation in which you try to build popularity and/or profit, carefully track the sales of items that are already good to top performers. You need to look for signs of "cannibalization," i.e., when a reformulated product begins to "eat" the sales of one or more existing high performers in the same category. This is not necessarily a bad thing, if the net effect is a greater combined profit. However, you want to avoid a situation in which your customers are switching to an item with a lower profit margin.

Finally, it's important to identify menu items that have lower-than-average popularity and produce a lower-than-average contribution to gross profit. These are also candidates for elimination, repackaging, re-pricing or replacing. If you choose to keep an item in this category, you should know the reason. Often, these items are important to a particular market segment (like kids) and should stay on the menu to help you remain competitive.

A Few More Words on Menu Pricing

Among the factors that must be taken into account when pricing your menu is concept, food cost, gross profit, market, location, economic climate, personnel, competition, and value as perceived by your guests. Focus on the following: Menu item value is critical, and a determination that's difficult to establish since there are so many disparate factors involved. So, don't be afraid to ask guests and employees alike what they would pay (or sell) for a particular menu item.

One of the most pervasive and preventable mistakes in the restaurant business is presenting guests with a price list menu, that is a menu that has all the prices listed on one side, usually with dots lining up the items with their respective cost to the guest.

The cure for this problem is simple: Tuck the prices into a paragraph. Don't highlight the price; don't make it another color, or type size, or style. Just end the description with a price without a dollar sign and move on.

You need to study your market and customers before setting prices, which requires judgment and observation. Apply common sense. If you would not pay that price for the item, most likely your customers would feel the same way. But realize that pricing menu items can rarely be completely objective. In addition, avoid the temptation to underprice a menu item. Since success in this business is often measured in pennies, underpricing can be as much of an error as overpricing. You don't want to pass on legitimate profits any more than you want customers grousing about your pricing, and eschewing your business for a competitor they perceive to offer better value.

As an example, consider a cup of beef bouillon. The food cost of a 5-ounce cup is about 10 cents. If it were priced to achieve a 40 percent food cost (a markup of 2.5 times its raw food cost) it would be underpriced at 25 cents. Since this item is usually served in white-tablecloth operations, the "custom-

Cash cows. Sometimes referred to as Plow Horses, these items are high-volume with below-average profit. Items that have a high competitive nature will probably fall into this category (particularly items that don't differentiate your menu from a number of other restaurants, including popular standbys like burgers). When working with cash cows on a menu, you will never want to highlight them, but instead bury them in the middle of a category. Cash cows are like milk in a grocery store -- making your guests read other items on the menu to find them may get them to trade up to something better for you.

Dawgs. Every restaurant has a few, some have a lot. Dawgs underperform in both profit and popularity, so if you cut an item this is often a great place to start. But before you start cutting Dawgs, you will need to look a little further first. If the items represent more than 25 percent of your overall business in a category, you may want to invest some time rethinking the items to see if you can increase their appeal. Also, cut items that are orphans first, as they are items that will hold your inventory ransom. An orphan is a product you inventory for only one menu item.

ary price point" could be $3.95 and it would not be considered overpriced by patrons. In fact, one technique for boosting the profitability of your menu is to offer low-cost, but popular items. The margins can be extraordinary, and boost the profitability of the house significantly.

Again, you need to look at each item separately, and determine which price seems reasonable. Applying a single markup method or marking up each item to return the same profit will result in items being overpriced and underpriced over what the customers see as "customary" in the market. If, for example, your cost to produce a common menu item like a hamburger was twice the cost of other restaurants, your price could not be twice the price of your competition. Your cost is excessive and needs to be addressed rather than shifted to your customers through excessive pricing; they simply will not pay it. You can only charge the "customary market price" for a hamburger unless you turned it into a "specialty" item. Markup is tempered by factors other than your food costs and profit targets.

It's Business as Usual

Regardless of the skill of the salesperson or the elegance of the pitch, ultimately, every product's key selling proposition is the perceived value to the customer. Any time people buy any product, be it a house, a quarter horse or a hamburger, they first do a simple calculation in their heads. They consider the product's function and price and decide if the two are close enough together to offer what they consider good value. If the function is too low to support the price, they won't buy. Or, if they are confused about the value of the offering, again the result is no sale.

Real Restaurateurs, *Real People*

Stories about people who realized their restaurant dreams

Farm-to-Table

In talking with Ivor Chodkowski about his restaurant 'Harvest' in Louisville Kentucky, you might think you heard him wrong when he discusses the size of the kitchen versus the size of the dining room. You might ask him to repeat himself just to be sure (as we did) and then you'll be in awe (as we were).

The dining room seats 100 people and is about 1,800 square feet. That's spacious and reasonable. But the kitchen is a mind-blowing 3,500 square feet.

Look at it this way: Experts recommend 30 square feet of building space per seat. So a 100-seat restaurant should be around 3,000 square feet. Again, using average recommended space calculations, the back of the Harvest,, including kitchen and storage, should be around 1,200 square feet.

But there's nothing average about Harvest, its owners or its success.Harvest is a brilliant example of the farm-to-table concept. Anyone who has worked in the kitchen of those restaurants knows that the space and staff required for prep work is often more than double that of other restaurants. Chodkowski knew that, as did his partners, all farmers in the Louisville region.

More than 80 percent of what is served at Harvest is raised within a 100-mile radius of the restaurant. Chodkowski doubles as a farmer himself and raises chickens, turkeys, hogs, black beans, corn, radishes and a few other vegetables.

The primary partners and a number of secondary investors had all met over the years at some of Louisville's numerous farmers' markets. Chodkowski and a few others had even worked in area kitchens doing some prep work on their produce, and they knew a good-sized kitchen was important. For almost four years, they talked about the concept and looked for the right space at the right price.

During that time, they also developed a funding source. Many entrepreneurs may be familiar with a crowd-funding website called Kickstarter, where individuals may post their ideas and solicit financial support from individuals. Kickstarter launched in 2009, but Chodkowski and his partners had set up a similar concept of their own in 2007, eventually raising the $500,000 they felt they needed to launch Harvest.

With money in hand, they finally found their ideal location in Louisville's East Market District, more popularly referred to as NuLu, and what's become the hottest spot in the city. A restaurant had last occupied the two-story space, but it had been sitting empty for about 18 months before the Harvest team signed the lease.

A significant stumbling point came when the remodeling began and the kitchen plumbing had to be brought up to a new sewer district overflow code. It could have been a lot more expensive, but the unexpected $10,000 outlay cut into plans to add a patio to the restaurant.

Chodkowski was able to use the kitchen's existing hood, dishwasher and gas line, but just about everything else had to be replaced. They bought some items used, but others were brand new. A half-dozen prep tables, a huge bread mixer, and refrigeration took up a lot of space, thus requiring them to knock out the wall that formerly separated the kitchen and dining area.

Today about 30 people can work simultaneously in the back-of-the-house with more ease than most restaurant kitchens offer teams of lesser size. That's one reason for the restaurant's success, says Chodkowski. The intense workload flows smoothly in a well-appointed space. Employee stress and turnover is also minimal, thanks in part to their good working space. Most of the BOH employees are fulltime and the 20 or so front-of-the-house people are part-timers.

Of course, customers only see what happens up front. The farm-to-table concept is emphasized with farmhouse style tables made of reclaimed wood, much of it from old tobacco barns in the region. Centerpieces include bundled wheat and locally-poured candles made of soy wax from locally-grown soybeans.

Customers seem to especially like the photos on the walls of the farmers who have contributed to the meal before them. Each photo is accompanied by a short biography identifying the farmer and what he or she raises. Another wall is dominated by a large map of the region with pins representing each farm that partners with Harvest to bring this concept to life.

To continue the flow of diners, the Harvest team hired a local PR professional who helped them create flyers that are regularly distributed at area farmers' markets. In addition to a Facebook page with a growing fan base, Harvest supports the local NPR affiliate and advertises in print outlets that are distributed via local hotels. Such efforts receive about $30,000 from Harvest's annual budget.

The Who, When, Where, What and Why of Selecting a Concept and Location

Chapter 4

There is plenty of opportunity to enjoy profitable business ownership for smart independent operators who apply sound restaurant business practices and can provide guests a unique and memorable experience. The big question: Should you be one of them?

Before you start some work, always ask yourself three questions - Why am I doing it, what the results might be and will I be successful. Only when you think deeply and find satisfactory answers to these questions, go ahead.
—Chanakya, Hindu teacher and philosopher.

If there is any term with which you should be familiar when contemplating becoming a restaurateur, it is 'concept'. Most likely, you already instinctively understand its meaning in the context of the restaurant business. There are 'concepts' built around quick-service chicken sandwiches, Mexican cuisine, upscale steak menus, and family-friendly atmospheres. Choosing the right concept for your first restaurant requires both soul-searching and pretty high-level market research.

You need to find a find a restaurant concept that fits your goals, interests and, even your personality. There are operators who are perfect for executing a small Irish pub concept. Others can bring something special to a Main Street breakfast/cafe eatery. And some operators have the drive, vision and resources to compete in the casual upscale market or a replicable quick-service concept that could morph into a regional chain. Each concept has its place and can bring satisfaction and wealth to the right operator.

The other part of the equation is determining if your market can support and/or sustain your concept. This is critical, whether you are starting a restaurant from scratch or buying an existing operation. Does your market have the demographics, in terms of potential guests and labor, to make your concept work or keep an ongoing concept afloat? Where is the population growth in your region? Who are your competitors?

The "Five W' Formula

In journalism or police crime investigations, the "Five W" questions are used to help research, understand and explain just about any set of circumstances.

So, You're Thinking About Owning, Operating or Investing in a Restaurant...

47

Determining the Who? What? When? Where? And Why? behind a situation provides a complete picture of the conditions before you. Answering those five questions can resolve many of life's uncertainties, and doing so is critically important when deciding whether to open the doors of a new restaurant.

Why?

Of the five single-word questions, 'Why?' is key. Just why do you want to do this? Is it for the money? You want to be your own boss? You love food and want to combine that affection with a career? You're after a different lifestyle?

Understanding your real motivation is a critical component in opening a restaurant. It's a difficult business, one that demands not only time and money, but a great deal of personal involvement, from originating the idea to planning to opening and beyond. Actually the excitement, decision-making and challenges of the opening phase are the really fun part of the restaurant business. That's why so many people become serial restaurateurs; they love the challenges and the thrill of the chase. The day-to-day part of actually running a restaurant present different challenges and rewards.

But before you get into either phase, you have you answer the Why? Failing to answer that fundamental question reduces the chance of restaurant success substantially.

There are, of course, lots of good reasons to get into the business just as there are many ways to justify or rationalize any decision. Restaurants are actually quite akin to a marriage. Your commitment, your ready investment of time and money and your flexibility are all key to its success. And there are literally hundreds of details that need your attention seemingly without end.

One answer to the question of why you want to open a restaurant can be found in the personality and career of current restaurant operators. While every independent restaurateur operates individually, there are common traits that brought them all to the business and bind them to a foodservice career. Many operators, particularly successful ones, like to talk about their success just as most of us do about things we've accomplished in various aspects of life. And one of the best ways to learn why you want to do something is to ask someone who is already doing it successfully. Call it informal real-life career counseling. Listening to their comments along with other people's work experiences can help you frame your own insights. It's a mirror into your future.

When Lance Morrow graduated from college, a mentor told him in order to make money he had to 'own something or sell something.' That advice launched the first step in his career. For six years he worked at Merrill Lynch selling stocks and bonds to individual investors. But he always wanted to own his own business, and was given that opportunity during a homecoming weekend at the University of Missouri.

Lance was able to buy a building which is now the Field House, a college hang-out in which half the 20,000 square foot space is a bar while the other half is for play — shooting pool, tossing darts, dancing, pinball wizardry and live music. He grew his restaurant business from there to additional concepts as he developed his own systems and procedures. With an education in finance and skills in construction, Morrow remains mostly self-taught when it comes to the restaurant industry.

Scott Acker entered the business because he wanted a car and needed a job to pay for it. He began washing dishes at a local Coco's. His early observation was that cooks worked less than dishwashers, but got paid more. He says, "I thought I'd like cooking because it was cool, and I like to eat." He worked his way up from there and at 19 was a district manager for five units of a steak chain. He and his partners now own several restaurants and with his background is a huge believer in systems. "Ray Kroc is my hero," he says and adds, "You would think running a restaurant would get easier with experience, but it doesn't always."

Visiting with current owners and operators like Lance and Scott in your local area can help you focus on the 'why?' of the restaurant question. While some may hold back, most are happy to talk about their experiences both positive and negative. As you dine out — something every perspective restaurateur should do often — asking questions of the managers and servers can produce terrific insights. Certainly ask questions on slow nights (and every restaurant has those), since those are the times when the managers are eager to speak with their diners.

Some of the questions to ask:

* I've always been interested in the restaurant business, how did you get into it?

* What's the best thing about what you do?

* Are there a lot of issues you face in this business? What are some of those?

* Our family is thinking about an investment in a restaurant; what's your advice?

* How did you choose this location?

* Where's the best place to go to find out more information on the restaurant business?

These questions are topic starters and can lead to more in-depth conversations. But understand that most operators, as with most other business people, do draw the line on answering questions on sales and numbers of return customers. Those can easily be found in restaurant magazines, books and websites. So, the best way not to end the discussion on 'why?' is to refrain from being too 'nosy'.

What?

As in, what are you going to offer? What type of food? What type of atmosphere? What are the demographics of the people you want as customers and what do they want to eat in what kind of environment?

Many potential restaurant owners have an idea of the type of restaurant they believe will work. Their wives (or husbands or brothers or sisters or grandmothers) have a special recipe or they've seen a concept while traveling that might work in their home city. Don't underestimate this 'gut feeling'

You knew going into this business that the restaurant market is crowded with competition, from other independents to national chains. What is it about **your** restaurant that puts it in a class of its own?

~ *Restaurant Startup & Growth* magazine/ RestaurantOwner.com

So, You're Thinking About Owning, Operating or Investing in a Restaurant...

49

approach since it has worked again and again. The fun of the restaurant business is coming up with new concepts and there is no question that many entrepreneurs have made fortunes with their ideas. McDonald's and Ray Kroc are extreme examples, but also good ones.

Asking 'what?' helps you home in your ability to quantify how your good idea can be turned into a profitable business. It not a simple process: it takes research, time and the ability to understand that an idea for your new business can come from many different directions; the work to make it a reality is the hard part.

George Nichols' dream of opening a restaurant started after a successful career as a business owner in another field. One day he walked into Culver's, an ice cream shop, in Kansas and loved the look of the food, the service, the hospitality and the whole Culver's concept. He grew up on the concept of frozen custard and that was one of Culver's specialties. By immersing yourself in Culver's 60-hour, week-long training program, as Nichols then did, you quickly learn if that business is something you really want to pursue.

If you're approved after that preliminary screening, you're sent to an actual operating Culver's for three months and take course in the company's Learning Center. What's learned there is not the end of your Culver's education. Rather, you're then sent to various locations to learn about labor laws and leadership, to complement your hands-on training in day-to-day operations in the real world, a world in which George Nichols thrived

Family is often the inspiration for many in the restaurant business. Just ask Cathy Morelli. She took over the family restaurant business and opened a new location only a few minutes away from where her parents launched Augustino's Rock & Roll Cafe in Illinois. Even with years of restaurant experience behind her, Morelli was confronted by a host of new situations, from changed menu ideas to changing procedures and systems.

The point is that the ways to enter the restaurant business are many and are discussed in other chapters of this book. Deciding on the concept for your new location should be at the top of your checklist, and the most creative item on your journey to opening day.

Once again a starting point for concept selection is a review of existing approaches and then finding a niche where your ideas can be merged with practical business opportunities. One of the best ways to do this is by collecting menus in person or on the Internet. Menus are the showcase of any restaurant, the tabletop billboard for its products and services. The choice of concepts and foods available to an aspiring restaurateur are almost limitless, so a good selection of menus can help identify what concepts you want and don't want to embrace.

For example, if you are considering opening an ethnic restaurant, then searching the Internet to see what other similarly-themed restaurants are doing is an easy way to build ideas. If you're thinking of creating an Argentine restaurant in Kansas City, for example, searching the Internet for ideas around the country, or for that matter, in Argentina, can help you focus on the specifics of what your menu should look like and the plates you should offer. Without exception, those who open restaurants are people who pay attention to what others are doing. The very best way experience that is by dining out frequently and carefull observing, so you can re-combine ideas, presentations and procedures learned first-hand into something uniquely yours.

Your own town is the perfect place to start. What restaurants are popular and why? Researching the 'what' will never been easier.

Where?

You need to learn and understand your proposed 'Trade Area'.

Questions about the potential trade area demographics — that is, the particulars of the area from which you'll most likely draw your guests — include: How big is it? Is the radius of your business going to be one, two or three miles, or in the restaurant intended to be 'a destination,' drawing people from longer distances? How many people and rooftops are in that radius? How many cars go by the location on a daily basis and at what time of day? How's the access to your restaurant? What are drive times from your location to different area population centers in the region? How many competitors in the trade area? What other restaurants are coming to the area that can help build or take away from your potential sales? Is the area growing? How visible will be the site you're considering? What's the residential and commercial activity? How does your daytime and evening menus fit with each of these questions? These are challenging questions, taking time and effort to answer well. And they're only the beginning.

The idea of 'Build it and they will come' may work in the movies, but probably not in restaurant site evaluations. These forgoing questions and many more, need to be addressed as part of any site selection process since the answers can have a dramatic effect on your potential success. One key element to consider in trade area demographics is restaurant density compared to population density. If there are too many restaurants for too few people, the weakest eateries will go out of business. If you're in an area overpopulated with restaurants, you'll have to provide the diners with a product and experience so superior to the competition's, they'll choose yours over the others. That can be a difficult challenge for the newest kid on the block.

McDonald's method of site selection is a good role model for so critical an undertaking. Notably, their researchers focus on concentration. Their initial rule of thumb: one McDonald's restaurant for every 30,000 people. Today, the chain has dropped the number to 15,000 or even 10,000. For other chains, the equation is different. For any independent, the numbers will also be different. Nevertheless, estimating the support base as part of the trade area evaluation is important.

In the real estate business, 'Location, Location, Location' is what matters most. In the restaurant business, that's not always the case...but it matters. Sometimes a lot. You need to have food, drink and service that match the

We all can describe the Chipolte or Subway experience in a few sentences, in terms of the food and service. Can your guests do the same for your restaurant? Before you say that you are not looking to create a fast-food empire or even a small chain, consider the importance of being memorable.

~ Restaurant Startup & Growth magazine/ RestaurantOwner.com

needs of your potential guests in your trade area. Just having a good location does not guarantee success, but no matter how good your concept or your operation, it's very difficult to overcome the negative impact of a bad location.

The purpose of this chapter is to find tools that can significantly reduce the risk of selecting a bad location and enhance the odds of choosing the optimum market and location for a particular concept.

In today's interconnected world, the Internet is a good research tool. America is a data-rich nation with more statistics on record than any other country. National, state, regional, county, and city data are available with some keystrokes on your laptop. Population information by zip code, age demographics, income distribution it's all readily available, and most of the time it is free. Make the most of it as you plan your new venture.

And you can get help in making sense of the numbers. There are many companies that specialize in analyzing demographic data, pinpointing the per-capita income of the residents in a given location, for example. Real estate brokers use this kind of information, and often share it with prospective buyers to promote sales.

An operator looking at opening a new store in, for instance, Greenville, South Carolina, and who wanted to know who lives in Greenville, could get that information from the local real estate board. You can also obtain detailed data from organizations such as Trulia (www.trulia.com), which will do the demographics down to block by block and tell you how much money everybody makes who lives on that street.

Trulia (and other similar services) have changed the real estate business for those looking to relocate. Enter the name of a place where you're considering buying a house, and the site will give you detailed demographic information about the neighborhood residents.

Area demographics is the heart of the matter — the keys to the kingdom, if you will — for restaurant operators looking to open or expand. "You've got to know the demography, the ethnicity, and whether or not you want to take a chance on something because the demography says it's a young group and they all go to college at these 10 colleges. You want to know age, ethnicity, and even topography. Is it a location that's easy to get to on foot or bicycle?

When data mining, use your imagination regarding what you want to know about the market to make your location an appealing choice for your target guests. The chains are doing it. And for the most part, they are doing it well. Independents wanting to compete need to employ some of the same methodology.

There are numerous other sources that can be used to flesh out any information you need to understand a general location and then delve down into specific potential sites. The Internet can save time by allowing you to type in real estate business properties and sites for sale and receive instant results.

All of the major real estate company brands have commercial divisions that are delighted to share their listings of available restaurant properties.

Real estate developer information packages always include valuable data on the surrounding areas. Much of the information is based on the U.S. Census, along with privately gathered data, and all of it can be useful in providing an overview and helping to solidify business plans. The realtors all have extensive websites, too. And the Internet listings through sites such as Loopnet.com, localagent.com, commercialsource.com, cityfeet.com Zillow and hundreds of others show potential property locations.

Local and city governments, particularly the larger ones, have a wealth of information on traffic studies, development areas, sales tax receipts and other data. They use this information to plan roads, sewers and other public services. Here again, prospective business owners need to dig through this data field and ask questions. The key is matching your concept with the information you've learned from searching the area demographics.

Another good starting place for information is the U.S. Census Bureau. The address is: thttp://www.census.gov/main/www/access.html. The interactive data tools shown on the website's opening page will give you an idea of the wealth of information available. Because of the depth of bureau's data, most all other demographic research starts here. A sampling of the information available through the bureau:

• Data Visualization Gallery — A weekly exploration of Census data used to promote visualization and make data accessible to a broader audience.

• 2010 Census Interactive Population Map — Use this tool to explore 2010 Census statistics down to the block level, compare your community with others, and embed charts on your web site.

• The American FactFinder — This interactive application provides statistics from the Economic Census, the American Community Survey, and the 2010 Census, among others.

• QuickFacts — State and County QuickFacts provides frequently requested Census Bureau information at the national, state, county, and city level.

• Easy Stats — quick access to selected statistics collected by the U.S. Census Bureau through the American Community Survey.

• County Business & Demographics Map — use this interactive map to explore Census data through a mash up of population and economic data.

• Economic Database Search and Trend Charts — Easy access to Economic Statistics using drop-down menus. Create tables in ASCII text and spreadsheet format. Display customizable dynamic charts.

• Glossary — Simple definitions of key Census Bureau terms.

• Cen stats — Applications available include: Census Tract Street Locator, County Business Patterns, Zip Business Patterns, International Trade Data, and more.

• Online Mapping Tools — using TIGER and the American FactFinder

• U.S. Gazetteer — Place name, and ZIP code search engine.

• Business Dynamics Statistics (BDS) — This tool shows tabulations on establishments, firms, and employment with unique information on firm age and firm size.

So, You're Thinking About Owning, Operating or Investing in a Restaurant...

53

- Visualization Tools — Visualize BDS data across multiple dimensions:
  - Geographic — Thematic Map
  - Cross Sectional — Bar Charts
  - Time — Time Series
- DataFerrett — a tool and data librarian that searches and retrieves data across federal, state, and local surveys, executes customized variable recoding, creates complex tabulations and business graphics. Current Population Survey, Survey of Income and Program Participation, American Community Survey, American Housing Survey, Small Area Income Poverty Estimates, Population Estimates, Economic Census Areawide Statistics, National Center for Health Statistics data, Centers for Disease Control data, and more.

DataFerrett's newest tool — the Community Economic Development HotReport — provides community and business leaders speedy access to information on counties and the Employment & Training Administration's Workforce Innovation in Regional Economic Development (WIRED) areas across the U.S.

- The Local Employment Dynamics partnership offers a variety of data tools including the following:

  - QWI Online: Select and find out about NAICS-based or SIC-based Quarterly Workforce Indicators by state, geographic grouping, industry, year and quarter, sex, age group, and ownership.

  - OnTheMap: This tool shows where workers are employed and where they live through an interactive and geographically flexible mapping interface. The maps, charts, and reports also provide detailed worker characteristics such as age, earnings, NAICS industry sector, as well as information on race, ethnicity, and educational attainment.

  - Industry Focus: This tool lets you determine the top industries for your local area and your local workers, focus on a particular industry to see how it ranks among top industries, and also look at the characteristics of those who work in that industry.

- Census 2010 EEO Data Tool — Using the web-based tool, you can select tabulations for various levels of geography based on residence or workplace. The data estimates available present information for various occupation groupings by race and ethnicity and sex.

- Research Data Centers

  - Secure Census Bureau Research Data Centers across the country offer qualified researchers with approved projects the opportunity to perform statistical analysis on selected internal microdata from the Census Bureau and other statistical agencies.

- Software to Download

  - Extract Software — General purpose data display and extraction tool that works with Census Bureau CD-ROMs recorded in dBASE format - (for: PCs and compatibles with CD-ROM player)

- VPLX Software — Variance Estimation for Complex Samples (for PCs and compatibles and UNIX)

- CSPro (Census and Survey Processing System) is a public-domain software package for entering, tabulating and mapping census and survey data.

- IMPS software — The Integrated Microcomputer Processing System (IMPS) software performs the major tasks of census and survey processing.

• Direct File Access

- Census 2010 datasets

- Census OUTGOING File Directory (HTTP) — Pickup files from Census Employees.

• Access Tools at Other Sites

- Integrated Public Use Microdata Series — iPUMS (University of Minnesota).

Warning! This census data searching can be time consuming. There is so much information and ways to slice, dice and access it you can spend hours analyzing and playing with the numbers. For example, one of the interactive maps on the website allows you to select your county to find the percentage of male versus female, ages of county residents, populations by race, family type housing and a variety of other parameters down to the block level.

Anyone seriously considering opening any retail business, restaurant or otherwise, should take a look at this free resource to understand the basic composition of their potential trade area. If you're constructing a business plan for investors, this information can help you provide perspective of who you'll be selling to and why your concept and location will work.

Another government source not to be overlooked is the Small Business Administration (SBA), whose website (www.sba.gov) has extensive information on helping individuals open and grow local business. Created in 1953 as an independent agency of the federal government to aid, counsel, assist and protect the interests of small business concerns, the SBA provides information and assistance for all types of businesses including restaurants.

The agency also links to www.business.use.gov, which offers comparative data on other businesses located by zip code. This data is limited and can be out of date as businesses come and go in specific areas, but it is another information source that can be used in your research and business plan.

How the Chains Select Sites. The restaurant chains are experts in picking the right place because they sign long-term leases and location is one of the few aspects of a restaurant you can't easily change. That's why their professional staffs and outside consultants spend so much time studying traffic movement, site visibility, area population density, and rental and lease factors.

H.G. Parsa, Ph.D., FMP, Barron Hilton chair in lodging and professor of hospitality management of the Daniels College of Business at the University of Denver in Colorado, says the rule of thumb for most restaurant busi-

You establish **relationships** through recognizing the great things that are happening in your restaurant on every shift every day.

~ *Restaurant Startup & Growth* magazine/ RestaurantOwner.com

So, You're Thinking About Owning, Operating or Investing in a Restaurant...

55

nesses is to keep real estate costs below 7 percent of projected revenue. "The next thing they usually look at," he says, "is how much it's going to cost to remodel or renovate; and development cost. All of that together should not exceed that 7 percent." Again, they project revenue, and decide if the rent factor is sustainable. If this sounds simple, bear in mind that many prospective restaurateurs don't go through this analysis with sufficient rigor, and suffer the consequences after they open their doors.

Other rules of thumb from Restaurantowner.com point out that rent should be around 6% or less as a percentage of total sales and total occupancy cost (rents, utilities, insurance) should be 10% or less as a percentage of total sales. Sales to investment ratios (Annual Sales/Startup Costs) for a lease hold restaurant should be at least 1.5 to 1, while for an owner owning the land and building, the ratio should be 1 to 1.

While it wouldn't be easily replicated, McDonald's strategy can offer lessons for even the smallest independent.

"McDonald's has a beautiful strategy," Parsa says. "They purchase real estate before it becomes expensive. They know land is cheap now, but that it's going to go up two, three, four years from now," if for no other reason than that the presence of McDonald's draws other major players.

"Once McDonald's comes," Parsa continues, "that's an attraction in itself. Other businesses will come, and the other businesses will pay higher rent and real estate than McDonald's." In short, the Golden Arches function like the proverbial Golden Goose. They can quickly improve the value of the real estate.

Parsa says, "When I was working for Wendy's, they asked me, 'How do you think Arby's and other companies find a new location?' I told them, 'Very easy: Look for where McDonald's is putting its restaurants and follow them,' and that is what they do." This is certainly an easy approach for the independent because it is simply a matter of locating the big players to see where they are building. Then the trick becomes seeing if the concept will match the location the big chains have chosen.

But in spite of its market cachet, McDonald's is not arbitrary about its location choices. And here is where you can emulate the chain, albeit on a smaller, less sophisticated scale, if you are willing to invest some shoe leather.

"I can speak to how McDonald's does it, since this is what I used to do there," says Melanie Smythe, principal of Candacity LLC, a consultancy based in Richfield, Wisconsin. "The regional development team drives to the potential market and maps out the trade area. They review demographics of the potential customer base by looking at who lives/works within the boundaries and travels to the area." They then compare surrounding trade areas for existing locations to make sure there is no overlap or, if there is, that it is not detrimental to the nearby locations. They also review the competition within and around the trade area.

"They look out over five to 10 years of development increases or decreases if it is a shrinking market," Smythe says. "They then assign potential sales figures and review the cost of going into business to determine if it is a viable site." If the location does, in fact, meet those thresholds, it is then reviewed by committee. If approved, it is offered to potential franchisees.

Sure, most independent operators can't afford teams of real estate specialists hunting for the next great market area. That said, you can hedge your bets to some degree by taking a trip to your town or city planning department and look at the local zoning map.

Perhaps there is an affordable parcel near a large tract of undeveloped land. Is it zoned for high-density housing, single-family homes or commercial use? Ask planning department staffers if they can tell you who is eyeing the land.

Anyone can join the local chamber of commerce, Kiwanis, Rotary, etc., and attend its functions. Developers and real estate people comprise a significant portion of the membership of these organizations. Don't be afraid to join and then "ask around." You might learn, for example, that a retirement community will occupy that dusty field across from a strip mall in a couple of years, and thus provide a good stream of future business for your coffee shop concept.

Just as this kind of research can help you spot opportunities, it can help you avoid blunders. A mistake successful chain operators avoid is settling alongside bad neighbors. Independents need to learn the same lesson.

For example, if you're selecting a location that's right next to a recycling plant, which could come with frequent truck traffic and pests. You most likely would not want to have a four-star restaurant on a street where a high school empties out right in front of your door. On the other hand, plunking a fast-food restaurant down at a bus stop so that commuters would be lingering right in front of your door — and perhaps have the impulse to grab a sandwich or cup of coffee to go — might be an excellent idea.

A recurring question about site selection centers on whether it's good to have competitors nearby. A rule of thumb is that you want to be where there are more rather than fewer restaurants. That's because not everybody makes a destination restaurant their choice for the day. They might say, 'OK, let's go to Joe's.' and when they got to Joe's it's packed. In such a case, those same would-be customers might want to go across the street because another restaurant is over there. If you're standing in front of Joe's and it's packed, and you have to get in your car and drive somewhere else, it might make you less inclined to go there next time. That's one theory. Another has to do with population density. That one holds if there's not enough population density for the number of restaurants in an area, it's almost impossible for the weakest one to stay in business.

Diners, in short, want to go where the action is. They may be willing to travel way off the beaten path for a favorite destination restaurant but if they do it's probably not going to be a chain. There are plenty of chain units at convenient locations. Whether you plunk down your business among chains

So, You're Thinking About Owning, Operating or Investing in a Restaurant...

57

or apart from them, as an independent, you have to make sure you differentiate from their food and service offerings.

Said another way: You can't complete with IHOP by emulating IHOP! If guests want Harvest Grain 'n Nut pancakes or Bananas and Cream Belgian waffles, they will gravitate to IHOP, regardless of whether you are next door or across town. You have to offer something special they can't get at a chain — in terms of atmosphere, menu or service — to make the cut.

About Previous Restaurant Locations. It seems like the perfect solution. Move into a current restaurant location that has gone dark for one reason or another. There are plenty of these available. There is a natural turnover in any marketplace including among restaurants. People retire, fail financially, pass-on, burn out, or for whatever reason, padlock their doors. The locations become available with almost everything in place including kitchen equipment, hoods, even tables and chairs.

Occupying this space with your own concept can be a good option, but it can be a risky venture as well. With more than 40 years of experience in the restaurant business, Kevin Heaton knows that. But with two successful restaurants within a five-mile radius and a solid presence in the community, Heaton thought he could pull it off.

"I thought with my operation experience and ability, I could pull it off," says the owner of The Rusty Horse Tavern in Parkville, Missouri. "I liked the challenge of making it better, but this location was a mistake." (Heaton eventually sold the tavern.)

After 16 months of operation, The Rusty Horse was paying its bills, but not making money yet. And that's not good enough for Heaton, a no-nonsense businessman who saw an eight-percent growth in his other restaurants during the same period.

The Parkville location is problematic for multiple reasons, all completely out of Heaton's control. First, the restaurant is in a utilitarian shopping center with little foot traffic. A hardware store, a veterinary clinic and a grocery store are among his closest neighbors. The view from the patio includes a lot for the local school district's fleet of yellow school buses.

However, parking is plentiful and the shopping center is at the intersection of two major highways. Visibility from the highways is limited. City ordinances prevent additional signage where they would be most beneficial.

But Heaton believes that the biggest factor preventing the restaurant's growth is the fact that other restaurants in this spot failed.

"The public has a trust factor and they've been burned in this location before," he says. "They often want to wait and see if the place makes it before they commit and that's hard for even the best operator to overcome."

One of Heaton's biggest challenges in getting the restaurant open was simply cleaning it. The previous operators had been cited for code violations on a number of occasions and the back of the house was disgustingly filthy.

For winning concepts, consistency in design, menu and execution of daily operations makes for a successful guest experience and that is what creates customer loyalty.

~ *Restaurant Startup & Growth* magazine/ RestaurantOwner.com

Neither had those operators taken responsibility for basic maintenance, so although the mechanical, electrical and plumbing were all in place, all required investments of time and money to get them in good working order.

However, in stepping into this location, Heaton has a problem that many restaurant operators might envy — the kitchen measures 1,500 square feet, a cavernous back space for a 3,500 square foot restaurant that seats 130 people. As it happens, that's a problem, too.

"You could park a big car in the walk-in cooler," he says. "It's way too big for our operation, but it's cheaper to use this one than purchase new. It's simply a waste of space."

The Rusty Horse Tavern is a burger joint, while Heaton's other operations are pizza restaurants. He tested the burger concept for several months of 'Burger Thursdays' at one of the pizza locations and received enough positive response to move forward with the concept.

The tavern opened with 20 items on the menu, but that has evolved and Heaton's are now on the third re-write with 43 items listed. In hindsight, he wishes he had started with a little lower price point and grown to his current price structure.

"I don't see that as a negative, but a result of our managers listening to the customers," he says. "We know the burgers are good, but we hear that customers want more healthy options as well and that's the direction we're moving, without losing the basic burger that the concept is about."

So that was the beginning of marketing The Rusty Horse — just talking it up with customers at the two pizza locations and utilizing the word-of-mouth marketing strategy. The risk of that practice, however, is taking away customers from one location to fill the other. Heaton did not see any serious impact on the pizza operations, but it is a risky practice.

Heaton implemented a social media campaign. A direct mail campaign did not produce the desired results, but he found that stories in local print publications have generated more traffic. If he had the budget, Heaton would have preferred to advertise on television.

If he had it to do all over again, Heaton says he would have invested another $250,000 and built a brand new restaurant in a prime location. But he was lured into the lower start-up price and a location with relatively 'good bones.'

His advice to others looking at a space where other restaurants failed: "Don't do it. Pay the money for an A location and make it yours."

Trust the Wisdom of Your Gut. Angela Phelan, senior vice president of The Clarion Group, a business consultancy, based in Kingston, NH, says she learned a lot about researching chain locations in the 1980s while she was working on tenant development for the South Street Seaport in lower Manhattan. When this historical site opened, 20 different chain restaurant operators said they had to be there. For most, she says, their decision was based on, "'Where is the hot location in town?' Everybody thought that the Seaport would be a good thing."

The person who gave Phelan the best lesson on the power of intuition to choose a location — "and it has been borne out over the last 25 years," she says — was Louis Kane, then the president of Au Bon Pain. "The reason I got to know him was that his first store was in Cambridge, right on Harvard Yard, and that did very well. Then he decided he wanted to come to New York. Like a lot of people, he thought that the South Street Seaport would be a very good place to be." Kane opened his store in a second-floor location.

"I always loved his products, and I couldn't understand why he wasn't doing well," she says. "Since my job was to understand how the operators could do well I spent some time looking at traffic patterns and whatever. Finally I called him up and I said, 'You don't know me Mr. Kane, but I'm in charge of tenant relations and I think your store is in the wrong place.'

The pair met, and before long Phelan suggested a new location, and asked Kane to come take a look at it. According to Phelan, he told her, "When I'm doing a deal, no matter how good the numbers look, if I don't have that gut instinct that it's the right place then I either have to move it or I don't go there in the first place.'

Gut instinct might be an important factor in selecting any location. Says Phelan, "Operators crunch all the numbers and look at how many people are going to walk across that sidewalk a hundred times a day." Kane told her it had to feel right to him, including being on the "sunny side of the street."

Kane's store ultimately moved to a location down on the main level, in a much more obvious traffic pattern. That said, he took the time to evaluate the new location personally.

At that point, Kane was an experienced chain operator; but his lesson holds great wisdom for all start-up and growth operators. Even if you have little experience in the restaurant business, you and your partners, family and friends have experience dining out. You know where you would travel for a given dining experience.

Remember the age-old management axiom: "When all else fails, trust your gut. It will never intentionally deceive you."

Words of Wisdom: Hire a Professional Site Evaluator

Consider hiring a professional site profiler; they're worth the money in several ways. Because real estate development is such an important and complex activity, entire businesses have developed to service the needs of those seeking help in selecting the correct locations for everything from gas stations to hospitals to restaurants. It's a big business and one worth looking into even for the smallest of independents.

Because in most cases these companies do not also sel real estate, they have no vested interest in promoting one location over another. That means they work for you and not someone trying to sell you a location. Jim Fisher of IMST Corporation specializes in helping evaluate potential sites for a variety of retail businesses, including restaurants. IMST doesn't seek out sites, but uses its experience and computer models to evaluate the viability of a particular site for a stated use.

Continued on page 61

Continued from page 60

Fisher says one of the biggest traps for prospective operators is their falling in love with a particular site location — "a site land love affair," is his terminology — even though it is not well suited for the intended use. An unbiased evaluation of potential locations is the best approach for owners and investors who hope to actually profit from it.

Professional evaluators have seen thousands of deals at all levels and back that experience by developing models and algorisms of what has worked and what has not. They also have developed sources for finding information that is often unavailable, unknown to others or difficult to access. Like all professionals, they have trade secrets that add value to what they're offering and those can be very beneficial when you're about to about to lay your investment dollar on the table.

The costs of these services run between $3,500 and $10,000 plus travel costs for personnel to visit the location — a relatively modest expense when you consider the total investment of opening a restaurant, particularly if that involves any building or substantial remodeling.

Finding these independent real estate site evaluation companies can be confusing since many real estate firms that offer such services as well. But, as noted, first and foremost, realtors are in the business of selling property and thus may not be as unbiased as you would like. You need an independent firm that does sales forecasts, feasibility studies, market analysis and property research.

This independence is one reason banks and investors like to see a professional site evaluation. It gives them confidence that their investment carries less risk because it has been studied and reviewed by an organization not 'married' to the site. This alone can be worth the upfront expense and can also save you from yourself. If one of these professional groups gives a 'thumbs down' on the location, they may be saving you a lot of money and heartbreak

When

Timing is everything in this business. Once your research phase is completed, financial arrangements are concluded, and it's time to begin the actual process of opening the doors and inviting customers inside, that's when the real dollars also begin to move rapidly out of your pocket.

Pulling all of the elements together can and will be challenging, but that's part of the fun. It becomes less enjoyable when things start to fall behind schedule, since the money will continue to flow out. Delays are inevitable and building a budget that takes these contingencies into account is key. Restaurant TV programs may show a facility being built or remodeled in a day or two, but in reality the process takes a lot more time and more resources. The fact is most restaurants do not open on their planned schedules. It's just part of the process. Even large chains that have repeated the opening process often find delays in inspections, licenses, deliveries or any number of things that are required to start serving meals to the public. We know of one well-respected chain in the South Florida area that forgot to apply for a liquor license for a new facility in a very upper scale location and its opening was delayed several weeks as a result.

Every year thousands of new independent restaurants do open their doors. New restaurant business licenses are issued all year long and setting

So, You're Thinking About Owning, Operating or Investing in a Restaurant...

61

> A good leader ensures he or she is surrounded by talented people, to whom he or she listens as well as directs. Every person in your operation, from dishwasher to general manager, has a unique view of your operation and each has valuable lessons to share. Remaining open to others' ideas and constructive criticism, regardless of the source, are powerful ways to lead.
>
> ~ Christopher Koetke

an opening date is the first step. Then working backwards with a solid opening checklist is a key to your opening success. RestaurantOwner.com compiled a checklist of some 300 items that can guide in a systematic way the timing of a restaurant startup. RestaurantOwner.com members can access the "Restaurant Startup Checklist" (and others) at:

http://www.restaurantowner.com/public/DOWNLOAD-Restaurant-Checklists.cfm

Who

The final "W" may be the most important to any restaurant startup. Who is going to do what? The answer is made all the more important because the diversity of skills needed for a restaurant to be successful. After all, a restaurant is both a manufacturing plant and a retail operation and needs personnel skilled in those respective areas.

There are lots of ways things can go wrong, which in the trade is known as being "in the weeds".

During Prohibition, aspeakeasy would often stash extra liquor behind the restaurant and if the place became very busy, a manager would have to retrieve fresh bottles from the "weeds" to continue serving customers. The saying has carried over to current restaurant slang and is used to let everyone know that things are falling behind. Always being in the weeds is a sign that the operations may need some fine tuning.

The chain restaurants have developed step-by-step systems that, along with their limited menus, provide them the ability to hire people with fewer skills than are commonly found in employees at independent operations. Their specially designed equipment and limiting any one worker to doing only one or two things on one or two parts of their menu is a completely different work environment from most independent operators. It's also why the chains, along with their buying power and low-wage policies, generally show a much higher profit margin than do independents with their multiple menus and more complex operations.

To a large degree your staff "is" your independent restaurant. The quality of the interaction of the staff with your guests is just one of many areas where your people can either make or break your business. Your staff not only has a lot to do with the success of your restaurant, but with the quality of your life, too. Dealing with people can be agony or ecstasy, the source of your greatest frustrations or your most gratifying accomplishments.

Most of us never got any good people training along the way. Bill Marvin, the "Restaurant Doctor" says, "When we go into management positions, we're just expected to understand what people are all about." The problem is that most of us don't intuitively know what makes people tick, and as a result, get involved in all sorts of counterproductive and self-defeating approaches in managing and dealing with people.

In the past, some operators succeeded despite a severe deficit in people skills because they could simply draw from what seemed to be an inexhaustible supply of disposable labor. If an employee didn't work out, you could count on plenty of other applicants eager to fill that slot. Those days are gone, and today you need good people more than they need you.

This is one reason why creating, and using, job descriptions is important in the independent restaurant environment. Not only do job descriptions help any operator control workflow, they are also invaluable in the hiring process. Job descriptions give you a benchmark by which to communicate your expectations and evaluate performance, both good and bad. To make these important tools useful, they need to accurately describe to an applicant the details of a position before they are hired. The person needs an accurate picture of what the job entails up front so, if hired, they can be a successful employee in your restaurant.

The key jobs in any restaurant include the General Manager, Assistant Managers, an Events Manager, Kitchen Manager, Servers, Dishwasher, Line Cooks, Prep Cooks, Bus People, Host/Hostess Bartender and in larger operations a Human Resource Director.

Complete job descriptions with checklists and qualifications can be downloaded from www.restaurantowner.com and used as templates or starting points for each position in your restaurant. Training manuals for each position are also part of restaurantowner.com service. It is important for your job descriptions to accurately represent the unique activities, responsibilities and expectations for each position. Here are some position summaries that can be expanded to help formulate the type of information that should be constructed for your specific needs:

General Manager. Oversees and coordinates the planning, organizing, training and leadership necessary to achieve stated objectives in sales, costs, employee retention, guest service and satisfaction, food quality, cleanliness and sanitation. The person holding this position must understand all policies, procedures, standards, specifications, guidelines and training programs. It is the general manager's responsibility to ensure that all guests feel welcome and are given responsive, friendly and courteous service at all times.

A key part of the position is to ensure that all food and products are consistently prepared and served according to the restaurant's recipes, portioning, cooking and serving standards.

The general manager is responsible for achieving company objectives in sales, service, quality, appearance of facility and sanitation and cleanliness through training of employees and creating a positive, productive working environment. The person controls cash and other receipts by adhering to cash handling and reconciliation procedures in accordance with restaurant policies and procedures.

So, You're Thinking About Owning, Operating or Investing in a Restaurant...

63

Treat Your Staff Well

How you treat your staff is the way they will treat your guests. While treating your people well is no guarantee that all of them will pour out exceptional service to your guests, just exhibit a little disrespect and condescension their way and see what you get. It's not only unreasonable, but also dangerous for restaurant operators to ignore or pay little attention to how their employees feel they're being treated. The working climate management creates has a huge effect on the level of care your guests receive.

The general manager is responsible for making employment and termination decisions and fills in where needed to ensure guest service standards and efficient operations. The person must continually strive to develop the staff in all areas of managerial and professional development, and also prepare all required paperwork, including forms, reports and schedules in an organized and timely manner.

In addition the general manager ensures that all equipment is kept clean and kept in excellent working condition through personal inspection and by following the restaurant's preventative maintenance programs. Job duties include inspections to see that all products are received in correct unit count and condition and deliveries are performed in accordance with the restaurant's receiving policies and procedures. It is also the general manager's responsibility to oversee restaurant policies on employee performance appraisals are followed and completed on a timely basis.

Other important elements of the job are scheduling labor as required by anticipated business activity while ensuring that all positions are staffed when and as needed; meeting labor cost objectives; being knowledgeable of restaurant policies regarding personnel; and administering prompt, fair and consistent corrective action for any and all violations of company policies, rules and procedures.

A general manager must also fully understand and comply with all federal, state, county and municipal regulations that pertain to health, safety and labor requirements of the restaurant, employees and guests. And whomever holds that position is responsible for developing, planning and carrying out restaurant marketing, advertising and promotional activities and campaigns.

Assistant General Manager. Oversee and coordinate the planning, organizing, training and provide the leadership necessary to achieve stated objectives in sales, costs, employee retention, guest service and satisfaction, food quality, cleanliness and sanitation.

The person in this position must understand completely all policies, procedures, standards, specifications, guidelines and training programs. The assistant general manager has many of the same responsibilities as the general manager and needs to make sure all guests feel welcome and are given responsive, friendly and courteous service at all times and that all food and products are consistently prepared and served according to the restaurant's recipes, portioning, cooking and serving standards. The position requires the administration of prompt, fair and consistent corrective action for any and all personnel violations of company policies, rules and procedures, and offering advice and suggestions to the general manager as warranted.

Chef/ Kitchen Manager. Directly responsible for all kitchen functions including food purchasing, preparation and maintenance of quality standards; sanitation and cleanliness; training of employees in methods of cooking, preparation, plate presentation, portion and cost control and sanitation and cleanliness.

Of course this is a key position in any restaurant and particularly so in any independent operation. This job requires special knowledge and is critical for a wide variety of reasons including food safety and motivating customers to return. The position oversees and directs that all food and products are consistently prepared and served according to the restaurant's recipes, portioning, cooking and serving standards.

Critical to the position is making employment and termination decisions including interviewing, hiring, evaluating and disciplining kitchen personnel as appropriate; providing orientation of company and department rules, policies and procedures; and overseeing training of new kitchen employees.

Maintaining paperwork is also an important part of the job, ensuring that all invoices, food counts forms, reports and schedules are kept in an organized and timely manner. Also a key responsibility is keeping all equipment clean and in excellent working condition through personal inspection and by following the restaurant's preventative maintenance programs.

Working with owners and other managers to plan and price menu items is critical to the position, as is establishing portion controls, sizes and systems and preparing standard recipe cards for all new menu items. The chef/kitchen manager creates ordering systems according to predetermined product specifications thereby ensuring delivery in correct unit counts and condition and in accordance with the restaurant's receiving policies and procedures.

Controlling food cost, usage and waste and maintaining proper inventory levels and conditions are as critical to this position as the ability to consistently prepare standard recipes.

Managing, scheduling and training kitchen personnel, and then providing performance appraisals on a timely basis are things expected of the chef/kitchen manager. To do all that means the person must be knowledgeable of restaurant policies regarding personnel and then administer prompt, fair and consistent corrective action for any and all violations of company policies, rules and procedures.

Servers. Provide friendly, responsive service to create an exceptional dining experience for all of our guests. The servers' primary objective is to show guests such a marvelous time that they will want to return again and again. They must welcome and greet guests, make them comfortable and assure them they'll be personally cared for and informed of specials and menu changes.

Good servers should be able to make recommendations that they genuinely feel their diners will enjoy and also answer questions about the food, beverages and other restaurant functions and services. They must be able to take food and beverage orders from guests, enter orders in the point-of-sale system that relays orders to the kitchen and bar, and to deliver food and beverages from kitchen and bar to guests in a timely manner.

Servers Are Your Sales Force

For all but quick-service restaurant concepts, servers play an important role in not only insuring guest satisfaction, but driving revenue. They should be intimately familiar with the menu, to help patrons choose items that will best suit their tastes, and suggest appetizer, drinks and desserts to complement their entrees.

So, You're Thinking About Owning, Operating or Investing in a Restaurant...

65

They are expected to perform side work at the start and end of each shift as required by service station assignment and to maintain clean service areas while monitoring their guests' dining experience. They need to ensure guests are satisfied with the food and service and respond promptly and courteously to any of their requests. Servers are required to be ready and willing to assist fellow servers as situations arise and to assist the bus person with clearing and resetting tables when needed.

Preparing and double checking a customer's final bill, presenting it to the guest, making changes to those charges, if applicable, accepting payment, and processing credit card charges are particularly important roles for the servers since it is during those exchanges that customers frequently decide to return, or not. Thanking the guest for dining and inviting them to return is a final step in the service requirements for this position.

As directed by the restaurant manager or immediate supervisor, servers also need to be available to fill in as needed to ensure the smooth and efficient operation of the restaurant.

Line Cook. Prepare, portion and then accurately and efficiently cook the meats, fish, vegetables, soups and other hot food products. Also perform other related duties including plating and garnishing of cooked items.

The line cook's job includes preparing a food items for cooking in broilers, ovens, grills, fryers and a variety of other kitchen equipment and assuming complete responsibility for the quality of products served. That means the cook must know and comply consistently with the restaurant's standard portion sizes, cooking methods, quality and kitchen rules, policies and procedures.

A qualified line cook must stock and maintain sufficient levels of food products at line stations to assure a smooth service, and must portion the food products prior to cooking according to standard portion sizes and recipe specifications. The cook must also maintain a clean and sanitary work station area to include tables, shelves, grills, broilers, fryers, pasta cookers, sauté burners, convection oven, flat top range and refrigeration equipment.

Proper plate presentation and garnish set-up for all dishes is important to generating customer satisfaction and is a key to a successful line position. The line cook must also handle, store and rotate all product properly. During slow periods, line cooks assist in food prep assignments and later follow checklists for closing the kitchen with the assistance of other kitchen staff. The person holding this position should have a minimum of two years experience in kitchen preparation and cooking and at least six months experience in a similar capacity.

Prep Cook(s). Prepare and cook meats, seafood, poultry, vegetables, sauces, stocks, breads and other food products using a variety of equipment and utensils, according to the daily prep list. Mustcomplete kitchen opening and closing checklists and refer to daily prep list at the start of each shift for assigned duties. Must understand and comply with consistent standard portion sizes, cooking methods, quality standards and kitchen rules, policies and procedures, while always maintaining clean and sanitary work stations, including tables, shelves, walls grills, broilers, fryers, pasta cookers, sauté burners, convection oven, flat top range and refrigeration equipment.

Prep cooks must always report equipment and food quality or shortages problems to the chef/kitchen manager. They should use their restaurant's standard recipe cards for preparing all products and not rely on their memory or that of other employees to accomplish that.

They also perform other related duties as assigned by the kitchen manager or manager-on-duty.

A minimum of one year of experience in kitchen preparation is typically required for this position and at least six months experience in a similar capacity.

Prep cooks should be able to communicate clearly with managers and kitchen personnel. The job is physically challenging, and applicants should be able to reach, bend, stoop and frequently lift up to 40 pounds and work in a standing position for long periods of time (up to 5 hours).

Dishwasher. The job title says it all...almost. The person must wash and clean to the highest standards plates, glasses, knives, forks, spoons, pots, pans and cooking equipment, all the while keeping the dish room and equipment clean and organized.

It's that person's responsibility to load, run and unload the dish machine and keep it functioning at proper temperatures to ensure sanitary wash cycles. Failing that task puts the entire restaurant at risk. In addition, excessive breakage issues or the incorrect application of washing and sanitizing chemicals can have an important negative effect on restaurant expenses, so maintaining order is keenly important as bussers and servers deposit used glassware and utensils.

In addition, dishwashers are generally responsible for bagging and hauling trash to the dumpster, and it's important for the restaurant's cost controls that they are alert to and retrieve any utensils, glasses or plates or equipment that might been unnecessarily discarded.

Generally, no previous restaurant experience is required for this position, but being able to work in a hot, wet, humid and loud environment for long periods of time and to lift, reach, bend and stoop is a key.

And a note for operator: overlooking the importance of this position can be expensive.

Bus Person(s). Serve guests with bread, water and butter upon their arrival, and provide refills as needed. Remove used tableware between courses; clear and reset tables after guests leave.

Money follows passion — not the other way around.

~ David Garland

So, You're Thinking About Owning, Operating or Investing in a Restaurant...

67

After receiving their assigned services area at the shift start the bus persons should promptly greet guests as they are seated and bring bread, butter and water to table. They are responsible for removing used tableware between courses, providing tableware for next course, and clearing and resetting tables after guests are done. They should also check surrounding areas for necessary cleaning. In most restaurants they, along with the host/hostess, inspect assigned restrooms every 30 minutes and clean as needed. They need to respond appropriately to guest requests and communicate those to the appropriate server, as needed.

It is key that they communicate with servers and the hostess to assure efficient seating, table utilization and customer service. They assist the servers as needed with food delivery, especially with large parties and during peak periods. They should always thank guests as they are leaving. While no previous restaurant experience is required for this position, they need to have a working knowledge of the predominant language(s) of the guests.

Also, bus persons need to be able to lift, reach, bend and stoop and work in a standing position for long periods of time.

Host/Hostess. First impressions count and this position is generally the initial contact with guests. They absolutely need to warmly welcome guests on their arrival. In many ways this position controls the flow of the restaurant so it's important to hire and train those assigned to it to efficiently manage and tseat guests to a table that best serves their wishes in a timely manner. They need to keep guests informed of wait times and situations that may delay their seating. When possible, open the front door for guests entering or leaving the restaurant with a smile and friendly attitude.

When immediate seating is limited, the Host/Hostess should record guest names and the number of people in their respective parties and then make sure they alert the appropriate guests when their tables become available. The host/hostess needs to provide guests with accurate estimated waiting times while trying to accommodate special seating requests for guests whenever possible.

In addition to seating guests based on guest preferences the host/hostess must also balance customer flow in server service stations. Upon seating, they offer guests a menu and inform them of their server's name and inspect table for proper presentation and completeness. They must communicate and relay messages to servers and bus persons as needed.

Upon the guests departure, they must thank them and invite them to return. While no previous restaurant experience is required for this position, proper personality traits and training are critically important and the applicant must be able to communicate clearly and effectively in the predominant language(s) of guests. Host/Hostess must have exceptional grooming habits.

Bartender. Provide timely, accurate and friendly service while preparing the highest quality beverages for guests. Good bartenders are an excellent addition to any restaurant's customer environment. A bartender not only takes beverage orders from guests and servers and prepares and serves alcoholic and non-alcoholic drinks consistent with the Restaurant's standard drink recipes, but also recognizes and acknowledges our regulars, learns their names, and engages with them.

Additional bartender responsibilities:

• Record drink orders accurately into the register system immediately after receipt.

• Accept guest payment, process credit card charges and make change, if applicable.

• Wash and sterilize glassware.

• Prepare garnishes for drinks and replenish snacks and appetizers for bar patrons.

• Maintain bottles and glasses in an attractive and functional manner to support efficient drink preparation and promotion of beverages.

• Clear and reset tables in bar area.

• Present drink menus, make recommendations and answer questions regarding beverages.

• Maintain cleanliness in all areas of the bar including counters, sinks, utensils, shelves and storage areas.

• Receive and serve food orders to guests seated at the bar.

• Report all equipment problems and bar maintenance issues to restaurant manager.

• Assist the restocking and replenishment of bar inventory and supplies.

• Be available to fill in as needed to ensure the smooth and efficient operation of the restaurant as directed by the restaurant manager or immediate supervisor.

Pulling together complete job descriptions and a training manual for each position is important to systemizing the restaurant. Restaurantowner.com contains a number of resources that present this information in a useful and practical format.

Camaraderie and cooperation between both sides of the house is necessary for a smooth operation with good morale.

~ *Restaurant Startup & Growth* magazine/ RestaurantOwner.com

So, You're Thinking About Owning, Operating or Investing in a Restaurant...

69

Naming Your Restaurant   Chapter

Establishing your presence in the community takes a great deal of time and effort. You have the cost of creating marketing materials, menus and signage to consider, as well as the time and effort to research the name to ensure you are not infringing on another restaurant's trademark.

Hanging a sign on a cow that says "I am a horse" does not make it a horse.
~ Unknown

There are numerous guidelines for selecting a name for most businesses, most of which are broken regularly. The name for your business should not be vague. "Blue Sky" evokes a pretty image on its face; however, it has taken on the meaning of a business idea that is simply a big dream without substance. More practically speaking, as a name for a business, it does not tell you much about its products or services. Is it a florist or a pharmacy or what? You would at least have to add those descriptors to the name, such as Blue Sky Pet Grooming. Still, we have numerous notable exceptions to the rule against vague business names. McDonald's doesn't tell you much about the concept, but it is a proverbial household name.

As discussed later in the chapter under "Trademark 101" an "arbitrary and fanciful" name such as Starbucks can be powerful once it is associated with a certain company.

The Cheesecake Factory offers a lot more than cheesecake, and Jack-in-the-Box sounds like a toy store, yet both concepts have done pretty well. You should consider, however, that it can take a lot of advertising, luck and time — of which you'll likely have a limited supply — for people to know what these names represent. Even top chain concepts such as Burger King, Red Lobster and Taco Bell certainly don't leave it completely to chance that folks will know what they offer — i.e., hamburgers, seafood and Mexican cuisine, respectively.

On the other hand, you do want your name to stand out in the marketplace, and not be what is known in the trademark world as "generic"... Tony's Pizza is a fine name, unless there are already five of them in your city. And we've all seen restaurants named after the owner, and nothing more, such as "Jack's Place". While that kind of suggests a restaurant and might be a source of pride for Jack, its owner, you have to consider the headaches you might encounter if there were, let's say, a strip club by the same name down the street.

Great names tend to be easily pronounced and memorable. This rule tends to be ignored by ethnic restaurants in particular. Ichiban means "first" in Japanese, and is a great name for a sushi restaurant. Diners whose taste in fine Asian food is more sophisticated than their grasp of linguistics might struggle with the moniker ("I think it is called itchy something"). If folks are lined up outside the door, of course, the owner doesn't care how the guests pronounce it.

While there are no hard-and-fast rules to naming a restaurant, once you pick one, it is nearly impossible to change it.

So Where to Start?

You will rarely go wrong if you bear in mind that your concept drives everything — your décor, your menu, your style of service and your name. If you are a white tablecloth French restaurant, the name "Jean-Paul's on Main Street" is certainly passable. Cindy is a lovely name for a woman; however, "Cindy's Grill" tends to suggest a more casual restaurant with a lower price point. That is not to say that at some point the community may come to associate Cindy's Grill with the finest seafood in town. It's just that many diners will have to cross the conceptual gap between the down-home name of the restaurant and the elegant décor, haute cuisine and high prices. Ideally, the name you pick for your restaurant should be compatible with the experience you are trying to create within.

You also have to consider the local culture when selecting your restaurant's name. A quirky moniker that would be appreciated in a college town or urban area might be lost on older residents in a small Midwest town. While you might be particularly hip and sophisticated, remember that your restaurant needs to be a good fit for the guests you want to attract, rather than simply an extension of your persona.

And, if you have any hopes of expanding your concept as a franchise, your trademarked name will be one of your most important assets. If this is your aspiration, you need to consider how well the name will work in a larger geographic area. Consider Bojangles. The folksy-sounding name seems to work in its primary geographic region, the Southeast. As a QSR (quick-service restaurant) that specializes in chicken and biscuits, the concept might not have the same strength in San Francisco as it would in Raleigh, North Carolina.

Focus Your Efforts

Many restaurant consultants suggest that you employ focus groups to explore different names you have in mind. There are marketing consultation companies that provide this service. They assemble a group of people who represent your target market, and elicit their reactions and responses to certain ideas via a moderator. You could manage this process yourself with a handpicked group in the community; however, there is a skill in doing this

Act as if it were
impossible
to fail.

~ Dorthea Brande

well, without leading the participants or introducing bias. Your friends and family might not be willing to be completely honest with you.

In any event, you will want to step outside yourself in creating a name. The name you conjured up at three in the morning in a fit of insomnia might be absolutely brilliant, but you'll want to get objective feedback from others. If the name is a good fit for the concept, it will be apparent to others, as well.

A common strategy in today's highly competitive restaurant market is to add a "modifier", a phrase or a few words below your restaurant's name or logo that clarifies your restaurant's concept or proposition. You can use your modifier on your signage, on napkins, shirts, and menus. It would be the catch phrase on the other side of the colon. For example, consider "Willies: Burgers, Beer and Big TVs." It tells you a lot about the restaurant, as does "River Run Inn: Steaks, Seafood and Wine."

Typography

How you present the restaurant's name communicates as much, if not more, than the name itself. As an example consider these different ways of depicting the same restaurant name:

A. **The Shore Café**

B. THE SHORE CAFÉ

C. The Shore Café

Which version seems the most upscale, the least expensive or the easiest to read from a distance? Fonts with serifs — those little flourishes that you see at the ends of strokes in fonts like Times Roman — are considered more fomral than san-serif fonts like Helvetica or Arial. Example B and C above both use serifs, but the forms of the letters express a very different feel. Example B seems more formal to most people, partially because of the uniformity of the letter heights and the narrowness of each letter. Thin and tall fonts are viewed as more feminine and refined than fat, heavy fonts. The font used in example C seems much more playful and fun, due in part to the flourishes on each letter. The drawback of this kind of font, however, is that the whimsical curls and letter angles make this hard to read from a distance. It might be perfect for your promotional literature and menu, but not translate well to signage.

Qualified graphic artists spend a great deal of time thinking about type. There are a number of fonts from which to choose. You should contemplate the typeface you use for the name of your restaurant at least as carefully as the name itself.

When all is said and done, remember this: Your restaurant won't fail or succeed on its name alone. If it did, the Bucket of Blood Saloon in Virginia City, Nevada, couldn't have flourished for more than 100 years.

Owners Tell How They Selected Their Restaurant's Name

While we can't guarantee all of the restaurants that follow will still be in business when you pick up this book, here are some back stories on how prominent restaurants picked their names, according to their owners.

Endolyne Joe's, Seattle. The name sort of walked in the door while the restaurant was under construction. This 80-year-old guy walked in and explained that the area was a turnaround point for the first municipal streetcar that used to run in West Seattle; it was the end of the line, hence the "Endolyne" part. Then we came upon a poem written in 1926 talking about the streetcar driver of the No. 2 line, a ne'er-do-well and ladies' man named Joe. And that was it: Endolyne Joe's was born. Recently, our group named its sixth, soon-to-open Seattle restaurant The Hi-Life, to evoke a sense of relaxation and "you've arrived." ~ Jeremy Hardy, partner, Chow Foods

Fifth Alarm Firehouse Pub, Byron, Illinois. I have been a fire captain for 23 years. We were planning for my retirement from the fire department, and my wife and I had always had a notion to start a fast-casual restaurant in our town (not sure why!). An opportunity arose to purchase the old city hall building, which, in fact, housed our town's first firehouse. The fire department had moved to bigger quarters years prior and the city administration had moved out of city hall to a new municipal building down the street. The building had been empty for six months or so. We purchased the building and did extensive renovations to open it up. We chose the name Fifth Alarm Firehouse Pub.

I know it's a bit of a mouthful, but we felt the name was appropriate for the building and for my profession as well. Not sure what you know about fires but the largest fire needs the greatest amount of alarms. Each alarm brings more equipment and manpower to the scene. The tradition in the majority of the United States is that the fifth alarm is the most alarms a fire chief can call for a fire. A five-alarmer is a bad one. Ever heard of five-alarm chili? Now you know why. ~ Randy Hogan

Taco Box, Clovis, New Mexico. Ours is Taco Box and it was at one time a franchise, but is no longer. We did not name it. I think the original owner wanted to incorporate the Taco from Taco Bell and the Box from Jack in the Box. The original building was also in the shape of a box, more or less. In our town, Taco Box is Taco Box and for the most part is known. But more often than I would like, people, when wanting to say our name, Taco Bell comes out of their mouths. I don't think it has hurt, other than I get ticked when I hear someone call us by the wrong name.

We also had two other concepts, both short-lived. We chose cute, but I thought not too cutesy names so that customers would still take us seriously.

Continued on page 75

One was a soup, salad and sandwich place named M.T. Belli's (pronounced "empty bellies") and the other Doughsy Doughs (pronounced "dozey doze"), which served baked goods. Those names just popped into our heads (one into my bride's head, the other into mine). No real thought process. ~ Tom Martin

D&R Depot, LeRoy, New York. When I picked the name for my restaurant, I wanted to capitalize on the fact that my restaurant was housed in a former passenger train station. I thought train stations have a natural draw for people. I didn't think I could use a real train name, so my husband and I chose to use our initials to suggest a train name. But because D & N, to us, sounded choppy, we went with my husband's initial and the initial for my nickname.

I now have a lot of fun with my customers who ask what our restaurant name stands for. I tell them the D&R stands for my husband's name and mine, and when they ask what our names are, I say Don and Nancy, and walk away. Either the customer accepts that answer without question, or has a delayed reaction — "wait a minute" — and then I tell them my nickname — Rebel — was used instead of my first name. ~ Nancy Nickerson

Angelo's, Washington, Pennsylvania. Way back in 1939, my grandparents, Angelo and Giacomina Passalacqua, opened a small neighborhood tavern. With all the nearby glass, steel manufacturing and farmland just outside town, the place became a very popular stop for area workers. The little tavern grew and my grandparents began to serve their customers real Italian spaghetti and fresh Italian bread. In those days, the place was called the West Chestnut Spaghetti Inn, which is a pretty terrible name. My grandfather passed away in 1953, and my grandmother retired in 1958 and turned the business over to my dad and aunt. My father named the restaurant after my grandfather, posthumously. It's been Angelo's ever since. The bad news is there are probably thousands of Angelo's across the country and I don't own them! ~ Michael Passalacqua

The Kings Arms Pub, Kentville, Nova Scotia. The name of our pub is The Kings Arms Pub with no apostrophe on the "S," which means that most people think it's misspelled but actually it's not. We wanted a true British pub and put a lot of effort into ensuring that the atmosphere was as close to a British pub as possible — large brick fireplace, stained-glass windows, and, of course, a large mahogany bar! Then in order to tell people that we were a British pub, we wanted a name that would indicate this. Obviously England is associated with kings and so we named it the King's Arms Pub, but we took it one step further to ensure a bit of uniqueness to our name. We are in the County of Kings and so to put a bit of a twist on the name we decided that the Kings in our name would be after the county we are in and not a possessive on the King's Arms. ~ Stephen Shaw

Continued on page 76

An organization's ability to learn, and translate that learning into action rapidly, is the ultimate competitive advantage.

~ Jack Welch

So, You're Thinking About Owning, Operating or Investing in a Restaurant...

75

Continued from page 75

Raccoon River Brewing Company, Des Moines, Iowa. This is a brew pub; Raccoon River is a prominent river downtown. The originator of the name is John Hickenlooper who is the mayor of Denver and the owner of Wynkoop Brewing Company. He likes names with two O's in the middle — Raccoon, Wynkoop, Hickenlooper. My other restaurants are Centro, which means the center, indicating the center of town in Italy. Centro is in the center of a downtown redevelopment district. With Forty Three, the original restaurant was on 43rd Street. We kept the name when we moved it downtown. ~ Paul Rottenberg

ToST Lounge, Seattle. We brainstormed name ideas with friends, which symbolized the spirit of our establishment. My partner and I opened our establishment because of our love to entertain, and expose people to new musical, food and drink experiences. ToST (as in toasting a drink) symbolizes our philosophy in life to take time out to celebrate the milestones, no matter how big or small. We decided taking the "a" out of toast would decrease confusion with a breakfast-themed establishment.

An artist friend of ours came up with the visual treatment of the letters. We saw it on paper and really liked it. One side note regarding branding ... I would recommend that others let professional sign makers do the job. My partner and I designed the sign and had a metal worker build it. It's aesthetically beautiful, but illegible in daylight! Although we didn't have the money for a large neon sign at the startup of our business, I think it would have been wise to squeeze the $10k from someplace to have it made. ~ Tanea Stephens

Trademark 101

More and more small-business owners are learning the value of trademarks in their business and are seeking ways to protect them. Trademark protection is becoming more prevalent, and everyone who wants to reap the rewards of their popular name or slogan is lined up to protect their — at least, perceived — valuable intellectual property.

Your first question might be, what is a trademark? A trademark is any word or a series of words, slogans, design, or symbols that are used in commerce to identify your goods and services. Some well-known trademarks are Microsoft; "It's the Real Thing" and the Nike "swoosh" symbol. In selecting a trademark, choose words that are not overly descriptive of your goods or services. For example, Exxon and Xerox are strong trademarks, but "Pretty Nails" and "Quality Cleaners" are not.

If you have been using a particular company or product name for some time, it is important to register it as a trademark so that others can't use it without your permission. A competitor who uses a name similar to your company's or product's name may create confusion among potential customers and may affect the reputation you have worked so hard to establish. Without a trademark registration, you can't demand that the competing company stop using the name. You have a choice of either continuing to use your name and risk confusion, or changing to a new name and starting over with building your name recognition.

For an established business, which has invested significant time and money in building a brand, and creating and purchasing advertising and promotional materials, this would represent a significant and unacceptable cost.

And if you have any hope of franchising or licensing your concept, having a protected trademark is vital. Without the assurance that the business's name will remain distinct in the marketplace, you offer very little to prospective franchisees who want to succeed on your reputation.

Don't wait until your brand is a household name to begin the process of protecting it. Even if you do not have a long history of using a particular name for your business, you may want to register it earlier rather than later to show that you are the first to use it, and also to make sure you are not infringing on an existing trademark. It would be a business disaster to spend time and money promoting a new name for a product line and then receive a cease-or-desist letter from a trademark owner demanding that you stop using its trademark.

There are two places to register a trademark. First, you may register it with the secretary of state in your state. In Texas, for example, the application form is available at the secretary of state's Web site, and the filing fee is $50. However, a state registration is valid only in that state. If you are doing business in multiple states, you should consider registration with the United States Patent and Trademark Office (USPTO). If you have any dream of franchising or licensing your concept, registering there is critical. One of the key assets, in these cases, is the use of the trademark. Unless you have muscle to keep your mark protected and distinctive, the rest of the deal has little value.

A federal trademark registration is valid and enforceable in all 50 states. You may apply for a federal trademark registration online at www.USPTO. gov; the filing fee is $375 per trademark (as of publication of this edition) for one international classification. In addition, you may apply for a trademark that you plan to use in the near future; this is called an "intent to use" trademark application, which allows you to "reserve" a trademark for future use. Once a federal trademark registration has been approved, you may use the ™ symbol to signify that the trademark is a federally registered trademark.

You can navigate the process yourself; however, an attorney who is familiar in trademark law can advise as to whether you have a strong mark, i.e., how likely it is to be approved by the USPTO. He or she will also help you keep track of important filing and renewal dates, and what to do if your mark is contested by another business.

You should strongly consider working with a knowledgeable intellectual property lawyer to guide you on the legal process of selecting and register-

> Some people regard private enterprise as a predatory tiger to be shot. Others look on it as a cow they can milk. Not enough people see it as a healthy horse, pulling a sturdy wagon.
>
> ~ Winston Churchill

So, You're Thinking About Owning, Operating or Investing in a Restaurant...

77

ing your trademark. In general, you want to avoid "generic" trademarks, as you might not be able to register them. "The Pizza Restaurant" is an example of a very generic mark. "Arbitrary and fanciful" trademarks tend to be the easier to register and protect. "Kleenex" is a good example. It has come to be a household name for a brand of tissue; however, on its face, there is nothing about the mark that suggests the type of product.

A trademark represents your business, your reputation, and the goodwill you have established with clients and consumers. Your brand is valuable and it is worth taking the time and effort to protect it.

How to Create a Winning Restaurant Business Plan

Hard work, great food, and the will to succeed are not enough. You need proper training, established operational procedures, and a creative marketing plan, before you open. These may be more important to a successful opening than menu design or table and chair selection.

Strategy without tactics is the slowest route to victory. Tactics without strategy is the noise before defeat.

~Sun Tzu

A business plan is your roadmap for the future of the business. Not only does it provide direction, it requires you to consider all the pitfalls and opportunities of your prospective enterprise, well before you open its doors. It is your script of how the business ought to be.

Without it you are unlikely to receive funding from anyone other than the most trusting or unsophisticated sources of financing. In short, many restaurateurs agree that having a sound business plan was the single most important ingredient in making their new business a reality.

So why do so many restaurateurs forsake this critical step, without which many entrepreneurs wouldn't even open a lemonade stand? Unfortunately, some operators don't understand how crucial a well-planned opening is to the success of their concept. For one, restaurateurs often want to get the ball rolling quickly. Too many operators put all their planning into simply getting financed. They then want to open the doors as fast as possible to create cash flow.

Where to start? You can wade through thousands of articles, software programs and books that can be purchased on the Internet or in the business section of your local bookstore/coffee bar. Some of these guides are valuable, although you might have to dig a little to find information created specifically for restaurateurs. This chapter is not meant to be the first and last word on the business planning process; however, it does provide an overview of the key, basic components of a strong business plan. We'll address the basics here, except for how to create financial projections, which is covered in Chapter 7.

The story of
my restaurant...

So, You're Thinking About Owning, Operating or Investing in a Restaurant...

79

So, Who's Going to Read It, Anyway?

Most business plans address the same basic areas; however, there are a variety of ways to organize and format them. The overriding goal is to structure your plan in a logical and easily understood manner. Consider that it will be your roadmap for development, and prospective financiers — be they institutional lenders or "friends and family" investors — will want to review your plan as part of their due diligence, before they open their checkbooks. Consider the ways that your business plan will be used before you begin writing. These include the obvious:

- Acquire investment capital.
- Get a bank loan.
- Obtain lease space.

And the not so obvious:

- Convince your prospective managers to believe in your concept.
- Gain respect and confidence from prospective employees.
- Allow management to concentrate on execution
- Avoids planning "on the go".
- Create a blueprint for operating your restaurant.
- Help you determine whether your plans make financial sense."

If you want to achieve your objectives, keep your business plan simple, but make it easy for its readers to find the answers to specific questions they may have. (As with any good reference, you will want to provide a table of contents that outlines the content in the plan.)

For most business people, the most daunting aspect of creating a business plan is the writing process. Most folks have a deadly fear of the blank sheet of paper or screen. This is the part where many would-be operators and experienced restaurateurs struggle. For successful operators, their expertise, in many cases, stems from their ability to conceptualize their dream of owning a successful restaurant. But when it comes to documenting their dream, the enormity of the task can be overwhelming.

"Creating a business plan for the first time is too daunting of a project for most newbies," says Dave Ostrander, who is known as "The Pizza Doctor." "Even we 'Old Grizzlies' often shudder at the task. It takes big hunks of time and lots of research to create a great one. Anything less than great has a big chance of being turned down."

That's a lot of pressure. Relax. You might not be Hemingway, but once you have adopted a structure for your business plan, "fleshing out" the content will flow more easily than you might expect. Address the following points, and you'll find that the skeleton of the plan will take shape.

Mind you, there is no shame in hiring assistance from a consultant, for whom writing a business plan is routine. Not only is the consultant producing a much needed document, but is helping to plan the operational strategy and opening process as well. Consider this icing on the cake.

Regardless of who drafts the final version of your business plan, have another set of eyes — preferably someone who understands the process — rigorously proof it.

The common question that gets asked in business is, 'why?' That's a good question, but an equally valid question is, 'why not?'

~ Jeff Bezos

While this is not Ms. Crabapple's English composition class, typos and misspellings reflect poorly on your attention to detail. Is this enough to cause a lender to deny funding or a prospective partner to lose confidence in your diligence and ability to execute a complex project? Maybe not, but don't take that chance.

The Executive Summary

Almost every business plan, regardless of business type, includes a one- to four-page introduction that gives the reader a summary of the business plan components to follow. The executive summary should be written last, after you have completed the other components.

The summary should effectively convey your identity, your concept, why the concept will be successful, and your plan to make it a reality, its cost, and the anticipated return on investment.

Use this opportunity to capture the reader's interest, and as a sales tool for your business plan. Avoid too many details in this section. Details will be addressed later. Discuss only the key aspects about your restaurant concept. Remember, some readers never make it past this part of the business plan. A well-written summary can convince the reader to thoroughly explore the rest of the plan.

Some plan advisers suggest that a confidentiality statement precede the introduction. After all, much of the content you provide is confidential and cost you a lot of time, effort and expense to produce.

Description of the Business

Legal structure. Establish early on the ownership structure and capitalization plan of the proposed restaurant. This section should include a brief description of the legal organization. For an independent business, this will typically be an S-corporation or limited liability company (LLC) (rather than sole proprietorship or partnership) since these "entities" allow for multiple ownership interests and can shield managing investors from personal liability for claims against the business. (See Chapter 9).

Site lease or purchase. If a definitive site has not been chosen, list the area or city in which the restaurant is to be located. Arguably, location is more important to a restaurant than it is to most any other business. Informed prospective investors will look at site selection very carefully.

Also, the financial consequences, including tax considerations, of a lease versus purchase is critical in any new venture. A detailed explanation of the rationale for selecting either is warranted in the business plan. For example, a significant attraction of the deal might be the investment value of the real estate. This section can be updated, if needed, once a site has been selected.

Capitalization. Give an overview showing the estimated capitalization needed to open the restaurant and the planned sources for funding it. Keep this section to the point, and don't clutter it with minor issues. Detailed pro-

So, You're Thinking About Owning, Operating or Investing in a Restaurant...

81

jections and investment requirements will be explained in the "Investment Analysis and the Financial Projections" sections of your business plan.

Business concept. As critical as this aspect is, writing your concept description is typically the most fun. What you want to do here is to paint a picture of what the experience will be from the guests' point of view. Just as a menu can whet one's appetite, creating an image of your restaurant concept can pique a reader's interest.

While you might envision serious investors and bankers as dispassionate number crunchers concerned only with income projections and returns, in fact, they need to be sold on why your business is a great idea. They need to be convinced that the concept should succeed in appealing to diners. Remember, everyone can understand what makes a restaurant enticing. If you can't get them excited about your concept, don't expect them to invest.

Writing a vivid concept description is a lot like telling a good friend about a fantastic new restaurant you have visited. Use descriptive, enticing language to bring the following features of your concept to life:
    * Service style; e.g. fine dining, casual upscale, fast-casual or quick-serve.
    * Size and seating capacity.
    * Décor and furnishings.
    * Operating hours and meal periods.
    * Atmosphere, ambience.
    * Lighting and music.
    * General menu theme.
    * Points of difference or unique selling points.
    * Related products and services such as catering, home/office delivery, and retail.

In addition to describing the food, be sure to mention interesting design elements, unique furnishings or other attractions. And don't forget the service. A good descriptive summary of the service style, as well as service promptness, is necessary to properly communicate the conceptual image of the restaurant.

The writing style you use should resemble that of a restaurant critic, albeit one who has only positive things to print about your restaurant. Descriptive remarks about the overall atmosphere you want to project help to solidify the conceptual picture you are trying to create. Your narrative should inform the reader of other key factors such as the restaurant's price point, hours of operation and service style. Alcohol service, if provided, should also be noted.

Be sure to express any unique selling points or points of differentiation the restaurant may have to other restaurants in the area. Typical distinctions are often made for signature dishes, ethnic cuisine new to the area, unique service styles or unusual décor.

You should also inform the reader of the size of the restaurant and its seating capacity. Make sure to mention the presence of a bar or banquet room and any significant factors about them. Finally, be sure to enlighten the reader about additional services the restaurant may offer such as catering, home/office delivery or retail merchandise.

Sample menu. Include a sample menu in your plan. A well-written and attractively designed menu can help to sell your concept. Whether your concept is a fine table dining or a quick-service fast-food restaurant, the menu is your No. 1 selling tool.

Customer perception, though influenced by several factors, is largely formed based on the appeal of the menu, whether it is a printed menu or a menu board. If you are opening a quick-service concept, consider the inclusion of your menu board design. And remember, it is not the number of items you have on your menu, but the design, variety and appeal that make an eye-catching menu.

Building design and layouts. Architectural drawings, floor plans, and artist renderings can also help you create a visual image of your concept. Include visual components of the concept, if available.

Management team overview. The success of any business relies on sound management. Don't believe it? Talk to any venture capitalist. A good story is just a good story. Venture capitalists want to know who is going to execute and drive the plan. A lot of great business concepts have been turned down by investors, both "friends and family" and institutional lenders, because the prospective managers did not seem to possess the experience, skill, education, and/or discipline to make the business work.

The restaurant business is no exception. Controlling costs, managing employees and servicing customers requires experience and talent. This section of the restaurant business plan is intended to convey the background and experience of the managing partners or owners as well as key management personnel who will operate the business. You should include a résumé-styled summary for each person in the restaurant's management.

Résumés. The summary should begin with the name of the person and a brief description of the role or position that person will occupy in managing the business. Provide a summary the person's experience or qualifications. You might choose to insert actual résumés in this section or list them in the Appendices section of the business plan.

Management agreements. Though not mandatory, these may be used to lay out the expectations of the manager, the incentive plans, if any, and a termination strategy. You should disclose if there are to be any management agreements in place between the company and owners, hired employees, or third parties. Include a copy of the management agreement, if available, either here or in the Appendices section of the plan. It is also acceptable to state that while a management agreement will be in place, none has yet been drafted. You should consult with your attorney before carrying out management agree-

> Sometimes when you **innovate**, you make **mistakes**. It is best to **admit them** quickly, and **get on with improving** your other innovations.
> ~ Steve Jobs

ments, since they are binding on the organization, and are a frequent source of litigation. Furthermore, you might not want to enter into an employment contract with certain managers, and instead, keep the relationship "at will."

Business Environment Analysis

Many restaurant entrepreneurs share an exceptional attribute that enables them to visualize a restaurant concept they fervently believe will have popular appeal to the dining public. After all, passionate belief in their concept is the driving force that can turn a dream into reality. However, passion must be balanced with reality when it comes to creating a sound business plan. In-depth market research is needed to substantiate that conceptual assumptions are in line with market conditions.

There are four basic factors to consider in your market analysis. First, you need to be aware of current industry trends and customer spending habits. Next, identify your target market, the niche to which your concept appeals. Third, compare the customer base for the chosen location with your target market. Finally, identify the local competition that may contend for the same customer base.

Industry overview. There has been a dramatic shift in dining habits over the last 20 or so years. The change has been gradual, reflecting the ongoing evolution of the industry. In the United States, the National Restaurant Association (NRA), www.restaurant.org, has been the premier source for identifying changing trends in consumer habits. Each year the NRA publishes, among other things, its annual "Restaurant Industry Forecast" which provides a glimpse of the industry through anticipated sales, customer spending habits, dining traits and operational and industry workforce trends.

The U.S. Bureau of the Census, the Department of Labor, and The Library of Congress are also good sources when analyzing population growth, ethnicity mix, labor and economic conditions. However, organizations such as the NRA and restaurant-based publications provide more relevant information about our particular industry. Given the projected growth of the restaurant industry, this aspect of your plan paints an optimistic future of your chances for success in a very competitive business.

Target market. Careful evaluation should be used to determine the preferred target market that your concept best appeals to and how that relates to the overall restaurant market with respect to diner demographics, preferences, and habits.

Use this section to describe the ideal (targeted) customer profile for the concept. Consider the demographic characteristics for your ideal customer such as head of household age, income, household size, ethnicity, single or multifamily housing.

Identify the preferred market size of residential and business population and the proximity to your restaurant's location. Establish desirable traffic count thresholds or a preference for a specific industry such as tourism. Determine the importance of traffic generators for your concept such as malls, theaters and universities.

Location analysis. Since most business plans are created before a site has been selected, the location analysis may be limited to the general area or city for the proposed concept.

As suggested earlier, site selection is often considered the most crucial aspect of the business planning cycle. The location analysis should describe market conditions that exist in the location (or general area) you have selected. Information gathered and displayed here should include demographic statistics, description of local industry and economic outlook, location traffic counts, traffic generators, and proximity to residential and business populations.

You should also draw comparisons between market conditions for the selected location, and the targeted market characteristics of the concept. List the surrounding neighborhoods, points of interest, and area businesses.

Demographic and other information about a specific market can be found through various sources, including Web sites. Contact the local chamber of commerce, the U.S. census bureau, the departments of labor (U.S. and state), and the county comptroller's and clerk's offices.

Often the most useful information will come from your real estate broker. Brokers have access to demographic information that is more specific to the immediate area surrounding the location. They can provide you with reports for one-, three- and five-mile radii. Real estate brokers oftentimes subscribe to services that specialize in collecting and analyzing data that is not publicly available.

Competitive analysis. Researching the local competition, in terms of proximity and similarities to your concept, is an important factor when estimating your market share. The competitive analysis should show the extent of market saturation, the type of other restaurants in the area, and restaurants deemed to be in direct competition with your concept. List the unique aspects of your concept that give you a competitive advantage over each.

Marketing Strategy

A comprehensive business plan includes a sound marketing plan. Investors and bankers want to know you have a proactive plan to grow your business. You can't rely on instant popularity and simple word-of-mouth marketing just because some restaurants, but not many, open their doors to instant success.

Use this section to paint a picture of your restaurant's marketing strategy before and after you open the doors. Distinguish your plans for the grand opening marketing from ongoing marketing.

Give an introductory summary of the marketing philosophy that will guide your marketing program. This introduction should convince the reader that

A positive culture means happier, more productive employees, lower turnover and better company performance and results. Owners, employees and even customers have a much better chance of getting what they want in restaurants where a positive, high-performance culture is maintained.

~ Restaurant Startup & Growth magazine/ RestaurantOwner.com

So, You're Thinking About Owning, Operating or Investing in a Restaurant...

85

a well-thought-out, workable plan is in place. Use a descriptive, enthusiastic approach to verbalize the plan.

Over the years, restaurateurs have found creative methods to market their concept. Some of the methods you may want to consider are:

Build a customer database. The cornerstone of direct marketing efforts is to build a customer database. Operators have used imaginative tactics to gather names such as business card drops or promotions that entice guests to sign up.

Frequent diner programs. Otherwise known as loyalty programs, automated frequent diner programs are now available with many POS (point-of-sale) systems. There are also a variety of services available that help you track and reward repeat customers.

E-mail campaign. E-mail as a marketing tool has been a growing phenomenon for a few years now. Unfortunately, spammers have infiltrated this market to the disdain of all. Nevertheless, e-mail can be an essential part of your direct marketing plan. It's inexpensive and promotions can be created quickly without the time and cost associated to produce and distribute mailers. Promotions can include monthly newsletters, specials, announcements, etc.

Direct-mail campaigns. Direct mail remains a highly effective tool to reach new customers. It can also be very effective when used in conjunction with a well-maintained customer database. Simple practices, such as mailing birthday and anniversary cards to existing customers, help to build customer loyalty.

Community/charity involvement. Community involvement helps build name awareness as well as loyalty. Diners tend to frequent establishments that give back to the community. Sponsoring charities has always been a great method to build support for your restaurant and provide help to others. Contributions can be financial or the use of your resources such as your banquet hall for meetings or serving equipment for events. Other community efforts include supporting local sports teams, churches, and fund-raisers.

Building business relationships. Building solid business relationships can lead to big bucks for aggressive owners. You can build tourism traffic by establishing relationships with hotel concierges. A strategic relationship with a major employer can help to draw lunch traffic from employees or from executive suites. Catering revenue is enhanced when you know who books the catering. Meal delivery to area businesses at lunch provides them with timesaving convenience and helps promote your restaurant and adds to its bottom line.

'Four-walls' marketing. In-house marketing is one of the most effective tools you have to keep existing guests coming back. Think of ways to promote your restaurant from within such as table tents, menu inserts, displays or signage, suggestive sales tactics or frequent diner promotions.

Public relations (PR). Effective public relations take creativity and work. You may choose to handle this aspect of marketing yourself or hire a PR firm. Whichever method you choose, briefly describe how PR will be handled.

Advertising. All restaurants advertise in one form or another. Simple signage with the name of your restaurant is advertising. Whether or not you are a proponent of advertising, your plan should be described here. Some operators may use this section to express a view against excessive advertising, choosing instead to bolster other marketing techniques. Either way, investors or bankers will be interested in your viewpoint, if only because advertising can be a huge expense.

Web-based marketing. Last, but not least, in this market you should be able to describe how you will use your web site, the Internet and social media to promote your business. Every successful restaurant needs a web site, as this is often the first place prospective guests will venture to size up your concept. Facebook and even You Tube have become a standard arsenal in startup restaurant marketing. You should also consider how you will deal with the online discount programs and user review sites.

Operations Plan

The operations section of the business plan should convey a general description of how the restaurant will be operated on a day-to-day basis. Most chain restaurants have systematized their operations. The system is then documented in an operating manual that the management team and employees must follow. This way everyone is on the same page.

Although it is not always realistic to complete an operating manual before the business plan is written, it is important to acknowledge the systems and controls you intend to put in place. Documenting the systems and procedures can take place during the opening process.

The operations section may be the most critical to the success of your restaurant; not so much from the investor's and banker's perspective, but as a comprehensive plan to share with management and employees.

Key considerations for describing your operations include:

Staffing. This section should list the staff positions, the number of people needed for each position and the average rate of pay for the position. List any recruiting plans or services you will use to attract potential staffers. Describe the hiring standards and interview process that will be used. This is not intended to be a labor cost projection.

The standard and expectation is that everyone comes to work expecting to play at the top of their game, every day. Every job in the restaurant is important and serves a noble purpose: the restaurant's mission to delight guests and encourage them to return with their friends and family.

~ Restaurant Startup & Growth magazine/ RestaurantOwner.com

So, You're Thinking About Owning, Operating or Investing in a Restaurant...

87

Training. Provide an overview of the training programs that the staff will undergo. Include in-house training and third-party training for subjects such as a state-mandated Alcohol Awareness Program servers may have to attend. Be sure to reference employee handbooks, training manuals and training tools.

Daily operations and production. This section should describe, in summary, the day-to-day operations of the restaurant from opening to close. It should convey to the reader that management has a sound plan for operating the restaurant. Briefly explain operational issues such as scheduling, departmental job functions, ordering and receiving, menu production, service, general safety procedures and maintenance.

Customer service. Describe plans for establishing service attitudes and policies. Include an overview on how customer complaints will be handled and how the restaurant will go about getting customer feedback such as surveys or through mystery shoppers.

Suppliers. You should list suppliers for specialty products that will help make your business unique. Show contingency plans for replacing key suppliers. If your concept relies on unique products like Florida stone crabs, Maine lobster, or imported items, then you'll want to have a backup plan readily available.

Management Controls

Operating a restaurant on a day-to-day basis requires established systems that help control costs and maintain excellence. Unfortunately, some startup restaurateurs open their doors unprepared to handle the daily challenges.

Incorporate management controls, tasks and support systems into your plan. Don't put off making operational decisions until a general manager or chef is hired. It is important that you acknowledge in your plan some of the basic controls such as:

* POS system to track sales
* Time and attendance tracking
* Scheduling
* Operations checklists
* Ordering procedures
* Inventory control
* Cash control procedure
* Security measures
* Safety policies
* Liability reviews

Administrative controls. Establishing systematic administrative procedures is equally important as putting in place management controls. One might view management controls as tools for management whereas administrative controls are tools to measure management's performance.

Administrative tasks such as accounting and payroll processing are vital to the financial success of restaurants. Many owner-operators use a bookkeeper, accounting or payroll service to handle some of the administrative tasks such as the preparation of daily and weekly reports, profit-and-loss (P&L) reporting, bank reconciliations or payroll processing.

Investment partners may want to know "who is guarding the henhouse?" To address their concerns you might consider the incorporation of these financial controls:

Daily cash control. Adopt a system whereby sales and receipts recorded by the POS system will be compared with actual cash and credit card deposits on a daily basis. Establish acceptable over/short amounts. Monthly totals should be compared with actual P&L statements for accuracy.

Weekly prime cost report. Prepare a weekly report that shows the gross profit margin after the cost of goods sold and labor cost has been deducted from the sales revenue. The prime cost, depending on the type of restaurant, is expected to range on average from 55 percent to 65 percent. Proper control of the prime cost is the single most effective measure of management's ability to operate the restaurant. Weekly monitoring allows for quick reaction to adverse cost ratios.

Purchasing records and account payables. Establish a system to process and record invoices and credits daily. Reports detailing cash expenditures, payments by check, and accounts payable transactions should be readily available. Consider how check disbursements will be prepared and to whom check-signing authority for the general operating account will be given.

Accounting system/service. Allow for the timely preparation of monthly financial statements, including the monthly P&L and balance sheet. The plan should state who will prepare the reports, such as the bookkeeper, CPA or accounting service.

Payroll processing. Provide an overview on how payroll checks will be processed. Consider how often checks will be issued such as weekly, biweekly, or semimonthly. Acknowledge your preference of preparing payroll in-house or to have a payroll processing service.

But Keep it "Under Your Hat"

When submitting a business plan for review by potential investors, bankers, and prospective partners, you should consider having reviewers sign a confidentiality agreement. In the critical planning and negotiating stage

Doing your best means not accepting average and doing just enough to get by. When confronted with a problem, look for a solution. Seek constructive feedback on how you can get better.

~ *Restaurant Startup & Growth* magazine/ RestaurantOwner.com

of a new operation you need to protect your trade secrets and confidential information. Chain restaurants use them in standard practice, and independent restaurateurs should consider them as well, particularly if the concept is novel and involves significant proprietary market research.

Developing a business plan takes time and effort, but it is well worth it, as the final, polished document will give you, and your investors, confidence that you really can reach your destination: creating and running a successful restaurant.

Take responsibility, be dependable and accountable. Do what you said you'd do, be on time and in the right frame of mind. When you see a problem, don't ignore it. Own it and solve it. Don't pass on inferior work for someone else to fix.

~ Restaurant Startup & Growth magazine/ RestaurantOwner.com

Real Restaurateurs, *Real People*

Stories about people who realized their restaurant dreams

And Baby Makes Three

The neighborhood around American University at the top of New Mexico Avenue in Northwest Washington. D.C., is prime real estate. The university's 12,000 students surround the location and within blocks are dozens of high-rises that are home to many of the capitol's young and energized up and coming lawyers, legislative aids, lobbyists and the like.

It's an area deserving of a good restaurant, which is what the landlord — American University — was looking for when it approached Bill Fuchs, owner of Wagshal's, an institution in the nation's capital since 1925.

Wagshal's Deli is where all of the movers and shakers in D.C. have eaten at some time or another — Supreme Court Justices, elected officials and party leaders. Prior to security increases after 9/11, Wagshal's regularly delivered to the White House.

The deli is within the same shopping center as Wagshal's Market, where fresh cut meat, imported wines and other specialty items fill the shopping baskets for those who appreciate quality food products. Also a block behind the shopping center is Wagshal's prep kitchen where the catering component of the business is handled, including making birthday and wedding cakes.

It's all nice and neat and convenient, which is why Bill Fuchs was at first a little hesitant to expand. But a new generation is entering the family-operated business, and Fuchs wanted to make sure that there was enough of an operation to keep everyone engaged. "We didn't want to replicate what we have, because that can be risky, so we asked ourselves what would happen if the Deli and the Market had a baby," says Fuchs.

Also inspired by frequent business and leisure trips to Spain and Portugal, Fuchs wanted to recreate Barcelona's famous Barquerio, an open air market filled with deli style dining experiences.

So looking at the 4,000 square feet of open space in what was once an administration building and knowing that he had the resources of Wagshal's prep kitchen and deli about two miles away, Fuchs signed the lease and began making the baby, which he christened simply "Wagshal's on New Mexico."

A key component of this new look comes from the display of fresh fresh meat and produce, with the latter positioned indoors or outdoors, depending on the season. But Fuchs

wanted a friendlier interaction between guests and his employees than a typical deli counter would allow. What he wanted was a different kind of display case and, unable to locate one in the U.S., his search took him back to Portugal. There he found it: a unit about 40 inches high and 36 inches deep, with an all-glass top. The display case is similar to what you find in a jewelry store, only this one was refrigerated.

There's little storage in this type of cases," says Fuchs, "so a lot of time is devoted to replenishing from our bigger refrigeration units. But the upside is more intimacy between the customer, the product and our clerks,"

Wagshal's refrigerated cases are clustered according to product, thus creating a friendly, neighborhood feel to the communications and transactions. The interior of the building is largely open, with very few walls and partitions. Terra cotta tiles, reclaimed barn wood and 14-feet high arched windows contribute to the old world feel that Fuchs wanted.

Other than several refrigeration units, Wagshal's on New Mexico does not have a back-of-the-house area to speak of. All of the menu items are prepared at the deli and prep kitchen two miles away. Deliveries take place several times a day via electric vehicles.

The menu options are the exact same as at Wagshal's Deli, which Fuchs says "gives me some comfort by minimizing the risk to our solid reputation." Fuchs recognizes there's nothing like this in Washington, D.C., and that indeed, few first time operators could accomplish this type of concept.

"This is really only possible because we have so much support off-site and because of the reputation that Wagshal's has developed over nearly 90 years of business in this city," he says.

Because of the long history of Wagshal's in the city, news of the third opening in 2013 generated a lot of print and social media buzz. The buzz was increased by the bright window graphics that covered the windows during construction. Vivid depictions of produce, fresh meat and an energetic vibe let those passing by know something exciting was about to happen.

The company generates a monthly newsletter for its regular customers and has also had a solid presence on Facebook and Twitter for years, so no specific marketing for the new location was necessary.

How to Create Realistic Financial Projections for Your New Restaurant

Chapter 7

Some would argue that the financial projection is the business plan. Why bother building a restaurant if it's not going to make any money? For potential investors and lenders, the financials are often viewed as the heart of the business plan and this section will get a lot of attention and even scrutiny from them.

Money is only a tool. It will take you wherever you wish, but it will not replace you as the driver.

~ Ayn Rand

An experienced operator recounted his career in the early 1990s when he was recruited to be the general manager and eventually managing partner for a beautiful, upper-casual steak-and-seafood concept. He joined the venture in the midst of construction, about three months before opening.

"Having had success in several nightclub ventures, the general partners spared no expense when it came to design and construction," he recalls. "Thick red leather booths encased in rich mahogany trim set the tone for the dining room ambience that our $1.8 million budget mandated. A constant flow of change orders and delays, including more Italian marble and a $41,000 brass and polished stainless steel revolving door entrance, contributed to ballooning cost overruns. Although the enhancements served to entrench the restaurant as a must-visit destination, the added expenses resulted in a final cost of $2.4 million to get the restaurant open.

"Overshooting the budget by nearly 33 percent meant that additional financing would be needed to pay for the excessive expenditures. Not only was the ROI (return on investment) projection shot, the partners were only able to raise an additional $200,000, leaving $400,000 in payables for which they expected to settle from cash flow.

"A quick rework of our break-even point revealed that we now needed to do $75,000 in sales per week just to break even. Needless to say, this restaurant concept, regardless of how good the food was, how great the service, and how magnificent the ambience, was now a prime candidate for failure due to underfunding."

So, You're Thinking About Owning, Operating or Investing in a Restaurant...

93

Fortunately, he was privileged to have had a "fantastic team of managers, staff, and supportive partners," he said, adding "We worked together to lower our break-even point, increase the sales volume and finally, after three long years, achieve a highly profitable restaurant that is still serving fine steaks and seafood today."

Not surprisingly, scenarios such as this are played out every day in the restaurant industry. And unfortunately, the vast majority of underfunded restaurants don't have the luxury of an experienced staff and sufficient revenues to withstand such dramatic shortfalls in their financial projections.

Let's focus on perhaps the most important aspect of your business plan: the financial projections. The process begins the moment your concept has been defined. As with every undertaking, you need to determine the right questions before you seek answers. These include:

* How much will it cost to build?
* Where will the funds come from?
* What are the projected sales?
* What are my break-even sales?

If you plan to invite partners or investors to participate, then you'll also need to answer the following:

* What is the return on investment?
* What is the sales potential?
* What are the growth expectations?
* What is the potential liability?

The answers to these questions can only be found by diligently preparing a realistic set of financial projections, accompanied by an investment analysis and a growth plan.

Money Talks

Some would argue that the financial projection is the business plan. Why bother building a restaurant if it's not going to make any money? For potential investors and lenders, the financials are often viewed as the heart of the business plan and this section will get a lot of attention and even scrutiny from them. This is where they have the opportunity to evaluate the financial viability of the venture and — all-important — gain a sense of the risk and return on investment potential the venture is likely to offer.

Even though you may have years of hospitality experience and are an expert at operating a restaurant, lenders and investors want to know you understand the financial side of the business as well. Showing knowledge of the numbers lets them know you see the big picture and are capable of not only running a restaurant but that you also possess the skills to build it as a successful business.

Although you may not have a financial background, you'll need to understand the numbers on the various schedules and statements that make up the financial projections section and be prepared to answer questions about the assumptions used to create them.

In fact, writing the financial projections section of a business plan might require you to seek outside assistance from a financial consultant and/or accountant. Still, don't be frightened by numbers if you don't have a financial background. As you plug through the process, you will become more comfortable with the concepts and the calculations. Creating financial projections is the hardest part of the business planning process, but offers a huge payoff. Arriving at realistic and achievable financial projections is perhaps the biggest confidence builder in the startup phase of a restaurant. You know that if you can maintain a realistic sales volume and control known costs at a certain level, you can make a go of it.

The Capital Budget

The first step, and one of the most critical, is to develop a capital budget for your venture. The "capital budget" is a detailed schedule showing all the various expenditures, construction, startup and preopening costs required to get the restaurant open for business. Adequately identifying and estimating the costs of the project at this stage is absolutely crucial. As already noted in this book, one of the main reasons for restaurant failure is undercapitalization, i.e., running out of startup capital before operating activities have a chance to generate an adequate cash flow to sustain the business. Don't place your restaurant (and future) in jeopardy by not having enough capital to complete your project according to plan or start out in a big financial hole.

Here are the major categories of the capital budget:

Land and building. If the owner/operating entity is planning to own the land and building (versus leasing a facility), the actual or estimated cost of the land and building should be included here. Also include any related acquisition costs such as closing costs, sales commissions, and finder's fees.

Leasehold improvements. In a leased facility, enter the estimated cost of constructing the leasehold improvements less any landlord contributions. Leasehold improvements will include the cost of demolition (if any), construction of walls, ceilings, electrical, plumbing, HVAC, fixtures, flooring and any other hard costs associated with the interior and exterior structural and mechanical components of the building. Also enter any landlord allowance or contribution for the construction of the leasehold improvements, as this will reduce the eventual cost of the leasehold improvements.

Bar and kitchen equipment. Based on your menu, prepare a detailed list of the bar and kitchen equipment you'll need. Obtain actual bids and be sure to consider the cost of delivery, installation and setup. If possible, reference a detail of the bar and kitchen equipment and place it in the appendix of your business plan.

Bar and dining room furniture. If possible, reference a detailed drawing of the bar/dining room furniture and place it in the appendix. Obtain actual bids and be sure to consider the cost of delivery, installation and setup.

Professional services. This section includes costs like vural, engineering, design, legal, accounting and other professionals and consultants whose services will be used. Obtain cost estimates from these professionals based on the scope of services you plan to have them perform.

Organization and development. A variety of costs are placed in this category, including deposits on utilities, sales tax and lease, permits and licenses, menus and other similar costs. Obtain cost estimates from suppliers or other authoritative sources.

Interior finishes and equipment. This section includes interior items such as kitchen small wares, artwork, décor, sound system, POS and other similar items. Obtain cost estimates from suppliers or other authoritative sources.

Exterior finishes and equipment. Items such as landscaping, exterior sign, parking lot and other similar costs are included in this category. Obtain cost estimates from suppliers or other authoritative sources.

Pre-opening expenses. Preopening expenses are standard restaurant operating expenses that are incurred before opening. Included are costs such as food, beverage and supplies inventory needed for menu development, training and opening as well as utilities, interest expense, uniforms, marketing and payroll costs of management and staff. It's common to hire the chef or other management personnel from one to three months before opening, depending on the need for their involvement in the development and startup activities. Hourly staff normally begins training one to two weeks before opening.

Working capital and contingency funds. Very few restaurants are profitable during the first few months of operation. Some restaurants that are quite successful today took a year or more to reach profitability. Some provision should be made in the capital budget for working capital to cover possible operating deficits after opening. It's quite rare to open up a new independent restaurant and start out making a profit in the first month of operation.

It is also important to have a contingency built into the capital budget for change orders and cost overruns. There will always be surprises and unplanned costs when opening a restaurant. Cover yourself by having a contingency equal to at least 5 percent to 10 percent of the total project cost.

Sales Projections

Projecting a realistic and achievable sales volume is at the heart of every restaurant business plan. Nearly all of the restaurant's expenses, as well as the profit, cash flow and return on investment are affected directly by sales volume.

> New restaurants also get bombarded by every coupon merchandiser, directory, magazine, newspaper, and a litany of other marketing opportunities. You need to create your own marketing plan, or enlist a marketing consultant before deciding on the various vehicles by which you'll market your restaurant.
>
> *~ Restaurant Startup & Growth magazine/ RestaurantOwner.com*

To estimate sales volume in a to-be-developed restaurant, both the average check per guest and guest counts by meal period should be objectively analyzed and projected.

In most restaurants the number of guests served can vary dramatically by meal period and day of the week. For example, many restaurants do as much as 50 percent or more of their weekly sales on Friday and Saturday. This makes it important to consider expected guest activity for every meal period in a typical week.

To get a sense of the level of business that can be expected, it helps to become very familiar with what kind of customer activity existing restaurants experience in your immediate market area. Spend some time in these restaurants and through observation and casual discussions with employees and even managers, inquire about their busy and slow times. Ask about how many table turns they do on different days of the week. Are sales trending higher or lower than last year. If you're tactful and friendly, it's often amazing what information they'll share.

Three sets of sale projections should be prepared:

* Conservative (worst case)
* Moderate (anticipated)
* Optimistic (potential)

The last thing you want to do is build your financial projections and business plan around a best-case scenario. The value of an "optimistic" projection shows you how well the business could perform if all the planets are aligned. It creates some excitement for you and your investors, regarding the potential of the enterprise. A more reasonable strategy is to attempt to build your business plan around a worst-case scenario. We don't suggest that you be pessimistic; however, if you can execute your concept and launch the business based on a conservative sales projection, you are more likely to weather the startup phase of negative cash flow, which is almost inevitable.

Labor Projections

Hourly labor cost is one of the largest expenses in any restaurant. Don't just assume that your hourly labor cost will be some certain percentage of sales just because of what other restaurants are doing. There are many variables that affect hourly labor and they can be different even in what may appear to be very similar restaurant operations. Take the time to project your labor cost by position for each meal period in a typical week based on the level of business activity you actually expect.

Taking into consideration each meal period's covers (number of meals served) and sales volume, estimate the hours and number of employees needed in each position to adequately staff the restaurant.

As a rule, management salaries should not exceed 10 percent of sales. A general manager's salary often runs from 3 percent to 4 percent of gross annual sales. If you're the owner/operator and you're also running the res-

The Importance of Job Descriptions

The first step in getting your restaurant kitchen organized is to create a list of duties and responsibilities for each kitchen job position. Job descriptions help your employees understand the expectations and results you look for from their job performance. It's also a good idea to include the skills, training and qualifications needed to perform each job. Job positions and stations typically differ from one restaurant to another and should be unique to an operation.

~ Restaurant Startup & Growth magazine/ RestaurantOwner.com

So, You're Thinking About Owning, Operating or Investing in a Restaurant...

97

taurant, you can, of course, pay yourself what you want. For purposes of the business plan, however, it would probably be prudent to keep your compensation within the 3 percent to 4 percent of sales. Your compensation should not become a contentious issue to your lenders or potential investors or detract from presenting the profit potential of the restaurant in the best possible light.

A typical rule of thumb for table-service restaurants is to keep hourly labor (gross payroll) at or below 18 percent to 20 percent of sales. Hourly labor cost on busy nights can be as low as 11 percent to 12 percent of sales, whereas on slow nights, it can be as high as 22 percent to 25 percent. The goal for the week, however, in most cases would be to shoot for an hourly labor cost of 18 percent or less.

Employee benefits include the employer's portion of payroll taxes, workers' compensation, medical and other employee insurance premiums as well as other employee-related expenses. Employee benefits often run 5 percent to 6 percent of gross sales and 20 percent to 23 percent of gross payroll.

Assumptions

On the assumptions page, enter the estimates of the remaining operating costs and expenses. We highly recommend you purchase the National Restaurant Association's (NRA) Industry Operations Report as a way to conduct a "reality check" on numbers as compared with industry averages. We also recommend following a restaurant-specific chart of accounts. The following are the major cost and expense categories included in assumptions:

Cost of sales. Estimate cost of sales as a percentage of the corresponding sales category. For instance, if your sales projections list food, liquor, beer and wine sales estimates, based on expected costs and anticipated menu prices you should have a good idea of what the respective cost percentages will be for each. If your sales projections show that you anticipate $100,000 in sales per month, and you have calculated an average food cost of 32 percent, then the food cost portion of your projections will be $32,000.

Please note that when showing percentages for cost of sales, you should show the percentage in relationship to the specific revenue category, not overall sales.

Direct operating expenses. Direct operating expenses usually run 4 percent to 6 percent of gross sales. Some of the direct operating expenses you'll want to include are:
* Auto expense.
* Cleaning supplies and services.
* Extermination.
* Flowers and decorations.
* Kitchen utensils.

* Laundry and linens.
* Licenses and permits.
* Menus and wine lists.
* Paper supplies.
* Security systems.
* Tableware and small wares.
* Uniforms.

Music and entertainment. Depending on the concept and the type of music and entertainment used, expenses in this category can vary significantly. According to industry averages, music and entertainment costs run from an almost negligible amount to as much as 2 percent to 3 percent of sales when live entertainment is employed on a regular basis. Among the costs of music are licensing fees to the performing rights organizations.

Marketing. Marketing includes expenses associated with promotions, advertising and marketing programs and materials. Industry averages show that most independent restaurants spend between 2 percent and 4 percent of sales on marketing-related items.

Utilities. The cost of utilities can vary widely depending primarily on the location, local utility rates and prevailing climate conditions. Most restaurants spend from 2 percent to 4 percent of sales and from $4 to $9 per square foot per year on utilities.

General and administrative. In most situations, "G&A" costs run 3 percent to 6 percent of sales. One big component and factor in this category is the use of credit cards by your customers. Examples of G&A expenses include:
* Accounting services.
* Bank charges.
* Cash over/short.
* Credit card charges.
* Dues and subscriptions.
* Office supplies.
* Payroll processing.
* Postage.
* Professional services.
* Armored car.
* Telephone and Internet.
* Training materials.

Repairs and maintenance (R&M). R&M includes repairs and ongoing maintenance of equipment, building components and landscaping as well as the cost of equipment maintenance contracts. Restaurants in a new facil-

So, You're Thinking About Owning, Operating or Investing in a Restaurant...

99

ity with new equipment should have below-average repair and maintenance expenses for the first few years at least. As an industry average, R&M runs from 1 percent to 2.5 percent in most restaurants.

Occupancy costs. These include primarily fixed expenses associated with the facility housing the restaurant. Kitchen equipment lease payments (if any) should also be included in occupancy costs. A good rule of thumb is to keep occupancy costs at or below 10 percent of sales. It is often very difficult to generate an adequate profit and return on investment when occupancy costs exceed 10 percent of sales. As a general rule, rent should not exceed 6 percent of sales.

In most restaurants, occupancy costs run $12 to $22 per square foot. However, in many urban locations, particularly in upscale neighborhoods, occupancy costs can run much higher. Still, the 10 percent rule of thumb would hold. Our advice would be to not venture into any location in which you're not confident the restaurant will generate at least 10 times the total occupancy costs in annual sales.

It is extremely important to accurately estimate occupancy costs for the business plan projections. Get at least two estimates from competent professionals in the real estate and insurance industries to determine property (ad valorem) taxes and insurance costs. You can't afford surprises in this area.

Depreciation and amortization. Depreciation and amortization are non-cash expenses and represent the arbitrary write-off or expense allocation of capitalized assets like equipment, furniture and fixtures and preopening or startup expenses. Work with your accountant to determine your depreciation and amortization schedules for various capital improvements.

In the operating projections we recommend adding depreciation and amortization back to net income (and subtracting loan principal payments) to arrive at the amount of cash flow generated by the restaurant each year.

Income statements. Once you've completed the sales, labor, and assumptions projections, you are ready to complete the income statement portion of your plan. This section should include:

Summary 'profit and loss' statement ('P&L'). You should provide a summary P&L reflecting both monthly and annual projections for each of the sales projections levels (conservative, moderate, and optimistic). The summary P&L may be preferred over a detailed version by some people who aren't interested in all the details. It's concise, easy to understand and contains the key restaurant industry ratios most people will want to know.

Use the information gathered for sales, labor and your assumptions to formulate your income statements.

Detailed P&L. Provide a detailed income statement based on the moderate (or anticipated) sales projection. This format will show interested parties the detailed expenses that you anticipate. It also reflects that you have done your homework, and that you actually have a plan for operating the restaurant day to day.

Five-year projections. Many investors know that they can't realistically expect a return on their investment in the first year. A summary projection showing three to five years of profit and loss helps them evaluate the probability of their ROI.

Cash flow break-even. You can pretty much count on any potential investor or lender to ask the question, "What level of sales do you need to cover all your expenses?" By doing a break-even analysis you can not only give them an answer, but also show them exactly how the number was reached.

To calculate a break-even point you must first identify all of your fixed expenses. Next, add the percentages of all your variable expenses. Variable expenses include your projected cost of sales, credit card charges, a portion of hourly labor (the portion not included in your fixed costs) and possibly some for paper and other supplies.

Investment Analysis

Once you have completed your financial projections you will have a better understanding of how much and where you need to get the capital it will take to turn your idea into reality. The investment analysis should provide a detailed picture of the investment plan for the restaurant. It should incorporate the sources of funds needed to complete the project as well as a proposed return on investment analysis (ROI).

Source of funds. Funding sources include bank or personal loans, leases, investment capital from partners or owners, or funds from venture capitalists. Would-be investors and bankers will want to know what type of liability the restaurant will assume. For example, if you plan to use a large equipment lease as a means of getting equipment without having to spend the upfront capital, then you need to disclose that. Equipment leases, like bank loans, take a priority over investment capital when it comes to getting paid back.

Capital contributions. Most plans will have only one type of investor such as partners or shareholders. However, in some cases there may be multiple types of capital contributors. An ROI analysis should be presented for each separate investment role or group. Additionally, each investor role should have a brief description of the expected financial requirements, ownership percentage (if applicable), ROI, and an explanation of how that investment role could be affected by unexpected cash requests in the event they are needed.

An ROI analysis should show how long, based on the moderate projections level, it will take for an investment to be paid back. If the payback is anticipated to extend beyond three to five years, you may have a tough time getting an investor to buy into your concept.

So, You're Thinking About Owning, Operating or Investing in a Restaurant...

101

Growth Plan/Exit Strategy

An aggressive growth plan can be a double-edged sword. On one side, investors will want to know that if the restaurant is a huge success, they'll have the opportunity to participate in the expansion of the concept. The other side is, don't depend on expansion to make your restaurant concept an attractive investment opportunity.

Use this section of your plan to portray future expansion possibilities and opportunities. This section can also be used to explain exit options for investors who may want to cash out or remove themselves from ownership.

Plan to Succeed

Creating a great business plan requires a lot of work as well as knowledge. Go to seminars. Seek consultants' advice. Get the NRA Industry operations report. Join the National Restaurant Association and its state counterparts. Do your homework.

You may spend 80-100 hours a week at work in or on behalf of the restaurant once you get ready to open. Without a good plan you may have to work that many hours for months thereafter. Spend those hours now to be sure you have a good plan. Many restaurants fail simply for lack of a plan. Others fail because they didn't follow their plan or adjust it as needed.

When it comes down to it, you invest both time and money in getting a restaurant started. Earnest and diligent business planning, especially developing the financial projections, is one of the best ways to invest your time before opening the doors. The payoff can be a long-lasting and profitable enterprise. Plan to succeed.

Creating a business plan for the first time is too daunting of a project for most newbies.

~ Big Dave Ostrander

Break-Even: It's Like Having Your Own Financial Crystal Ball

Calculating how much sales a restaurant must have to cover all of its costs for a certain period of time, say a week or month, provides tremendous advantages for restaurant operators, including more restful sleep. Some of the advantages of knowing your "break-even":

It tells you the sales volume your restaurant needs every week or month to have any real chance of making a profit. Knowing only your sales volume can give you a good sense of whether you're making or losing money.

Knowing your break-even enables you to respond promptly to sales declines that may put the restaurant in an unprofitable position. During a sales slump, break-even acts like an early warning system. It can tell you that once sales slide past a certain point, chances are you're losing money and you have a real problem on your hands. It's much better knowing that sooner rather than later.

Break-even also gives you a tool to quickly estimate your profit or loss for a period of time, with knowing just your sales.

There are two basic types of costs in business. Those that stay the same regardless of sales volume like rent (unless you're subject to rent as a "percentage" of your sales) and property taxes, which are referred as "fixed" costs. There are also costs that go up or down in direct proportion to sales volume, a good example being food and beverage costs, which are referred to as "variable" costs. These numbers can be derived from your profit and loss statement (P&L).

The basic formula for computing break-even is:

Break-even Sales = Total Fixed Costs / 1-Variable Cost %

Don't worry if you can't determine your fixed and variable costs to the penny. Even arriving at "ballpark" figures will be useful. Let's say, for the sake of example, you determine your total fixed costs for a given period are $25,821, and your variable costs are 34.4% of your total sales.

Applying this formula, you will find that your break-even sales are:

Break-even Sales = $25,821 / 1-34.4 %

Break-even Sales = $25,821 / 65.6 % = $39,361

We recommend that every restaurateur purchase a copy of the National Restaurant Association's Uniform Systems of Accounts for Restaurants. Our team edited the 8th edition (most recent version as of this publication), and we believe it is an invaluable accounting and financial resource for restaurateurs and restaurant accountants and bookkeepers.

— Jim Laube

How to Find Investors
and Raise Startup Capital Chapter
for Your First Restaurant

How does one go about finding investors? What will they want in return? How much do you have to give up to a prospective investor? These are questions we hear over and over again. But these questions are hard to answer with a single, uniform response since investment relationships vary from one deal to the next. What works in one scenario doesn't necessarily work in another.

Before borrowing money from a friend it's best to decide which you need most.

~ Joe Moore

One of the greatest misconceptions of first-time restaurateurs is assuming that prior business experience and a good business plan will be sufficient to get a bank loan. They wrongly suppose that the restaurant, once completed, will serve as the primary collateral for the loan. Then they're unhappily surprised after the loan officer tells them that they have a good business plan, the restaurant concept looks like a "slam dunk," and the numbers are believable, but the only way they can get a loan is by putting up more collateral.

One operator put it like this: "Banks are not in the risk-taking business! I thought that being in the business for years as a manager, and the ability to show a proven positive cash flow would be enough. It was not. The banks were most interested in what would happen if I walked away. What are the real assets that they could get their hands on to protect their investment."

For some, this means they have to get a second mortgage, dip further into their savings, or get a loan against their retirement account. For others, they might seek a relative's help either as a guarantor, investor or lender.

This practice is evidenced by the results of two surveys conducted among members of RestaurantOwner.com. Respondents who spent $100,000 or less on opening their restaurant cited as financing sources, their savings accounts, home equity loans, borrowing from relatives and "maxing out" their credit cards.

But what if your restaurant idea will cost $200,000, $500,000, or even $1 million? The fact is, out of more than 400 survey respondents, the average spent to open their restaurant was around $450,000, and in both surveys

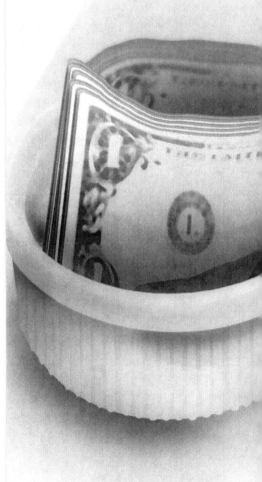

So, You're Thinking About Owning, Operating or Investing in a Restaurant...

105

the median spent was $200,000 to $225,000. The huge gap between the median (this means that half the respondents spent below this amount and half spent above this amount) and the average can be attributed to several respondents spending way more than $450,000 to finance their restaurants.

Seeking Investment Capital

If you have a concept that will cost hundreds of thousands of dollars to open, then chances are the financing methods mentioned earlier just aren't realistic options for raising that kind of capital.

So, if you don't have enough money, and you don't have the assets required to get a loan, the logical solution is to find an investment partner who does. RestaurantOwner.com survey results showed that once restaurant financing surpasses $300,000, there was a substantial increase in the number of respondents reporting that investors were a key part of the funding process.

Investors aren't Lenders

To gain a better understanding on finding an investor, let's first define the term, particularly that of "restaurant investor". You need to understand that, with few exceptions, investors aren't lenders. They are owners. That's right, regardless of your legal structure, the reality is that an investor is your partner, not your lender. Banks are lenders, not partners. Once you pay back any bank loans, the bankers are gone; they don't get any more of your cash flow.

Consider also that investors want a better return on their money than a bank might demand. The banks get a relatively low return in the form of interest. The reason it's lower is because they have collateral, which reduces their risk exposure. On the other hand, a would-be investor has only the assets of the business for security. In an industry that experiences a 60 percent failure rate within the first three years, restaurant investment is a risky proposition. Therefore, from an investment viewpoint the return needs to justify the risk.

For a restaurant deal to be attractive, the typical investor wants to see at least 20 percent annual return on the investment (ROI). However, that may not be enough to offset the inherent risk. You're much more likely to get a better response if you can offer 25 percent to 30 percent annual ROI.

Take note; at this point we're not talking about ownership percentage (equity). We're simply expressing ROI. It really doesn't matter if the investors are 5 percent, 50 percent or even 90 percent equity owners; they'll probably be more concerned with their prospective ROI.

Don't discount that many people consider owning a stake in a restaurant appealing and prestigious. That said, you have an ethical, and in some cases, legal duty to provide potential investors with enough information to create sound expectations about the potential risks and return of their investment. (See "Be Sure to Stay on the Right Side of Securities Laws When Raising Capital" on page 111.)

Finding Potential Investors

We don't want to discourage you, but the fact is finding someone to invest in your restaurant is likely to be a challenge. You may have heard or read about investment group terms such as venture capitalists, private equity firms, or angel investor organizations. In fact, conduct an Internet search on these terms and you'll find plenty of wealthy investment groups looking for "home run" ideas to invest in. If you're an established restaurant with franchise or growth opportunity, pursuing these types of investment firms could yield dividends. However, for startup restaurants, chasing these professional investment groups may prove futile.

You need to look locally for partners. Many entrepreneurs turn to family and friends for capital needs, but we recommend that you give this route some serious thought beforehand. While your restaurant idea may be your greatest passion, it's also risky by nature. Do you really want to risk their money and your relationship for this venture? Should things go badly, and in this business things go badly more than 60 percent of the time, sometimes family is all you have to fall back on.

Consider instead cultivating your existing business and social relationships. Run your idea by those in your network of acquaintances. Who knows, there may be an angel investor in your midst. The Angel Capital Education Foundation defines an angel investor as a high net-worth individual who invests his or her own money in start-up companies in exchange for an equity share of the business. Many are former entrepreneurs themselves and make investments to gain a return on their money, or to participate in the entrepreneurial process, or simply to "give back" to their communities by catalyzing economic growth.

If you plan on finding multiple investors, keep in mind that the Securities and Exchange Commission (SEC) and your state's commerce regulatory entity have strict rules when it comes to soliciting investment capital. Even though this is a private rather than a public offering, seek the counsel of an attorney who specializes in forming legal entities that have multiple investors and who can advise you on the formulation of a prospectus, if warranted. (See "Be Sure to Stay on the Right Side of Securities Laws When Raising Capital" at the end of this chapter.)

SEC regulations prohibit you from using any form of public solicitation or general advertising in connection with your search for investment capital. This means you can't throw a party, entice prospective investors to attend, and then solicit their investment with a PowerPoint presentation.

Before you start chasing prospective investment partners, you better have a solid business plan in hand. A sophisticated investor should be able to evaluate the merits and risks of the proposed restaurant venture. The first

So, You're Thinking About Owning, Operating or Investing in a Restaurant...

107

thing they're going to evaluate is you. The quality of your business plan will be a direct expression of your capabilities as an operator.

As discussed earlier, a good business plan should reflect your qualifications, experience and track record, and that of your proposed management team, if already selected. It needs to do a good job of detailing the restaurant concept and provide a convincing argument of how that restaurant concept can be successful in the intended market.

The business plan should include solid, realistic financial projections, including detailed startup costs, sales projections, profit-and-loss, and the expected ROI for the venture. You will be asked to validate your numbers, so be prepared to defend them with authority and financial understanding.

If you are searching for investment partners who can also contribute their business expertise as well as their money, then having a work-in-progress business plan may be acceptable. You may be an expert at running a restaurant — you should be very confident with financial projections as well — however, you may lack general business experience, such as structuring your legal entity, dealing with landlords, or getting bank financing. Experienced business partners can help fill these gaps and are more likely to have faith in the capabilities you do have if you're upfront about your shortcomings. They can help round out your business plan as the development progresses.

Be forewarned: If you plan on having multiple investors, having an incomplete business plan is a sure way to scare them off.

Structuring the Deal

A key consideration for investment will center on ROI and equity positions. The question we've heard often: "How much ownership should I give to an investor?"

The short answer is, "every deal is different." Typically, equity positions are influenced based on several factors, such as the number of owners (investors), capital contribution, liability and participation, to name a few.

First, let's view a single-investor scenario. If you think you're going to find an investor who will put up 100 percent of the capital, share full liability, and then settle for 50 percent or less equity, yoursearch may take a long time.

To enhance your own "sweat equity" position, you need to put up some capital as well. However, the ratio-of-equity ownership percentages do not have to equal the capital contribution. You can still put together a deal that ensures you have a greater equity interest by following this simple rule: The investors get their money back first.

For example, let's assume your venture will cost $500,000 to fund and you plan to invest $50,000 of your own money. You then seek an investment partner who will contribute $250,000 in cash and co-sign for bank financing for the remaining $200,000. To enhance your 50-percent equity position, you maintain a modest salary for running the restaurant, but you designate

> The experience is composed of the food, service and ambience. When you create some level of WOW factor in any of these variables, you have enhanced your chances of providing a memorable experience.
>
> ~ *Restaurant Startup & Growth* magazine/ RestaurantOwner.com

cash distributions to be commensurate with the ratio of capital contributions. In this case, the investor would get 83 percent ($250,000 ˜ $300,000) of the cash distributions as compared with 17 percent ($50,000 ˜ $300,000) for you until the original capital investment is paid back. This is simply an example; actual percentages will be determined through negotiation.

An example of structuring a partnership deal might be you and your operating partners forming an LLC (limited liability company) that serves as the "general partner" for the venture. Let's say you structure the deal so that the restaurant entity is separate from the real estate entity, creating an environment wherein the restaurant paid rent for the real estate. You divide the capitalization into, perhaps, 40 shares. Investors, as well as the general partner receive an equity position in both that equals the number of shares purchased. Cash distributions are structured to be equivalent with the equity position. On top of that, the general partner receives a management fee for operating the restaurant.

Disclosures

When partners are added at or near the inception of a venture, there are often no current financial statements to disclose, only good-faith projections. In this case, prospective partners should be provided financial projections that are more than just fanciful hopes and dreams. That is, there should be some rational basis to the projections that can be articulated either when answering a potential investor's questions (or addressing a jury in securities fraud litigation). For example, meal check averages should be similar to those in nearby venues of a similar service type (or based off the check averages of your other restaurants). Occupancy should be realistic, and not calculated on two full table turns per day (unless you're lucky enough to have that in an existing unit). Patio revenue should be adjusted seasonally to account for changes in the weather.

Using realistic financial projections will allow a more accurate calculation of the investors' anticipated payback period, which will manage expectations. You have little to no chance of hitting your target if your projections are not sound. That makes investors angry.

As for risk factors, many of the risks in a start-up venture seem like common sense. It seems strange that you would need to disclose the possibility that the business has no operating history, so there are no historical data from which to evaluate the investment, when everyone knows that is the case. But it should be disclosed. A host of similar disclosures (e.g., we might have to borrow money if we go over budget; we might go over budget if there are construction delays; there might be construction delays if there is a shortage of material; there might be a shortage of material if there is a natural disaster or war) must be made, in the eyes of the Securities and Exchange Commission, to protect the unwary investor from the profiteers tricking them out of their savings.

A Good Deal is When It's Good for Everyone

Successful investment partnerships don't happen by chance. They require planning and commitment. Involving a qualified attorney during the planning stage is a must. A good attorney can protect you against unforeseen pitfalls by addressing issues within the partnership or operating agreement such as what happens if additional cash contributions are needed or if one of the investors wants out or is in default of the agreement.

As lawyers might tell you, "The best way to plan for a good partnership is to plan for when it goes bad." Hopefully you'll find investors who are as enthusiastic about your restaurant venture as you are, and that it ends up being a good deal for all involved.

A Few Words of Advice for Restaurateurs with More Cash than Experience

Your decision to enter independent restaurant ownership probably stems from either a love of food, affection for entertaining, entrepreneurial longing, past business successes, or all of the above. Whatever the reason, we want you to know that this is an extremely challenging business that takes money, experience (both in business and in restaurant operations), and resolve. Chances are that you have three out of the four, lacking only in restaurant experience.

So, before you get too far down the development path and make too many mistakes, consider finding an operating partner who can bring the right type of restaurant experience to your venture. Not all restaurant experience is equal. In other words, just because someone may have a successful background in running a 16-unit Wendy's franchise, doesn't mean they are properly suited to open your $2 million casual dinner house.

Try to find an operating partner or general manager who has experience in a similar concept. Do background checks on any candidate, including references, and before you hand over the keys to your $3 million- to $5 million-a-year operation, do a credit check to see how the candidate handles personal financial affairs.

Once you think you have the right person, at least on paper, go into the interview process with the objective of establishing a comfort level with the prospect. We recommend you spend a lot of time together in a short period. Is this the type of person whose close company you enjoy? What do you have in common?

Keep in mind that there are a lot of great general managers, many of whom work for chains, who are looking for entrepreneurial opportunities themselves. They have the restaurant experience but not the cash or business ownership experience. Finding the right operating partner is the first step in turning your restaurant dream into reality.

Be Sure to Stay on the Right Side of Securities Laws When Raising Capital

Raising money from investors is easy. All you have to do is ask for it, explain how it will be used, give the investor part of the company and promise a fair return within a reasonable time. Right? Wrong.

When you use, or even want to ask for, other people's money as capital to finance your business, you cross the great divide that separates those who invest themselves from those who finance business ventures to obtain a return on their capital. In exchange for their money, investors expect a piece of the action — ownership of some part of (an equity position in) the company — since that likely will yield them a greater return than they would receive if they simply lent the money at some fixed rate of interest.

The seemingly innocent acts of accepting or even asking for other people's money in exchange for a piece of your company (for example, offering shares of stock in a corporation or a membership interest in a limited-liability company — both of which are securities) in exchange for startup or seed money, triggers federal and state securities regulations designed to protect unwary investors from unscrupulous profiteers.

In general, unless an exemption applies, every security issued must comply with securities registration laws, and doing so is often a fairly expensive and cumbersome process. Exemptions often key on factors such as a limited number of investors; residence of all investors in a single state; investor sophistication (as measured by wealth and income, with the upper end termed "accredited"); a pre-existing relationship between the investor and the company or its principals; the absence of any advertising or promotional information; and a commitment from all acquirers that the stock purchase is for their own accounts and is not being made as a securities dealer, with an eye to further distribution. State regulations often are referred to as "Blue Sky Laws" because that is all that some disreputable companies delivered to their investors in exchange for their hard-earned and often forever-lost cash.

Many of the reforms that continue to govern today (Federal Securities Acts of 1933 and 1934) were created in the aftermath of "Black Friday," the October 1929 stock market debacle. Consistent with former U.S. Supreme Court Justice Louis Brandeis's admonition that "Sunlight is said to be the best of disinfectants," by calling for specific disclosures and warnings, these rules partially level the playing field to help neophytes participate alongside more experienced investors.

Regulation does not mean that raising money is taboo. Rather they allow anyone inexpert in the area to retain an attorney who specializes in securities laws to guide them through the process, whether by way of registration, qualification or exemption. Depending on the complexity of the financing structure, the entire process can be fairly straightforward and involve minimal filing requirements or can be incredibly complex, requiring extensive disclosures such as those found in a prospectus or private placement memorandum.

The failure to comply with securities laws can have dramatic consequences, so take care to obtain legal advice applicable to the securities being issued or transferred and the company (issuer) issuing or acquiring them.

Please note that no book should be considered a replacement for qualified legal and tax advice. Each transaction has specific circumstances and issues that need to be considered individually.

Choosing a
Legal Structure
for Your Business

Chapter

L ike any business, a restaurant may be organized in a variety of ways, including, but not limited to, as a sole proprietorship, a corporation, a limited liability company, or a partnership. The choice of business entity, if any, used to conduct a restaurant's business has important legal and tax implications for it.

> *"Everything is o.k., until it isn't."*
>
> ~*Advice from a lawyer to his client (Anonymous).*

When you get into the restaurant business, your foremost concerns are basic: will it be successful and will customers actually come? Your attorney and CPA have the same concerns, of course, but they are focused on numerous details you might not have considered.

In this chapter, we look at some of the legal and tax issues that face operators in choosing the form of their business. Most likely you've heard the terms sole proprietorship, corporation, limited liability company, and partnership, but you might not be sure of their significance when starting a business.

The information in this chapter is not exhaustive, and we encourage you to have a good attorney and CPA at your side from the inception of any transaction involving starting or purchasing a business. Still, we believe the information that follows can help you have a more productive conversation with your advisors and help you feel that you have sufficient information to be an active participant in making the right choices for your enterprise.

The Legal Organization of Your Business

Restaurants may be organized in a variety of ways, including, but not limited to, as a sole proprietorship, a corporation, a limited liability company, or a partnership. Each has important legal and tax implications. The Internal Revenue Code (IRC) allows certain business entities to be taxed as corporations, partnerships, or choose to be completely disregarded (the "check the box" rules).

Sole Proprietorship. Doing business as a sole proprietorship means the restaurant is owned by a single, natural person, and any income and ex-

The LLC: Popular but Not Necessarily Perfect

The Limited Liability Company has become an increasingly popular choice of business entity for start-up businesses because it combines the tax advantages of a partnership as a "pass-through" entity and the "limited liability" of a corporation, in that the owners (called "members") of an LLC are generally shielded from personal liability for the LLC's debts and obligations. That said, you should consult with an attorney and tax adviser to determine if this is the best business form for you. First, LLCs are governed by state laws, which may vary from state to state. Also, there are tax and other reasons why a corporation might be advantageous for your business. Finally, you should understand that the limited liability protection that the LLC affords its members is not absolute; there are circumstances in which the members will be liable for company debts and obligations. Many of the details are beyond the scope of this manual; however, a competent business attorney can advise you on these matters.

penses related to the business will be reported on Schedule C of that person's personal federal income tax return. The restaurant does not file a separate tax return. The taxable income of the restaurant shown on Schedule C will be combined with the other components of the owner's taxable income and is subject to tax at the applicable individual tax rates.

If a sole proprietor of a business does not wish to operate under his or her name, the restaurant business may choose to do business under another name registered with the state's secretary of state or register of deeds (i.e., a "doing business as" or DBA name) but this does not change the manner in which the restaurant will be taxed. In addition to income tax, the taxable income of the restaurant operated as a sole proprietorship will be subject to self-employment tax. The self-employment tax rate is the equivalent of the combined employer and employee portions of the Social Security (FICA) tax. Your CPA can advise you on the current self-employment tax rate.

Corporation. A restaurant business may be organized as a corporation, whether it has one or multiple owners. A corporation offers the benefit of limited legal liability for its owners, but potentially at the cost of double taxation of the restaurant's income at business entity and owner levels. The Internal Revenue Code allows corporations to elect to be taxed under Subchapter C or Subchapter S of the code. The default treatment for a corporation is to be subject to tax under Subchapter C. A "C" corporation is treated as a different person separate and apart from its owners (the shareholders) for income tax purposes. Accordingly, a C corporation is required to file a corporate income tax return (Form 1120), and its income is subject to federal income tax at the corporate level.

When corporation income is distributed to shareholders as a dividend, both the corporation and the shareholders might be subject to income tax individually. Accordingly, doing business as a C corporation usually results in double taxation of the income of a restaurant business. A corporation, however, may elect to be taxed under Subchapter S of the IRC (a corporation making such an election is called an "S" corporation). An S corporation has the benefits of limited liability protection for its owners, but allows most income to flow through and be subject to income tax at the shareholder versus the corporate level. The Subchapter S election is subject to certain limitations, including the maximum number of shareholders and who can be a shareholder (only individuals who are residents of the United States).

Although an S corporation's income usually flows through to its owners for income tax purposes, an S corporation is still required to file a separate federal income tax return (Form 1120S). For an existing business organized as a C corporation, making an S corporation election can have significant income tax consequences, including the recognition of "built-in gains" on the corporation's assets.

Partnership. A partnership may be used when there are two or more owners of a restaurant business. Partnerships generally offer the advantage of a single level of taxation of the income of the restaurant business, but usually at the cost of a loss of limited liability protection for at least one of the partners (e.g., a partnership may be organized as a limited partnership, offering limited liability to its limited partners, but the general partner will not benefit from such protection). Income of a partnership flows through to its partners and is subject to income tax at the partner level. An advantage of partnerships over other business entities is the wide latitude afforded under Subchapter K of the IRC to allocate items of income and expense among the partners. The owners of a partnership can be any kind of individual or business entity. Partners cannot draw a salary from the partnership as can the restaurant's employees. This can be a significant disadvantage for the tax and retirement planning of the owners.

Although the income of a partnership is not subject to tax at the partnership level, the partnership must file a federal income tax return (Form 1065) for information purposes. Partnerships also must file a Form K-1, detailing items of income and expense flowing through to each partner to be reported on each partner's federal income tax return.

Limited Liability Company. Limited liability companies offer the benefit of limited liability protection for all of the owners of the LLC while retaining the benefit of being taxed at a single (owner) level. In addition, LLCs are not subject to many of the limitations of C corporations (any person or business entity can be a member). Unlike a partnership, an LLC under most state laws may have a single owner or multiple owners.

The default treatment of a single-member LLC is for the entity to be disregarded for federal income tax purposes. Accordingly, a disregarded LLC will not have to file any federal income tax return and all of its income and expenses will be treated as if they were incurred at the owner level. In effect, an individual who operates a restaurant business as an LLC will be subject to income tax in the same way as if the business were operated as a sole proprietorship (but with limited liability protection for its owner).

The default treatment of an LLC with more than one member is for the LLC to be subject to income tax as a partnership. A single or multimember LLC may elect, however, to be subject to federal income tax as a corporation. A single-member LLC electing to be taxed as a corporation has the option of subsequently making the S corporation election.

It should be noted that members cannot draw a salary from the LLC as can the restaurant's employees. The entity may wish to consider this factor by making the S corporation election which, among other advantages, will allow the members to draw a salary and potentially participate in any retirement plans offered to the restaurant's employees.

How Choice of Entity Affects the Purchase of Restaurant

Many restaurateurs get into the business by starting brand-new operations from the ground up. There are, however, those who either get their start or increase their holdings by purchasing existing businesses. These can be win-win deals for all involved.

The sellers are typically owners looking to retire and/or cash out on a successful concept, and are in the position to realize value created through hard work, creativity, and skilled management. The buyers have an opportunity to take over a successful operation with a known revenue stream, an established reputation, and a base of customers. The customers continue to enjoy a favorite eatery that changes hands seamlessly.

But between making an initial offer to purchase and being handed the key to the front door, the buyer has a lot to consider. These transactions can be complex from a legal and tax perspective for all parties; however, typically it is the buyer who is the most vulnerable. The seller often controls the transaction. The seller's attorney typically draws up the first draft of agreements, including the purchase contract, which contains warranties, representations, and indemnification language. To the unarmed buyer these might look reasonable at first blush. In fact, often there are liability and tax issues that the buyer might overlook, unless a competent transactional attorney and tax consultant are involved in the negotiation and drafting process to protect the buyer's interests.

'Asset' Versus 'Entity' Purchase

Prospective purchasers of existing businesses face the critical question of whether to purchase just the assets of a business (an "asset purchase"), or whether to purchase the actual business entity itself (an "entity purchase").

In an asset purchase — just as it sounds — the buyer purchases the business's equipment, inventory, rights to use its name, etc. Most often, the buyer creates a new entity, typically, an S corporation (S-Corp) or limited liability company (LLC) to operate the business going forward. In an entity purchase, the buyer purchases the business entity itself by acquiring all of the selling corporation's or LLC's shares.

In most cases, sellers prefer to sell the entire entity, while buyers prefer to purchase the assets only. From the seller's standpoint, the potential tax benefit of an entity sale is that the profits are considered 100 percent capital gains (assuming that he's not selling at a loss.) Capital gains are taxed at a lower rate than ordinary gains. On the other hand, if the seller sells just the assets, some of the gain may be ordinary, and some may be capital, depending on the assets. Not all proceeds from every asset's sale are eligible to be taxed as capital gains or loss. In any event, for the seller, tax planning in an asset sale is usually more complex than in an entity sale.

From the buyer's perspective, an asset purchase is preferable, since in an entity purchase, the buyer might assume the liabilities of the previous owner,

Hiring isn't child's play. In the typically high-turnover restaurant business, the pressures can be crushing. In the fray, you can easily lose sight of the legal issues, which frequently bite new restaurateurs who lack hiring experience and are uninformed about the relevant laws.

~ Restaurant Startup & Growth magazine/ RestaurantOwner.com

and could be at a tax disadvantage, for the reasons we discuss n detail later. In short, it's important that both buyer and seller understand these issues prior to entering negotiations.

For Example

Joe's Diner, LLC, has been placed on the market through a business sales broker. William "Will" Cook wants to be a restaurant owner, and he likes the location, name, and concept of Joe's Diner. As part of his initial due diligence, he learns that Joe's Diner, LLC, is a profitable enterprise.

Few restaurants are owned as sole proprietorships. Instead, they are more likely to be organized as corporations or LLCs, to shield the owner(s) from liability. Mr. Cook intends to create a new company, Cook Enterprises, LLC, to purchase the assets of Joe's Diner, including all rights to the restaurant's name, rather than acquire Joe's Diner, LLC, itself. The two owners of Joe's Diner, LLC, (i.e., the individuals who hold all of the membership interests in the company) want to simplify the transaction. They suggest that Cook purchase all the shares of Joe's Diner, LLC, (i.e., an entity purchase), and even sweeten the deal to encourage him to take this path.

Joe's Diner, LLC, owns all of the assets of the restaurant, including rights to the name. Cook thinks, "Why just purchase the assets of the company when it seems that buying the entire company would be a more seamless transaction? Anyway, I want to start running this place ASAP!"

Cook refers the matter to his attorney and tax adviser, who explain the pros and cons of each of these two methods. Generally speaking, most buyers prefer an asset purchase over an entity purchase for the following reasons:

• Cook can pick and choose among the seller's assets, buying whatever he wants, and does not have to purchase all of them.

• Cook would get a "full cost" basis for the assets purchased. This means he can begin taking full depreciation on all of the assets purchased, and can dispose of them without having to pay tax on any untaxed gain accumulated while they were held by Joe's Diner, LLC.

• Cook does not become responsible for Joe's Diner, LLC, as an entity. He doesn't have to file tax returns for Joe's Diner, LLC, as an entity, liquidate the entity, etc. He just owns the assets. The future of Joe's Diner, LLC, after the sale is not his problem.

• Cook may be able to avoid exposure for the liabilities of Joe's Diner, LLC, by purchasing just the assets of the company (instead of purchasing the company itself). When you purchase the company itself, you very often will "step into the shoes" of the former owners, becoming responsible for the seller's liabilities. If Joe's Diner, LLC, is facing pending litigation, for example, Cook could inherit it by purchasing the entity. That is why it is so important for a buyer of an entity to demand sufficient warranties and representations of all known liabilities, and seek broad indemnification for such in the purchase agreement. (Note that a buyer can also acquire responsibility for the seller's liabilities by buying just the assets of the business (especially where he buys all or most of the business's assets), but, without going into great detail, there is certainly a greater opportunity to avoid this result through an asset purchase rather than an entity purchase.)

By contrast, there are reasons why Cook might prefer to buy the seller as an entity instead of the seller's assets. These include:

• If Cook wants to continue operating the business as it is, buying Joe's Diner, LLC, the entity, itself makes for a more seamless transition for the buyer and is less noticeable to the customers of the business that new ownership is in place.

• Cook would not have to form a new entity (i.e., Cook Enterprises, LLC), get new taxpayer ID numbers, bank accounts, property tax listings, etc.

• Cook might not have to renegotiate contracts with suppliers, vendors, etc., of Joe's Diner, LLC. They might continue to do business with Joe's Diner, as if nothing has changed.

A Taxing Decision

As suggested in the forgoing example, among the advantages to the asset purchase from the buyer's standpoint, probably the biggest one pertains to taxes: The buyer would receive "full cost basis" for assets purchased. This is often the major influencing factor for the buyer.

Here's a simple scenario to illustrate when purchasing the assets of the business would provide a more favorable tax outcome for the buyer. Imagine that a single shareholder owns all of the stock of The Restaurant Inc. (TR Inc.), a corporation in which the shareholder has invested $100,000. In accounting terms, the tax "basis" in the stock is $100,000. ("Basis" refers to the original cost of an asset less depreciation. The resulting amount is used to determine gains or losses for tax purposes.) Depending on how much time has passed since TR Inc. purchased the assets, they might be fully depreciated. We would say that the shareholder's "outside basis" for his stock is $100,000, but that the corporation's "inside basis" for its assets is $0.

If this person wanted to "liquidate" TR Inc., (i.e., sell off all its assets), the shareholder would be subject to tax on $100,000, which represents the $100,000 value of the corporation's assets, less the corporation's "inside" basis of $0. This would be true whether the corporation sold its assets for cash and then dissolved itself, or the corporation dissolved and then all of its assets were distributed to the shareholder.

In purchasing TR Inc. as an entity (i.e., purchasing all of the stock of the corporation), the buyer would "step into the shoes" of the selling shareholder, and would be subject to this same tax result. So if the buyer later liquidated the corporation, the tax on this same $100,000 amount of gain would apply. The more immediate, and perhaps significant, tax consequences to the buyer is the inability to depreciate the assets. Again, the buyer steps into the shoes of the seller, who has already fully depreciated the assets.

But when purchasing the assets of the corporation (rather than purchasing the corporation as an entity) for $100,000, then the buyer would have a full $100,000 basis in these assets and would not be subject to any taxable gain. The buyer could form a new corporation and transfer these assets to that corporation. In tax terms, the new entity's inside basis and the buyer's outside basis in its stock would now both be $100,000. As noted in the previous example regarding Joe's Diner, LLC, the buyer can begin taking full depreciation on all of the assets purchased, and can dispose of these assets without having to pay tax on any untaxed gain accumulated while holding them. The immediate and future tax savings to the buyer realized by purchasing the business's assets, rather than the entity itself, could be significant.

But Sometimes Asset Versus Entity is a Nonissue

Here is where it gets a little confusing. In some cases, the "asset versus entity" question is a nonissue for tax purposes. For example, say the business you're purchasing is a sole proprietorship. The owner is a person who owns all the assets of the business and simply files a Schedule C on the tax return. Since a proprietorship is not deemed to be a separate entity from its owner, unlike a corporation or LLC, the purchase of a proprietorship is treated as an asset purchase for tax purposes, by default. Simply put, there is no entity to purchase in such a case.

Again, few restaurants are owned as sole proprietorships. Still, this scenario provides a useful illustration because a similar result could occur when the buyer is purchasing a single-owner LLC, in which the owner is an individual (as opposed to a single-owner LLC that is, in turn, owned not by an individual person but by another LLC or a corporation). That's because the IRS generally treats a single-owner LLC as a "disregarded entity" for tax purposes, as if it did not exist separately from its owner. So, if the one owner is an individual, and you disregard the LLC, then you are left with a sole proprietorship, at least for tax purposes. Thus, as logic would follow (or at least IRS logic), even if you purchased the LLC itself (i.e., its shares, rather than its assets), the purchase is treated as an asset purchase, tax-wise, by default.

Why should you care? From a practical standpoint, you might be able to gain certain benefits of an entity purchase and the tax benefits of an asset purchase, by purchasing the entity.

But what if the business you're buying is a corporation with one owner who is an individual? Here's a situation in which LLCs and corporations differ tax-wise: The IRS never treats a corporation as a disregarded entity for tax purposes, not even a single-individual shareholder S-Corp. As far as the IRS is concerned, a corporation is always "separate" from its shareholder(s), and is never automatically an asset purchase, as it would be in the purchase of a single, individual-owned LLC. So, when purchasing a corporation, regardless of the number of shareholders, you will probably need to structure the deal as an asset purchase to get full basis of the assets.

So, You're Thinking About Owning, Operating or Investing in a Restaurant...

119

Of course, many restaurant business corporations and LLCs are owned not by individuals, but by other corporations and LLCs, as subsidiaries. For example, ABC, LLC, a holding company, might own XYZ, LLC, a restaurant business. Therefore, when purchasing a restaurant, the buyer needs to know who or what owns the target business in the transaction to determine the tax ramifications of the purchase. The organization of the owner of the business can affect the inside and outside tax bases of the seller's assets and the buyer's tax exposure, if and when the buyer decides to liquidate the business.

Buyer be Aware

We hope you can see that a prospective buyer needs to bring more than an attorney into the transaction to review documents. Rather, the purchaser also should employ a qualified tax professional, such as a certified public accountant, both to examine the books and tax records of the selling company, and to determine if it is a disregarded entity.

Purchasing a business is the most complex and expensive transaction most individuals will encounter. Again, by enlisting the help of qualified professionals to assist with your due diligence, negotiations, and drafting, when purchasing a business, you can increase the odds that you'll avoid unpleasant surprises and disappointments after the deal is done.

Please note that no book should be considered a replacement for qualified legal and tax advice. Each transaction has specific circumstances and issues that need to be considered individually.

Real Restaurateurs, *Real People*
Stories about people who realized their restaurant dreams

Springing Forth from Disaster

When you open a coffee shop and cafe in a town named Greensburg, the name "Green Bean" is a natural fit. But anyone who knows Greensburg, Kansas, recognizes that "green" has a much deeper meaning — one that is attracting new businesses and opportunities to this rural community in the southwestern part of the state.

The seat of Kiowa County, Greensburg is a frequent stop for truckers and travelers along U.S. 54, a major east-west artery in the region, and U.S. Highway 183, a north-south artery from Canada to Mexico. Otherwise, Greensburg was just another little town out on the prairie, home to about 1500 people, until the night of May 4, 2007.

Then it was gone.

At 9:45 p.m., an EF5 tornado with a path nearly two miles wide and winds registered at 250 miles per hour, destroyed Greensburg — all of it. Only a grain silo and liquor store remained.

Within weeks, as leaders and residents of this community began talk of rebuilding, they recognized they had a unique opportunity. Six years after the tornado, Greensburg is now widely-recognized as the nation's model green community with more LEED-certified buildings per capita than any community in the world

And the building that houses "The Green Bean" is one of them.

Tim Kyle grew up in Greensburg and his wife, Kari, in a town a few miles away. The night the tornado hit, they were living elsewhere, working in the construction business. Of course, by 2008, the housing industry was so devastated it, too, seemed to have been hit by a tornado.

The Kyles had a young child ready for school and they wanted to move home, back to a small town where life made sense. And Kari had a dream of opening a coffee shop.

The problem for the couple and anyone else wanting to open a restaurant or any other business in town — there were no buildings left in which to operate, and most small businesses cannot afford new construction costs.

So, local residents set up a non-profit organization, Kowa County United, to construct buildings that would bring businesses back to the community in a hurry. Everyone was invited to contribute, giving $500 here or $1,000 there. They knew they would not get their money back, but their goal was to get their town back.

Any profits from Kiowa County United goes right back into construction of new buildings for small business owners. Rent for the Green Bean is a reasonable $450 per month for 1,500

square feet. Technically, the building in which the coffee shop is housed is not LEED-certified. Although all of the appropriate building measures were applied, the board of the non-profit chose not to expend funds on LEED certification, which it deemed unnecessarily costly.

The first building was simply called "The Business Incubator," a space large enough to accommodate ten businesses. It filled quickly, and The Green Bean was one of them, opening for business in November 2009.

The coffee shop was on a side street and the Kyles knew that they needed the visibility of Highway 54 since much of their success would depend on travelers stopping in for a good cup of java.

At the time another building that was adjacent to Highway 54 was under construction that would house nine businesses and the Kyles decided to move their shop into it. By March 2010, The Green Bean was open for business in its new location, in full view of those traveling on Highway 54.

"Of course, we wanted to get open and start earning an income as quickly as possible," says Tim Kyle, "but in retrospect, I wish we had just waited until March to open here,"

The Kyles spent about $6,000 of their $50,000 business loan on wiring, plumbing and building counters at the first location and then had to repeat the process in the new space just four months later.

The Green Bean is a success; despite the fact that only 20 percent or so of the business comes from locals in the vicinity of Greensburg. Most customers pull in from Highway 54 and 183, as the Kyles had anticipated.

Tim Kyle attributed that success to three things:

1. The Green Bean is the only coffee shop within a 100-mile stretch of Highway 54, with the exception of convenience stores and gas stations. The business is GPS-listed with Google, so anyone searching for hot cup will find it.

2. A billboard on the west side of town tells travelers that this is the only coffee shop for 100 miles. A billboard on the east side of town is in the works.

3. The media coverage about Greensburg's unique initiatives has been far and wide, including a three-season, 36-part Discovery Channel Planet Green series. Several episodes included The Green Bean.

At first, customers included gawkers and curiosity-seekers who came to see evidence of Greensburg's destruction first-hand, but now tourists and new business developers are coming to see and experience this model environmentally-friendly community out in the Kansas prairie.

"Our hope is that the town will continue to grow and as it does, we can grow the business," Tim Kyle says. "I would love to roast my own beans and become more coffee-nerdish, but for now, we're happy that we are where we are."

Selecting Professional Advisers

Find a restaurant that you like, owned by people who run a good operation, and find out who they are using as advisers. Customers often find good restaurants through word of mouth, and that's exactly how many independent restaurateurs find their accountants and attorneys.

There is nothing more hateful than bad advice.

— *Sophocles*

The best and brightest businesspeople in any industry surround themselves with smart advisers. There are a number of aspects to launching a new restaurant in which you will require highly trained specialists in the startup phase and beyond. Top executives and entrepreneurs have a team of lawyers, accountants and consultants on their teams, and so should you. Unlike a Fortune 500 CEO, you might not have the personal mobile number of some of the top advisers in the country in your phone's "favorites" list, but there's plenty of good talent out there eager to work for you.

Still, it's most likely, you'll need to do a little homework to find your dream team.

In planning your new restaurant, you've likely visited a number of local restaurants and others with similar concepts. You've talked with friends and neighbors about what they return to a particular restaurant over and over. You've taken notes and done research on what appeals to you in all aspects of the dining experience. Well, you should employ that same approach in selecting an attorney, accountant and consultant for your restaurant — the process is as fundamental as salt and pepper to the success of your business.

In fact, finding the right advisers should be at the top of your list when embarking on a business plan. Leaders in the industry agree that the right combination of legal, financial and professional advice introduced at the appropriate intervals of the startup phase make indelible differences in the first few years and in the long-term success of your restaurant.

Start With a CPA

Given that most restaurants that fail do so because of inadequate financial controls and projections, it's essential to spend some serious time looking

So, You're Thinking About Owning, Operating or Investing in a Restaurant...

123

at and talking about dollars and numbers with a professional who can also help you develop the best tax strategy, especially if you are purchasing an existing operation.

Many people who are drawn to the restaurant industry love to cook and love to entertain, but are not necessarily astute in accounting and financial matters. Similarly, many people when thinking of hiring professional guidance in the legal and financial arena envision a huge cost associated with the service. That's not necessarily so, particularly when the restaurateur can effectively communicate wants and needs in a clear and concise manner.

First, determine if you need an accountant or a CPA. An accountant is an individual who usually has a two- or four-year degree in bookkeeping and/or accounting and is familiar with general accounting principles. A CPA is certified by the American Institute of Certified Public Accountants, participates in ongoing professional development and is considered an expert in general accounting principles. A CPA is going to cost you more money, but can provide a greater range of services, from tax planning to investments and more.

Many accountants or CPAs will offer a first-time meeting or consultation at no charge. This is a good time to ask questions and determine if you are comfortable with that person. I don't want people who think like me," said one operator. "I want someone who is smarter than me on a subject and someone who will challenge me to think about these issues in a smarter way."

Then, you must determine what service you want the accountant to provide. Do you want this person to provide monthly ongoing services, such as bookkeeping, invoicing and paychecks? Many small-business owners are comfortable with handling such daily or weekly chores themselves, but others become easily frustrated and bored with tasks that take them away from the dining room or kitchen, the places of action in a restaurant.

You might save some money by doing this yourself, but if it generates frustration or takes away from your greater contributions in other elements of running a restaurant, perhaps you want to consider have a professional handle accounting and bookkeeping.

You may wish to consider an accounting firm with both noncertified accountants and CPAs. The former can handle ongoing work billed at a lower rate than the latter who can be called upon for any larger, more complex or comprehensive service, as necessary.

The good news for those who choose to do the monthly ongoing services themselves is that it's a lot easier than it used to be. For example, Restaurant-Owner.com offers a variety of downloadable forms and programs that simply walk you through the process. Other business financial accounting programs, such as QuickBooks or Peachtree, make accounting services much simpler and less time-consuming than ever before.

You should have your decision made about an accountant as soon as you get a bank account. Even if you can put forth financial projections, you should run it past a CPA for input and feedback.

"Whatever you do, don't ask your Uncle Bob or Cousin Charlie to do the accounting for you," Laube says. "You've got to have someone who understands the restaurant business and someone who will not hesitate to offer constructive criticism or point out problem areas for you."

A CPA is also in a better position to work with an attorney on legal issues and make recommendations on the intricacies and structure of your business. With exposure to small business and investor startup, a CPA can guide you on the more common ways of splitting the action before and after payout. An attorney can offer good advice after you present your proposed investment structure. "This is a make-or-break decision," says Laube. "Don't take it lightly."

Legal Eagles

Randy Rayburn had been in the restaurant business in Nashville for more than 30 years, opening 11 restaurants for other people before opening his own, The Sunset Grill, in 1990. But in doing so, he learned an expensive lesson about working with accountants and attorneys, an education that cost him $50,000.

"Basically, I made an investment in a restaurant that was never legally chartered," Rayburn says. "I had run it all past our family accountant, but if I had spent the money upfront on a good lawyer, I could have saved myself a lot of time, frustration and $50,000."

Rayburn's best advice to anyone in the startup phase of a restaurant is to find a good lawyer who specializes in the hospitality business, and don't flinch on spending the money. "This is someone who could save you your life's savings at the back end of the deal, if you spend some serious money upfront," he says.

And as when selecting an accountant, don't use the family attorney or your Uncle Bob or neighbor down the street. Lawyers are as specialized as doctors these days and that expertise is what you want. Depending on the situation, you might need someone well versed in labor law, real estate law, and litigation and business transactions.

That's a lot to ask of one attorney, although in many circumstances, a sole practitioner who specializes in business and commercial law can handle the majority of your needs. Just make sure that person is someone who knows when to pass your needs along to someone with more experience. Otherwise, a medium- to large-size law firm may have everything you need under one roof.

Finding the right attorney may be the product of first finding a good accountant. Rayburn has learned that good accountants familiar with the restaurant business often work closely with good lawyers with similar expertise. Other

So, You're Thinking About Owning, Operating or Investing in a Restaurant...

125

Between making an initial offer to purchase and being handed the key to the front door, the buyer has a lot to consider. These transactions can be complex from a legal and tax perspective for all parties; however, typically it is the buyer who is the most vulnerable. The seller often controls the transaction. His attorney typically draws up the first draft of agreements, including the purchase contract, which contains warranties, representations, and indemnification language. To the unarmed buyer they might look reasonable at first blush. In fact, often there are liability and tax issues that the buyer might overlook, unless he involves a competent transactional attorney and tax consultant in the negotiation and drafting process to protect his interests.

~ Restaurant Startup & Growth magazine/ RestaurantOwner.com

restaurant owners are also a good source for recommendations, as is the local bar association, HospitalityLawyer.com, and your state's restaurant association.

Very few attorneys will talk with you for very long off the clock, although some may waive a first-time fee. Your first communication, which will probably not be lengthy, will be over the telephone. To save yourself money in that first meeting, and all others down the road, you simply need to have a good sense of what you want and an organized list of questions or problems for the attorney. There's no need for you to attempt to "outsmart" the attorney, but you should be responsible for being well-versed on your needs and the direction you want your business to go. That will save everyone time and resources.

"Some of the best advice I've ever received from attorneys was deals to pass on and situations to avoid," Rayburn said. "By being prepared and using an attorney early on, I've learned I don't need an attorney as often."

Since opening the Sunset Grill in 1990, Rayburn has opened a second restaurant of his own. For his latest venture, Cabana Nashville, he has brought in his chef and general manager as partners.

"I'm beginning to look at retirement and an exit strategy from the business, so an entirely different set of legal papers and legal needs were required this time around," he says. But Rayburn is confident by meeting with the correct attorney early on and spending good money upfront, that he will encounter few problems down the road when he chooses to step away from the business.

Consulting Services

Your relationships with your accountant and attorney are going to be much different from the one you have with a consultant. While a consultant is certainly a business professional, you and this person should develop a more "warm and fuzzy" relationship than you have with the accountant and attorney.

"The best consulting relationship isn't just capable, it is compatible," says Chris Tripoli with A'La Carte consulting services in Houston. A good consultant is synonymous with a good listener. In any meeting, but particularly the first two or three, the consultant should be asking you lots of questions, taking lots of notes and truly listening to your vision of your business.

"There really has to be a meeting of the minds for the vision to develop and for your relationship to work," says Nashville restaurateur Rayburn, who has used a variety of consulting and design firms in opening his various restaurants.

The point of bringing in a consultant during the startup phase is as varied as each owner and property. Certainly, you should seek input from a consultant before signing any lease or making other long-term commitments.

"It should be at the point when you've finished thinking about things on your own and are ready to hear other opinions," Tripoli said. "And be prepared to hear things you don't like."

A good consultant, above all else, is going to create some discomfort as you bare your soul by laying forth your vision and plan. But raising red flags and making you doublethink every step is what that person is being paid to do.

"Much of the time, clients aren't as ready as they think they are," says Tripoli. "And the budget is never, never as complete and as detailed as it needs to be." Often, consultants will meet with you two or three times without charge, and you should be doing most of the talking. You should have also talked with other restaurateurs about consultants, as well as vendors, grocers, accountants and bankers. The restaurant association is always a good source, as is any university that teaches hospitality courses. A small, yet highly respected professional association for the consulting profession is Foodservice Consultants Society International, which lists its members at www.fcsi.org."

Consultants charge by the scope of their services, so questions you should ask should be based on your needs: marketing, staff retention and training, financing, concept, or whatever the need may be. Do you want the services of a consultant on a one-time basis, for a specific need, or just a monthly "checkup" of your overall operation?

Checking references, while important with an accountant and an attorney, is much more important with a consultant. Which clients have succeeded? Which have failed? What led to that failure? Asking those smart questions of any potential consultant, accountant or attorney, will go a long way toward helping ensure yours will be one of those restaurants that succeeds, and you will be in a position to make recommendations to others, rather than being in that list of those operators whose projects fail.

Where to Find a Good:

Accountant. Links to local and state chapters of the American Institute of Certified Public Accountants can be found at www.aicpa.org. Also check with your state chapter of the National Restaurant Association for recommendations of accountants with a history of working with restaurants.

Attorney. You may check on the professional conduct record of your attorney through listings with the local bar association and your state attorney general's office. A free source for finding peer-reviewed attorneys by region and specialties is www.martindale.com. Also check out www.HospitalityLawyer.com, which provides a list of attorneys by region who specialize in various aspects of hospitality law.

Restaurant consultant. A small, yet highly respected professional association for the consulting profession is Foodservice Consultants Society International, which lists its members at www.fcsi.org.

So, You're Thinking About Owning, Operating or Investing in a Restaurant...

127

Questions For Which You Need Answers When Selecting an Accountant:

☐ How many other restaurant clients has this person worked with?

☐ Has this person ever developed financial projections for a startup business?

☐ And were those business plans successful in raising money and actually opening the doors of the restaurant?

☐ Do they use the National Restaurant Association's Uniform System of Accounts?

☐ Can this person get your financials prepared using a four-week accounting cycle?

Questions For Which You Need Answers When Selecting An Attorney

☐ What is the attorney's area of specialization?

☐ How many attorneys and how much support staff does the firm have?

☐ How many hospitality clients does the attorney have?

☐ Is a list of clients available for contact by you to get their assessment of the attorney's performance?

☐ Is there any reason this attorney has been reprimanded or censured by a state bar professional responsibility board?

Questions For Which You Need Answers When Selecting A Consultant

☐ What services does the consultant offer?

☐ How long will it take to put in place consulting plans?

☐ What is the consultant's familiarity with your region and your concept?

☐ Is a list of clients available for contact by you to get their assessment of the consultant's performance?

How to Work Effectively with Family Members

A strong family business can be formidable. That's particularly true in the restaurant business where many independent operations are family-owned and -managed and successful. If this is your ambition, don't take for granted that your strong family unit can maintain its integrity when running a challenging business. It is critical that you learn to work effectively with those members, be they your parents, spouse, children and siblings and, more importantly, work at it every day.

I grew up in a family business... that really has provided the core of my belief in American small business, and in America's ability to grow and operate important businesses that can compete and be successful.

~Karen Mills

Divide and Conquer

Restaurant owners and their family members who have restaurant experience and culinary training before they open the doors of a new venture have a great advantage. It allows your family to learn "on someone else's dime." Some successful family operations made it a goal to have at least one member of the clan graduate from a culinary school and yet another received hospitality management training to learn the numbers and the operations side of the business.

This underscores the importance of creating a clear division of responsibilities for participating family members, with the understanding these roles can evolve over time. The last thing you ever want to do is fire a family member, which can create feuds and hard feelings that last for years. That's why it is important that each member of the family find his or her niche in the business, the place where he or she can contribute most effectively and gain satisfaction. Practically speaking, you can't have two head chefs and no accountant.

When the Magnolia Pancake Haus in San Antonio, Texas opened, owner Robert Fleming worked with his wife, Sheila, from the beginning. Sheila focused more on marketing and guest relations and Robert focused on in-house operations.

Establishing a clearly delineated chain of command is important in a family restaurant operation. "It is imperative that lines of leadership be estab-

So, You're Thinking About Owning, Operating or Investing in a Restaurant...

129

lished very early in the process of opening a restaurant," says Patricia M. Bowman, associate professor with The Center for Food and Beverage Management, The Hospitality College, Johnson & Wales University, Providence, Rhode Island. "Employees appreciate consistency in a restaurant as much as guests do. When the lines of responsibility are not clearly established with the family members themselves, it is difficult for the employees to know who is in charge."

The Flemings have made certain every employee knows the established "pecking order" in their restaurant. That was especially important as their daughter, Patricia, grew up in the business. "As our teenager was growing up and we were trying to keep her young and innocent, she was working around people in their 20s who took her under their wing like a younger sister," Robert said. "I had to tell her, 'they are not your friends, they're my employees and you take the family's side.'"

Opposites Attract

Dee and Ron Nusser own the 90-seat Brother's Bistro in Fallbrook, California, after selling three other locations. Because they have opposite management styles, the couple minimizes how much time they spend together at the restaurant, and they're very clear about who is responsible for which tasks.

Ron oversees the wine list, front-of-the-house employees, and all ordering. Dee is the executive chef, and she works with the back-of-the-house employees. She also handles catering and event planning, marketing, Web and menu design and financial books for the restaurant.

"Ron's always happy when I take care of things," Dee says. "I come from a banking background and am very conscious about labor laws and anything that pertains to paperwork. I am more of a solitary, studious kind of person. He's better with the employees than I am. You need to have a good yin and yang, as far as who has the talent to do what."

"If you can't separate responsibilities, forget it," Ron says. "Find out what each family member is good at and then designate who will do what. That's especially important in the restaurant business, because it is fast-paced."

Division of responsibilities also plays an important role in the Mirabile family's restaurant. Jasper Jr. co-owns Jasper's Restaurant, in Kansas City, Missouri, with his older brother, Leonard. The casual, upscale Italian restaurant serves Sicilian, Tuscan and Piedmontese cuisine.

Jasper handles the kitchen, menu development and marketing responsibilities, while Leonard handles office and financial matters and the front of the house. Although Jasper has become the restaurant's public persona through his cookbooks, media appearances, and cooking demonstrations, he and Leonard split all profits 50/50.

"He does what he does and I do what I do," Leonard says. "I take care of the business end and he takes care of the cooking. I don't think Jasper has written a check in seven years." Nevertheless, Jasper does look at the books frequently.

Communication is Key

Evan and Andrea Grier purchased Harry's Restaurant in Manhattan, Kansas, in mid-2006. To the existing restaurant, which had been a Manhattan fixture since 1989, they added a small delicatessen called Howdy's, which caters to the business community. Though new to restaurant ownership, both of the Griers attended and graduated from the hotel and restaurant management program at Kansas State University and they both grew up around family-owned businesses.

The couple divided their responsibilities early on, and they always try to frame their discussions against the goals and core values they have established for the business. While often working in the restaurant at different hours, they also built in several hours of overlapping time they spend there each day.

"It helps our quality of life because our responsibilities are clearly delineated," Evan said. "You utilize each person's strengths and liabilities. When Andrea and I do disagree, it needs to remain a business discussion. Problems tend to escalate when personal issues get brought into those discussions. Regardless of our difference of opinion, we're both trying to better the organization. When we disagree, the person with that responsibility has the final say."

Division of responsibilities," he says "helps in communicating with other members of the organization, too; it's absolutely vital because one clear message is being presented."

The couple takes a "team approach" to management of the restaurant, by using the expertise of longtime employees, and meeting with their core management group to communicate goals and objectives every other week.

Andrea says flexibility is important, too. She and Evan have changed their individual responsibilities as their business needs changed. "Not only should there be flexibility for the operational structure as the business grows and changes, but there needs to be flexibility for family members as their personal lives grow and change, especially if the family structure is such that there are teenage children working in the operation," Professor Bowman says. "As they discover careers and destinies of their own, they should be afforded the opportunity to leave the operation and grow on their own."

Same Kid, New Role

A tricky transition occurs when the restaurant owner's child suddenly becomes a "boss" in the business. In this case, it is important that employees understand your offspring's new roles and responsibilities.

Consider the case of the owner's son, who helped at the restaurant since he was 12 years old. When he entered his 20s, he began working full-time in the business in a management role. And that meant longtime employees had to adjust. It is preferable to have these discussions with staff prior to the change in leadership. It can take a little time for a long-time staff member to take orders from the kid who hung around the business doing odd jobs. Setting expectations ahead of time can prevent miscommunication and setting up family members and staff for failure.

"Fairness" is a watchword for operators who bring family members to work alongside non-relatives in the business. In short, family members should be evaluated the same as all other employees, which sends the message that all employees are equal and will be handled as such. But diplomacy can be a real challenge when employees also are family members.

Lindy Robinson, assistant dean for design and hospitality at Johnson County Community College in Overland Park, Kansas, says family-run restaurants must clearly establish how to respond when family members don't live up to expectations.

"It's important to all parties involved, to vocalize what their expectations are for the business, how to protect the bottom line, and what are acceptable behaviors; for instance, you can treat your in-laws to dinner but not your sorority sisters," Robinson says. "There's going to be emotion in the day-to-day operations, so maybe you schedule a weekly meeting to talk over issues and situations that arise. Practice open, honest communication."

The language used can make a huge difference in how well a message is received. Telling a family member that he needs more training to do his job effectively is far different from saying, "If you weren't my brother I wouldn't have hired you."

Learn to Separate Family Time from Business Time

Taking a break from the family business requires effort. It is important to make time for other family obligations as they arise, and to have activities and conversations that don't involve the restaurant. "Our home time is so limited, but we have a home life separate of being business partners," Evan Grier says. "At home we don't discuss restaurant issues."

Robert Fleming believes his family has become more adept at separating the business of the Magnolia Pancake Haus and family life in the last couple of years.

"We started the restaurant when our daughter Patricia was in the seventh grade, so we were growing the business while raising a child," Fleming says. "We serve only breakfast and lunch and we're finished at two, so we've been better able to make ourselves available for some of those 'kid things.'"

Looking to the Future

Selecting which family member will take over when the original owner steps down or away from the business can be a touchy situation. The decision needs to be based on who is most qualified. This means taking the emotion out of the decision, which is difficult when dealing with siblings and children. Professor Robinson says that sending a family member to a differ-

There should be quality in everything you do. The quality of ingredients, menu items, personnel and management decisions all affect the overall quality of the guest experience.

~ *Restaurant Startup & Growth* magazine/ RestaurantOwner.com

ent restaurant for several years of training can help reduce tensions among other family members if that person returns in a leadership role.

Fleming plans to work in the business for as long as "the Lord and my body allow me." But he doesn't presume to know whether his daughter, Patricia, will have any interest in working with the pancake house later on.

The Nussers' daughter has expressed no interest in running Brother's Bistro. Just because a child grows up in and around a family restaurant does not mean she/he will choose to carry on the family tradition.

"The industry is not for everyone," Professor Bowman says. "Family members may need an 'out.' A family is too important to be held hostage to a restaurant if you know in your heart of hearts that the industry is not for you."

Estate Planning Considerations for the Family-Owned Startup

One of the most important issues in estate planning, especially for small-business owners, is a basic one but one that often doesn't receive enough attention: Who will you name as your beneficiaries, what will they each receive, and when will they each receive it?

Sometimes the most natural decision in these matters can result in very poor choices, from an estate planning perspective. Married business owners, when asked what they want to do with their property upon their death, very typically will say that they want all their property to pass to their spouse, if living, and otherwise to their children equally.

If your spouse does not survive you, your first thought may be to simply leave all of your property (including the business) to your children equally. If all of your children are equally involved in the business, this may be fine. But this is usually not the case.

If some of your children are involved in the business and others are not, it may be an excellent idea to leave the business to the children who are involved and leave other property to the other children. By doing this, the children who are in the business won't be stuck having to deal with their siblings who aren't in the enterprise. This situation can create a mess for the children who are in the business. If children who are not active in the business own more than 50 percent of the business, then you are asking the kids who have stepped up to the plate to run the show to do so without control.

You also want to protect the children who aren't in the business from being "frozen out" of the benefits of being partial owners of the business. Many small businesses pay most of their earnings out as salaries, not as dividends or other equity distributions. Non-active children, receiving no salary from the business because they don't work there, may go year after year receiving nothing whatsoever from the business. For them, it may turn out to be an empty asset. It would be far better to give them other property instead.

If any of your children are young, you should provide for a trust to hold their shares until they reach a responsible age (perhaps 25 or 30). Lastly, you might have persons involved in your business who are not family members and who you think are important and should be able to stay on after your death. In this case, you might consider giving them a written long-term employment contract so that they will have security in their position after your death.

So, You're Thinking About Owning, Operating or Investing in a Restaurant...

133

As hard as it may be for you to actually talk to your family and business partners and associates about what you want to have happen to your property after your death, this is actually one of the best things you can do to ensure harmony and understanding among the folks you care about. Before you see your lawyer to draft your estate plan, sit down with your husband, wife, kids, partners and favored associates and discuss ideas or recommendations about things such as how they should run the business after your death, who they should hire or fire, who should be engaged to handle any necessary appraisals, etc.

Oftentimes this can be a tremendously valuable source of information to your beneficiaries, which will be lost if you don't take the time to do this. Plus, family members who have a chance to talk with you about your "testamentary" (legalese, meaning relating to your will) plans are far less likely to challenge things after your death, to question whether you were influenced by someone against your will, or to squabble with other family members over what you've left each of them.

It's time well spent.

Real Restaurateurs, *Real People*

Stories about people who realized their restaurant dreams

The Right Move

*W*hen do you know it's time to expand your operation, or perhaps pick up and move to an entirely new location?

For Duskie Estes and John Stewart of Sebastopol in Sonoma County, California, it was when they realized they were turning away more customers than they were seating each night. But more specifically, it was when the right location made itself available.

The husband and wife team has been working in the restaurant business all of their lives, and had been in business together for the past 12 years. They opened their first restaurant, Zazu in Santa Rosa, in 2001 and a second, Zazu on the River in Healdsburg, in 2012. But they knew they could do better by combining those efforts under one, much bigger roof.

For the better part of two years, they looked, talked to landlords and architects until one day they were approached by the developers of an interesting concept in Sebastopol.

The Barlow was born in the early days of the 20th century as a massive old apple processing facility with multiple barns, warehouses and offices. It had been sitting empty all of the 21st century, until recently when the old buildings were renovated to house artisan food producers, from bakers to coffee makers to distillers and wineries. Art galleries and organic food markets fill in more space.

Dustie and John negotiated a lease for space in the Barlow, about twice the size of their previous restaurant, and began designing their dream facility. They worked with an architect primarily to handle all of the permits, but Dustie and John did most of the "grunt work" of the design themselves.

"Because we are both chefs, we had some very specific ideas for our kitchen, particularly because we have spent 12 years working in the same kitchen," Dustie says. "We were determined to build in some elbow room."

Elbow room indeed. The restaurant is 3,600 square feet and conventional wisdom says that the kitchen should be no more than 800-900 square feet. Yet Dustie and John have a massive 1800 square feet kitchen. And just a month after opening, they were wishing they had made it even bigger.

John's specialty is smoking his own meat, particularly pork. Just about everything on the Zazu menu features pork. He applied for a permit from the Department of Agriculture to sell bacon and salami directly to customers. That takes up a lot of space. Plus, the building

that is now home to Zazu also includes an event space for catering and banquet services.

"We thought we had designed in space for growth and flexibility, but it disappeared fast," laughs Dustie.

Otherwise, they are quite pleased with all aspects of the design, both the front and back of the house. The dining area features butcher block tables wrapped around an open kitchen under high ceilings, a brushed stainless bar, barnwood siding, roll up doors, and gas-style industrial light fixtures.

John's advice for others building a new space from scratch is to really think through your menu ahead of time. "Think about the actual preparation of each item, where essential equipment and storage should be to make everything as smooth and convenient as possible," he says. "It's more than just putting a stove and a closet in a room together."

After a four-month construction period, they actually opened a week ahead of schedule, relying on word-of-mouth from their previous location and announcements via a 10,000 name e-mail list.

The previous location, half the size of the Barlow space, was located in a rural area, far from any foot traffic. It was a dinner destination only. In moving to the new space, Zazu did more than just double its space and business thanks in part to it being closer to an urban area and surrounded by other businesses that generate traffic to its front door. The restaurant is open for lunch, has an expanded liquor license and a growing catering business.

"We've gone from seating about 100 people a day to more than 600," says John. "The volume has really caught us off guard."

That's been the only problem for the restaurant — getting into the mindset of creating six times the product as the owners had done for so many years.

"It's a pretty good problem to have," says Duskie. "We feel pretty dang lucky."

How to Manage the Life Cycle of Your Restaurant

Like any other product, your restaurant concept also has a life cycle. In this chapter we will help you understand your restaurant's life cycle dynamics and prepare you for managing each phase as you move your concept along in the marketplace.

Today was good. Today was fun. Tomorrow is another one.

— *Dr. Seuss*

When first planning to open your restaurant, your goal is to get open, your strategy is to get open and all support tactics involve getting open. On one hand you can't wait to hear the register start ringing. On the other, you just know that you're going to forget something.

All in all, it's hard to think past opening day — until after opening day. Then your goal is to do a better job tomorrow. Your strategy is to learn from your opening-day mistakes. But there is no time to plan any corrective tactics. You close the front door at 11 p.m., get home around 1 a.m., and open the back door maybe seven hours later, often sleep-deprived.

You've likely been warned of the reactive life of a restaurateur, constantly caught up in managing the business for today with no time to get ahead of the learning curve. There is, however, a way to be a proactive restaurateur.

Now we will review the general phases of a concept's existence, as it emerges and evolves.

Preopening and Year One: The Realization, Organization, and Prioritization Period

In this phase you must transform your vision into a tangible and viable plan that can be put into operation. Here is where you realize, organize and prioritize every step of how your restaurant is going to function.

Realize. This is when you think "outwardly" about every conceivable internal and external factor that will affect how you will do business. You must include anything that could come into play regarding your concept. Even if a factor seems remote, you include it. You can always delete it in a later stage when you begin to organize and prioritize.

The challenge here is to imagine any variable that could affect the business and surprise you. By the way, when you first open a restaurant, most surprises are not good. So it is best to keep them to a minimum.

This is the time to brainstorm. Gather together anyone who will be involved in the business. If you know who will manage the restaurant, make sure that person is present for every discussion. You will want your manager and key staff members to have authorship in the restaurant's operating plan. If you have a confidante in the industry, enlist that person's input. This is also a good time to enlist the help of a restaurant consultant. Most consultants have checklists developed to ensure all the major factors leading to a successful concept introduction are considered.

Organize. This step involves reconsidering all the factors accumulated in the previous step and converge those into the main areas of the business. Categories would include, but might not be limited to:
* Concept development.
* Operations.
* Marketing.
* Menu planning.
* Accounting.
* Purveyors.
* Management.
* Staffing.
* Information technology.

Prioritize. Now list all of the variables listed in each category according to their effect on the business and the urgency to get started. For instance, in marketing, your priorities might look like this:
* Design logo.
* Design menu.
* Design signage.
* Design any collateral material (posters, table tents, etc.).
* Design grand opening ad.
* Determine media to use for the ad.
* Determine charity to support with opening.
* Develop PR campaign.
Additional personnel priorities might look like this:
* Write a profile of the management team, by position.
* Engage a restaurant recruiter for assistance.
* Hire a general manager.
* Hire a kitchen manager.
* Hire other assistant managers, with input from managers.
* Develop a policy-and-procedures manual.

Preopening and Year One is when you develop operating systems and procedures based on the most immediate priorities. Due to the complexity of pulling all the different pieces of the business together (investors, financing sources, real estate choices, menu development, décor and design, personnel, etc.), creating and following a checklist of every detail involved in getting opened is critical. There is no detail too small or insignificant if you plan to succeed from Day One. You don't want to be paying rent on a location 30 days before you are able to get open because you are waiting for your sign to be erected, your menus to arrive, or your liquor license to be processed.

Ideally, your schedule should include ample time for training, team building, and crew practice by arranging VIP meals before the grand opening. The maxim "Practice makes perfect" especially applies to opening a successful restaurant.

Implement. Rich Melman is chairman of Lettuce Entertain You Enterprises (LEYE), a Chicago-based operator of more than 100 restaurants, and a self-described "champion of the value of concept development." He once said, "Implementing your concept is like a first taste of a new recipe; it's exciting but may need a little tweaking to get just right." He also says, "The best restaurants open leaving a few bullets in their gun and never put everything out there in the beginning."

Melman says that with the many restaurants LEYE has opened over his more than 30-year career, each had the same goal: To establish the concept during the infancy period in a step-by-step process. He suggests first opening for dinner only, and build on that base of success, by adding a lunch program, private parties, to-go, catering, Sunday brunch, and a late-night program, incrementally as the market indicates.

Years Two and Three: The Time You Learn to Become More Effective and More Efficient

The goal in this phase of business is to gain CONSISTENCY — boldface, all caps and underscored — in executing your concept. On their first visit, most customers are usually understanding about little things not going quite right in a newly opened restaurant. And they are usually forgiving, as long as any discrepancy is handled immediately and politely. But as time passes, so does the forgiving spirit of your customers. Therefore, you must be as consistent as possible, as soon as possible. And that is the key reason that practice is so critical in the preopening phase.

During this second phase, continual training is vital. Some restaurant owners make the fatal mistake in believing once their restaurant opens, there is no longer need for formal staff training. New hires are simply thrown into the fray.

In truth, if you don't continue to train and coach your staff, there will be plenty of time for to do so later after your customers abandon your restaurant leaving few people to serve.

So, You're Thinking About Owning, Operating or Investing in a Restaurant...

139

Also during this phase you will experience staff turnover. Some will quit because you're too busy and they don't want to work that hard. Or some others will leave because business — and tips — are low. Obviously, in the latter case, your better servers will be the first to exit.

In fact, some owners quit training because they don't want to invest those dollars in a new crew member who might quit soon after. Jim Sullivan, an industry training guru, once made an excellent point regarding the tendency to cease training staff after a few employees defect: "Do you know what is worse than training a crew person and having them leave? Not training them and having them stay." Talk about setting yourself up for failure!

In addition to ongoing training and personal coaching, putting in place your daily operating systems is critical to supplying your staff with the tools they need to provide a consistent experience for your guests. The more consistent your service, the easier it becomes for your guests to clearly understand your concept, and then communicate all of their positive reactions to their friends. Your most influential and reliable form of marketing is word-of-mouth endorsements by your current customer base to new customers. And the more consistent the execution of your concept, the more likely your guests can explain why their restaurant experience was so great.

Years Four through Six: Learn to Excel

Just as the previous phase was about maintaining consistency, this phase is about "becoming the best." Period.

By now, systems have been in place and all operational processes have been refined to gain better efficiency. The prime costs of food and labor are the key targets of attention. The challenge is to improve these costs without your guests experiencing any negative results of the action, such as slower service, smaller portions, or seemingly reduced quality.

P&L (profit-and-loss statement) reviews by ownership and management should take place each week to determine if actual costs are in line with the budget, pinpointing areas needing help and creating programs for improvement. The focus is on improving the flow of sales dollars to the bottom line and the elimination of any debt.

In this phase, too many operators spend an inordinate amount of time trying to squeeze an extra tenth of one percent out of labor or food costs, when they could be attempting to find ways to put an extra dollar on the top line and flowing 40 percent to 50 percent of that dollar to the bottom. Once your sales are substantial enough to cover all of your fixed costs, any additional sales dollars are only subject to variable costs, including food, some labor and some incidentals like utilities, cleaning, and linen.

For example, if your weekly sales are $25,000, that one-tenth of one percent equals a $25 savings. If your average check is $10 and your customer count is 2,500 per week and you put in place a suggestive selling program for appetizers, drinks and desserts that averaged a per-guest increase of only 50

Although the skills aren't hard to learn, finding the happiness and finding the satisfaction and finding fulfillment in continuously serving somebody else something good to eat, is what makes a really good restaurant.

~ Mario Batali

cents, you'd increase sales $1,250 with a flow-thru of $625. So where is the time and effort better spent?

Year Seven and Beyond:
Re-energize Your Vitality

Now everybody in your market knows everything about your concept and restaurant experience. Your restaurant has been operating for years. You haven't changed it much, but your competition probably has changed since you opened. New concepts with new looks will intrigue your current customers and lure them away from visiting you. Your guest counts may start to drop little by little. Or a powerful chain with "marketing dollars to burn" may open and cut into your sales by as much as 10 percent to 20 percent.

Those guests you used to see three or four times per month now come in only once a month. They can choose among all the new, exciting concept entries in the marketplace, while yours has become the all-too-familiar place they've visited for seven years.

Most restaurant chains look to freshen up their design or décor every five to seven years. The extent of the change depends on the extent your rivals have improved the experience in your competitive niche. If you are an independent casual dining concept and The Cheesecake Factory, P.F. Chang's, Buca de Beppo, and a Sullivan's Steak House open in your market, after a while you may not have the menu variety, food quality or energized experience to which the casual diner has become accustomed.

After all, restaurant customers aren't afraid to "flash their egos" by being seen in places that are "in" and reflect well on their social status. They may still like your restaurant's concept, but your place isn't as top-of-mind as it once was. Most likely, the foundation of your business is sound; you just need a makeover. Again, the reference point to the degree of change needed is the competitive set. To what degree has competition changed the "playing field"?

If the new competitors' food and service aren't markedly better, you may just have to re-paint, re-carpet and re-pave to keep pace. Maybe freshen the menu or décor package. If a variety of different ethnic concepts enter the market, you may have to re-engineer your menu to provide more variety to complement the physical changes in your restaurant. If you don't, your current customers will get their Italian fix at Buca, Oriental at Chang's, and steak at Sullivan's. How many dining-out dollars will they have left to visit you?

Following are some varying degrees of change you may have to adopt to continue to compete in the marketplace:

Concept reinvention. In this situation the core concept is still sound and your reputation hasn't eroded. You just need to re-energize your restaurant to provide guests with a fresh experience.

So, You're Thinking About Owning, Operating or Investing in a Restaurant...

141

Remembering that today's price value equation is not just "food for the money," but rather the value of the entire experience (menu, décor, and service), you need to evaluate each factor and then adjust accordingly.

When brothers Raul, Roberto and Rick Molina were taking the reins of their 40-year, three-unit Mexican restaurant company after their father retired, they decided to look within their company to find the needs of their concept. After discussions with key staff and an extensive customer market survey, they learned what the "guest perceptions" were of their concept, how the buying habits within their marketplace had changed, and were better able to plan their re-energizing strategy. They decided that a combination of facility enhancements (design and décor), new furnishings, menu and in-house marketing modifications were in order. One year later they were enjoying the fruits of their labor, including same-store sales increases.

Another mature restaurant concept took a slightly different route to get to the same place. Brenner's, a family-owned steakhouse with a 40-year history was bought by a large restaurant chain. The national chain went about its research to confirm market conditions and customer perception and then set in motion a well-planned, meticulous facility improvement program meant to retain the established charm and tradition, while adding capacity and much-needed operational improvements.

The new owner kept the well-accepted steak and seafood menu, but added improvements to the wine list and service. These steps combined to create a re-invented mature restaurant that has been well-received by its patrons and looks ahead to many, many more years of success.

Concept re-Creation. In this case the concept has become "tired" and uninteresting to today's consumers. Even if you have a good reputation for the experience you offer, if that experience doesn't have the power to attract the masses, tweaking it will never pay off. If the location is still viable and you and your management team have a good reputation in the market, you need to create a new concept that appeals to the changing consumer trends in dining out.

When Rich Melman decided it was time to close "Bones" in suburban Chicago, he knew of its risks. The 25-year-old concept had a loyal following, but marketplace changes and two years of sales slippage helped to confirm his thoughts that the time was right and the location was ready for a concept change.

But reconceiving a restaurant's theme isn't always a guaranteed home run. Melman said he followed the same steps of concept development, research, testing and planning as if it were a brand-new "first time" restaurant. And, as we all know, opening new restaurants isn't easy.

"One of three things will happen, and two are not good," Melman says. "The new restaurant will either be wildly successful, because it is so well-received, barely successful because it may have missed the mark and will require more work, or fail." Bones turned into "L. Woods" and although there may be a few who miss Bones, there were many new customers and increased spending to make the concept change a success.

Melman reminds us that the best way to manage mature restaurants is to continually ask yourself, "What's next?" The answer may be a small tweak, new menu item, marketing tip or uniform change. Or you may find the market has shifted and your concept requires something new and different. Regardless, one thing is sure: There is always something next.

So, You're Thinking About Owning, Operating or Investing in a Restaurant...

143

What Will My Restaurant Be Worth Someday?

Chapter 13

You do not have complete control over the timing of many of life's events, including the need to evaluate your business. So, it's smart procedure to have your business's value assessed annually.

Price is what you pay. Value is what you get.

— *Warren Buffet*

If you were asked to estimate the value of your house, you might research listings and selling prices of comparable properties in your neighborhood or town. Depending on the current state of the housing market, you might be elated or dismayed over what you learn. However, if the value is lower than you anticipated, it's unlikely your response would be, "The market be damned, I expect top dollar," or "I'm getting divorced, and I need to get enough money to cover my alimony."

It is also unlikely that you would assume to recoup the cost of a swimming pool if you knew that buyers in your market do not value pools or may even consider them a liability. And while you might pay heed to "rules of thumb," such as what local economists say about average home appreciation (or depreciation) in your market, you would only use such information as guidelines to be weighed along with many other factors.

As with most assets, the value of a home is ultimately driven by the market, which sometimes favors sellers and sometimes favors buyers. So why do some restaurateurs seem to place so much weight on factors beyond what the market is willing to pay when determining the value of their businesses?

"Selling a restaurant is a more emotional transaction than selling a home," says Neal DePersia, a Cary, North Carolina, business broker with National Restaurant Associates. "Restaurateurs want to recoup their sweat equity." On the other side of the deal, however, prospective buyers are driven by the romance of owning a restaurant, and might not be truly objective in their purchase.

"As brokers, we have an ethical responsibility to give sound advice to sellers on pricing, and our message is not always what they want to hear," DePersia says. "The price is established by the market." That begs the question: How do you define market value for an independent restaurant? Unfortunately, there is no pat answer or formula.

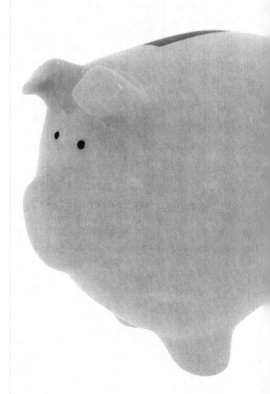

So, You're Thinking About Owning, Operating or Investing in a Restaurant...

145

While it may be difficult for the owner of an independent restaurant to assign a hard-and-fast value to his or her concept (the valuation of franchise units tend to be more predictable due to their uniformity and franchisor support), a practical number can be derived. There are a variety of factors that drive actual and perceived value of independent restaurants, they should be considered to allow owners to maximize that figure.

Before we delve into these factors, consider that the time to address these issues is not when you are under significant time constraints. You do not have complete control over the timing of many of life's events, including the need to evaluate your business. Have your business's value assessed annually. The slings and arrows of outrageous fortune might force you to sell your business on relatively short notice because of a setback or unexpected opportunity, and you'll be in a better position to do so if you have taken the time to carefully build your business and already know what it's worth.

Numbers Games

"Business valuation is more art than science," DePersia says. Based on experience, however, he and other restaurant experts have arrived at various valuation formulas, ranging from "rules of thumb" to fairly sophisticated methodologies. For example, DePersia has found that in his geographic market, a typical successful restaurant will list for roughly one half of its reported annual sales, and usually sell for 25 percent to 40 percent of the annual gross. Thus, a restaurant with $2 million in annual sales might list for $1 million and sell for $500,000 to $800,000. In the end, the restaurant's location, financial performance, age, equipment condition, and occupancy costs — whether a lease or real estate purchase — all impact value.

According to Craig Salvay, a business financial and valuation expert in Kansas City, Missouri, whether the valuation is performed for the benefit of an institutional lender or a prospective buyer, "the number people really look at is sustainable free cash flow," that is, your "net operating income adjusted for market real estate rent (where the operator owns the real estate), and reduced by both the cost of recurring capital expenditure (leasehold improvements, fixtures, furniture and equipment) and the cost of maintaining inventory, receivables and other current, noncash assets."

Revenue is telling, but it does not tell the whole story. Institutional lenders certainly are among the most detached and objective assessors of business valuation, and "no restaurant gets a loan based simply on its revenue," Salvay says. "Banks lend money based on sustainable free cash flow — the amount available to repay debt — and may lend up to and beyond 2 1/2 times that sustainable free cash flow, but usually not more than 60 percent to 70 percent of the value of the bank's appraised value of the leasehold improvements, fixtures, furniture and equipment.

According to Salvay, you determine the free cash flow of the business, first by determining the operation's net operating income; that is, subtracting operating expenses that are required for generating sales from the total sales related to your primary business. For example, for a restaurant's main business of selling food and beverages — "not toys, souvenirs, T-shirts and other incidentals," Salvay says — the expenses that are required for generating those sales include cost of labor, both direct (ie, wages and salaries) and indirect (ie, benefits, insurance, FUTA and FICA) and consumables, including food and paper products.

Complicating the detailed financial analysis required to determine the true free cash flow of a restaurant is that many independent restaurateurs may not report all of their income. "Unreported income can represent a high percent of the worth of the restaurant," DePersia says. However, "if the seller can't prove the income, he shouldn't expect to get paid for it. You can't have it both ways."

In determining the true sales volume of the business, smart buyers will want to look at the business's invoices or its bank deposits. For example, an out-of-town prospective buyer for one of the businesses listed by DePersia offered to work at the restaurant for free for a week to determine if the sales "added up" when compared with what was being reported by the owner.

DePersia also recommends running a business without burying personal expenses in the financial statements for a year, prior to selling, to help provide a more accurate and favorable picture of the cash flow. "Many restaurateurs try to expense a number of owner perks, such as automobile payments, cell phones for themselves and the family, etcetera," DePersia says. Moreover, these items are not always clearly identified on profit-and-loss (P&L) statements, but buried within line items such as "extraordinary expenses," which requires digging to determine the true value of the restaurant, in terms of income and cash flow.

Sustainable Revenue

Institutional lenders, investors and buyers are not only interested in the current value of the business, but its long-term prospects, as well. A good percentage of prospective buyers of independent restaurants are focused on whether the business will provide a reasonable living and service the debt of the purchase for the next 20 years.

A P&L (profit and loss statement) and balance sheet are merely snapshots of your business's financial status at a certain point in time. Sophisticated buyers and investors are concerned with the future of the business for the long haul. And that's why you need to consider the sustainability of your revenues in the valuation equation, according to Salvay.

"There are several key factors with which you need to be familiar in creating sustainable revenue," Salvay says. These include the physical condition of fixed assets, competition and location, all of which contribute to the perception of the restaurant's current value as well as its staying power. Maintaining your physical assets influences your ability to serve guests efficiently, as well as

So, You're Thinking About Owning, Operating or Investing in a Restaurant...

147

> No matter how great your marketing plan is, even if it brings in hundreds of new guests each week, if you have a bad product (e.g., inconsistency) all you will have accomplished is to more quickly let people know about it. So, before you schedule grand openings, drop big bucks on advertising, or spend a gazillion dollars on billboard advertising, make sure you are ready to serve your new guests in a manner that will make them repeat customers who will spread positive word-of-mouth endorsements.
>
> ~ *Restaurant Startup & Growth* magazine/ RestaurantOwner.com

maintains the morale of the staff. When DePersia contemplates brokering the sale of a business for a new client, his first order of business is to look at the size of the restaurant, its concept, menu, health scores, and condition of equipment.

On this note, you should be aware that improvements don't necessarily equate to improved market value. Consider an independent coffeehouse that spends more than $150,000 on improvements to its leased space. The results are beautiful and dramatic. Unfortunately, given the annual revenues of the business — for example, $250,000 per year, it is unlikely that it will ever recoup these expenses when it comes time to sell.

You need to look hard at the improvements contemplated, whether your space is leased or owned, to determine if they are necessary to your business. You also need to consider whether a future buyer will value the improvements sufficiently to help you at least recoup that investment at the time of sale.

The consistency and effectiveness of the business's marketing and customer service, among other things, will determine how well it fends off existing and future competition. Of all the factors cited by Salvay, location is the most crucial to sustainability, and one of the most difficult to change once you've picked a spot.

The Dirt on the Dirt

If you have the good fortune to own rather than lease your land and space, the valuation of your restaurant is going to be significantly influenced by the value of your real property. For the purpose of this chapter, we are removing real property value (other than the value of the leasehold, as we will discuss) from the equation, and sticking to the value of the business and its FF&E (furniture, fixtures and equipment).

Commercial real estate valuation is distinct from business valuation in some pretty fundamental ways. There is a larger market for 2,000 square feet of "store front" than, let's say, a "Thai restaurant" concept. Sales and lease information on the real property in which the restaurant is operating is much easier to find than business sales and income data on comparable restaurants in that market.

In any event, if you own your business's real property, you may want to know the value of your business as segregated from the real estate, as many operators sell their restaurant businesses, but retain ownership of the space and become landlords.

For those of you who, like most independent restaurateurs, lease your space, the value of your leasehold can be an important factor in the selling value of your business. "Most buyers and sellers underestimate the value of the lease," DePersia says. According to him, you create leasehold value in your business when negotiating the lease with the landlord. In a perfect world, the lease should be assignable to future owners; otherwise, the buyer will not receive the benefit of attractive terms and conditions you negotiated at the time you started or purchased the business.

Long initial terms (more than 10 years) with long renewal options are important. You might want to avoid going into partnership with your landlord, in the form of rent as a percentage of sales of your business.

That said, you need to be willing to negotiate for the best lease possible for the short and long run. Even if you are unable to negotiate an unconditional assignment and release from your leasehold interest, you and your attorney might be able to negotiate lease terms dictating that assignment and release "shall not be unreasonably withheld." In this case, the landlord would agree to be reasonable in his approval of any new tenant. This will provide the landlord some control over the risks associated with an assignment and give you the opportunity to assign a good lease to a qualified tenant.

In a growth market, the long-term value of your well-negotiated lease can be significant. For example, DePersia cited a restaurant for which the lease was negotiated when student enrollment at a nearby university was about 10,000. When the owners sold the business, student enrollment had swelled to 25,000, more than doubling the restaurant's market. For the new owners, the ability to assign the lease on its original terms was an attractive selling point.

Location

An important service offered by brokers — and one a seller should consider undertaking even when not using a broker — is conducting a demographic, competition and traffic study. DePersia hires a firm to create such custom reports for sellers. The value of this information — current and projected — is significant to smart buyers.

Choice of location is the single most important decision a restaurateur will make in terms of the business's sustainability of revenue, according to Salvay. He underscores eight key factors when evaluating a location:

1. Access. Going to a restaurant is rarely done on impulse; most often, it's a considered decision to travel to a particular place. So, ease of access to that place is critical.

2. Parking. Accordingly, if that trip is by car, convenient parking is critical. If guests know that parking near your restaurant is hit or miss, they may forgo your business for a competitor with ready parking, even if they prefer your food and service.

3 and 4. Visibility and Signage. These two factors are grouped because they both relate to your advertising. Restaurants that are tucked away from view or have limited signage due to overly restrictive signage regulations are at a serious marketing disadvantage.

5. Zoning. You need to know the kinds of structures and businesses likely to spring up around you. Will it be office and retail space or light industrial? The type of development in your area can affect the number of potential guests on any given day, or the willingness of guests to drive to your location.

6. Demographics. These are corollary to the issue of zoning. Make no mistake, the chains carefully study the current and projected demographics of a region. You can immediately tell more about the character of a town by its chain restaurants and big-box retailers than almost any other visible evidence. Are there enough office spaces in the area to attract the affluent working professionals who are likely to visit your hip, upscale bar and grill? Are there enough families with kids to make a themed pizza operation successful?

7. Competition. While you might think you want to be spaced far away from your nearest competitor, a factor which Salvay describes as the "agglomerative effect" favors the congregation of competing concepts, which is why you'll see competitor chain restaurants within a stone's throw of each other in busy shopping areas. The agglomeration of competing restaurants can draw people to the area, and actually allows the competing businesses to have more traffic than if they were more widely separated. (As with all generalizations about business, there are exceptions to this rule. A recent Cornell University study identified choosing a location saturated with competitors as a key factor in restaurant failure. This is one of the reasons that a sound demographic and traffic study is critical, in determining if the market can support your location).

8. Labor. Restaurants need access to labor and labor needs access to you. Most restaurant jobs are near or at minimum wage, and very likely a percentage of your workers will need public transportation to get to you. Otherwise, you may have to pay a premium to fill certain positions.

You Can't Control Wages, Just Productivity

Regarding labor and its effect on the value of your restaurant, Salvay says you should take measures to ensure that you maximize your rate of labor productivity, which is measured as a ratio of sales to wage hours worked. You have very little control over your cost of wages, which will be determined by the minimum wage and the local market for labor. You can, however, influence your workers' output by providing them with quality tools, an efficient layout — especially in the kitchen — and boosting morale through good training and a system of rewards. High labor productivity will be reflected on the financial statements as well as in a low rate of labor turnover. There is great value for a new owner to take over a business in which the staff knows how things run and are happy working in the organization.

No Pat Formula

So, the value of independent operations is driven by myriad factors and ultimately determined by whatever buyers are willing to pay or lenders are willing to lend, at any given time. Observed market multiples of sales or income, such as noted by DePersia, certainly give you a starting place in pricing your business.

Again, however, buyers are interested in how much money they can pull out of the business after they service their debt over the long haul. The amount hinges on the sustainability of revenue and the true income and free cash flow of the restaurant. Anything you can do now to improve these numbers will make your business a more attractive target for a buyer and a more acceptable risk for a lender.

While it's impossible to remove emotion when determining value — this is the restaurant business, after all — during the process, keep your head as clear as possible. And whether you intend to sell or finance your business this year or in 20 years, consider the following principles of restaurant valuation:

• Free cash flow is among the biggest indicators of the value of your business. You don't get paid for income you can't prove. Keep clean books.

• Show buyers and lenders that your business has staying power. Maintain a restaurant that can produce sustainable revenue.

• Your leasehold can have value to the next owner. Negotiate a strong lease from the start, and attempt to obtain long initial and renewal terms and assignment and release provisions that are favorable to you.

• Pick your location carefully, and with an eye toward the future. It is one of the most critical factors affecting business value, and one that cannot be changed easily.

• Unless they really improve the appeal of your restaurant, those antique chandeliers from Venice had better be something you really love. The next buyer might not want them at all. Try to make physical improvements that increase the asset value and sustainability of revenue of your business, such as replacing or repairing tired kitchen equipment and fixtures that are essential to your restaurant.

Real Restaurateurs, *Real People*
Stories about people who realized their restaurant dreams

Below the Ground-level Opportunity

In major cities like Chicago, where real estate is at a premium, a rooftop patio is a price-less restaurant commodity. Veronica Beckman and Brian DeNicolo knew that, which is one reason they chose the building they did in Chicago's River North neighborhood, and one reason they persevered when things didn't go as planned.

Their restaurant is Tanta, a Peruvian concept featuring internationally renowned chef Gastón Acurio. Following successful operations in Lima, Madrid and Barcelona, this is the first North American opening for Tanta, which means "bread" or "nourishment" in the Peruvian culture.

Tanta Chicago opened August 12, 2013, after more than eight months of renovation to the single-story, 10,000-square-foot, late 1800s-vintage brick building. Over the years the edifice had housed a variety of businesses and its previous renovations had been hit and miss in code and functionality. The building shared a structural wall with the adjacent building, which complicated construction issues. However, it was one of the few vacant buildings in the desirable River North neighborhood, so the challenge was weighed against the location.

By using the basement, the main level and rooftop, the design opened up 7,000 square feet of space on three levels. A skylight in the main dining room and use of natural stone, combined with interior/exterior landscaping serves to create a sense of openness that Beckman and DeNicolo wanted. During the planning process, architects and managers traveled to Spain and Peru to garner an essential understanding of the concept and culture prior to construction in Chicago.

"The multi-level concept was a concern and a challenge," says Beckman, "but it's working out well." They approached the project in two stages: the basement and main floor first, and the rooftop after that.

Imagine the worst of a basement in a neglected, century-old building and then multiply it by 100, and that was the condition of the space when Chicago Design & Construction, the renovation contractor, began work.

"Making a basement a public area often doubles the cost in fees and construction," says Mike Caravello, of Chicago Design & Construction, "but the walls and structure were sound, so we cleaned things up and made it into a very effective prep area, kitchen and office space." Public restrooms were also located in the basement.

The design required a two-story ventilation system for the stove hood and the installation of a sprinkler system. The contractor also built two new stairwells and an elevator. The basement houses two walk-in coolers and a walk-in freezer, along with a dry food storage area. The main dishwashing station and ice making station are also in the basement.

One serving line in the basement and two serving lines on the main floor eliminate the need for most of the staff to move between the basement and main floor. Upstairs the food moves through the back line to the front line for final preparation and plating and then through the front pass to the servers.

The fact that Tanta is a menu-driven concept and does not feature live bands nor a large bar menu improved Beckman and DeNicolo's ability to receive a patio license. That the location has few residential neighbors also moved the process along a little faster. However, as the rooftop makeover neared completion, the health department required a redesign, increasing costs by more than $5,000.

"We had just completed a vine-covered trellis over the bar when the health department told us it needed to be a more solid construction that could be locked down at night," says DeNicolo. So, the vines were replaced with galvanized steel, shouldering out the light and airy concept with hard permanance.

"There were no health department guidelines in this area, so although we had not violated any guideline, we were still not approved," DeNicolo recalls. "The health department was great to work with, but the lesson is to really talk through each component of the design concept."

The other challenge the Tanta team faced was training the staff. Because there are very few Peruvian restaurants in Chicago, even experienced wait staff were unfamiliar with many of the dishes, the peppers and spices, and the seafood common in these dishes.

"It's not like this was another take on burgers and fries," says Beckman. "We had to teach the entire Amazon culture in a three week period."

Because the training is so intense, Beckman recognizes that Tanta opened a little short-staffed. She wishes that the training would have taken place long before the opening night, but otherwise, the Tanta concept, from basement to rooftop, has met with success in the City of Big Shoulders.

So, You're Thinking About Owning, Operating or Investing in a Restaurant...

153

Estate Planning and Succession Tips for New Restaurateurs

Ancient Egyptians were often buried with their personal belongings and even pets as they ventured to the world beyond. But these days we barely exit with the clothes on our backs. If you care about your family and the future of your business after you leave the stage, the best strategy is to deal with the inevitable now, and then move on to a fulfilling, successful, and hopefully, long, long life.

In this world nothing can be said to be certain, except death and taxes.
~Benjamin Franklin

You're gearing up to launch a new restaurant, or you've already got one up and running. The future is bright, and your head is swimming with the day-to-day challenges of running a small business. The learning curve can be steep and the demands intense. Add the pressures of managing a family, a relationship, or just life in general, and your plate is more than full. But it's fun, it's exciting, and you're living your dream.

So, who wants to consider what will happen to your loved ones, business partners, and your restaurant if you fall out of the picture? No one, and you least of all. That's why most folks avoid planning their estates like they avoid root canal surgery. But if you're a business owner, your estate planning issues can get much more complicated than an average Joe or Jane with a house, 401(k), savings account, and life insurance policy to distribute at the end of the road. You are building a business and a potentially valuable legacy for your children and their children. In addition, you may have business partners, fellow shareholders, and associates who count on you and your restaurant in their plans.

Failure to properly address estate planning and business succession matters can cause brutal family squabbles with irreparable results, onerous tax consequences, and forever-lost opportunities to put the right people in place to run the business after your death. It can create unyielding financial hardship on persons charged with continuing the business, and, ultimately, can cause the failure of a successful entity you've worked so hard to build. In addition, there have been many lawsuits filed by siblings against siblings, and shareholders against shareholders because of poorly conceived or nonexistent estate planning. It's a pretty sorry legacy to leave behind, frankly.

So, You're Thinking About Owning, Operating or Investing in a Restaurant...

155

Choose the Right Business Entity

Here's an issue that can make a big difference for you now, in addition to helping with estate planning after your death. You need to choose the proper business entity for your business. (See Chapter 9: Choosing a Legal Structure for Your Business). Your choices are: sole proprietorship, corporation and partnership, or the relatively new structure — the limited liability company (LLC).

What is a sole proprietorship? It's a business conducted by a single owner, without the formation of a separate legal entity. Sole proprietorships are simple. They are good tax-wise, too, since they are not subject to income taxes as a separate entity. But the owner of a sole proprietorship has unlimited exposure to any liability generated by the business. That's not so good.

How about partnerships? A partnership is an association of two or more people to carry on a business for profit. Typically no filing with any state office is required to create a partnership. If two or more people start operating a business and sharing its profits, they've got a partnership whether they know it or not. The owners may have a written partnership agreement (indeed, they should), but this is not required.

From a tax standpoint, partnerships are excellent, because all income and deductions they generate "flow through" to the partners. The partnership itself generally does not pay any income taxes, even when the partnership is dissolved and its assets are distributed to the partners. And, if the partnership runs a loss, this loss will flow through to the partners, where they can use such losses to shelter other income from tax.

How about liability? Ah, there's the rub. As with sole proprietorships, partnerships typically subject their owners to unlimited exposure for business liabilities.

Enter the corporation. Corporations offer their owners shelter from liabilities of the business. The owners of a corporation typically run the risk of losing what they've put into the business, but not their individual assets, too. Corporations are separate taxpayers. If a corporation runs a profit for the year, it will pay income tax on this profit. This is the essence of "double taxation" (with corporate profits being taxed once at the corporate level, and again at the shareholder level if these profits are distributed to the shareholders as dividends).

Even if a corporation is able to avoid corporate-level tax on its yearly profits, it may face a whopping tax bill when it is dissolved. When a corporation is dissolved, it is treated as having sold all of its assets for their fair market value. A corporation can try to avoid all this by electing to be taxed as an "S corporation," which is is given quasi "flow through" tax treatment, but this treatment is not as complete as that afforded partnerships.

What if we could combine the liability protection of corporations with the tax treatment of partnerships? That's exactly what LLCs provide. LLCs offer protection from liability exposure that is actually somewhat better than that offered by corporations, and multi-owner LLCs are taxed just like partnerships. Perfect.

LLCs aren't just for multi-owner businesses. A single-owner business can be formed as an LLC, too. The owner of a single-owner LLC is taxed directly on the LLC's profits and losses, as if the LLC didn't exist. Thus, someone using an LLC will obtain full LLC liability protection, but will simply report the business income or loss directly on that person's individual tax return. An excellent arrangement for a single-owner business.

LLCs are growing dramatically in use and will likely become the dominant form of business structure in the coming years. They should be the first option that is considered when creating a restaurant's ownership structure, and in most cases will be the best choice. The primary exception to that is where a person is seeking to minimize self-employment taxes; in such a case an S corporation may be a good choice since there are no such taxes on distributions paid out as dividends.

How to Use Choice of Business Entity to Reduce Gift and Estate Taxes

LLCs (as well as corporations and partnerships) are all helpful in estate planning, for several reasons. One involves the concept of valuation "discounting" for gift and estate tax purposes. Discounting is used in asset valuation; that is, if you make a gift of property or if property passes through your estate at your death, that property must be valued for gift tax or estate tax purposes. (For this chapter, and in estate planning in general, "property" is used in its broadest sense, and refers to any asset in which you have an ownership interest. It can be real property, which is to say land, or personal property, which is to say basically, everything other than real property. It also includes retirement plans, life insurance proceeds, business shares, stocks, and rights to intangible assets, such as trademarks, which can be subject to estate taxes.)

If an LLC, corporation or partnership holds the property being transferred, then what is being transferred is an interest in the entity, not the property itself. If the entity is not publicly traded, there will be a valuation "discount" available due to its lack of marketability. Then if the interest being transferred is a minority interest in the business, there will be a "minority interest" or "lack of control" valuation discount. Other discounts may apply, and altogether these discounts may reduce the value of the property transferred by up to 50 percent, perhaps more.

For example, federal law allows you to give up to $14,000 of property per-calendar year to any person, completely free of gift tax. **(Please note, this is subject to changes in U.S. federal tax law. Consult a tax advisor prior to acting on the advice in this section.)** If you are looking to reduce the size of your estate by giving $14,000 each year to each of your children, obviously you will be able to give more property if you can get a valuation discount for the gifted property. With a 50 percent discount, you can give property otherwise worth $28,000 and still be within this $14,000-per-year exclusion.

So who wants to consider what will happen to your loved ones, business partners, and your restaurant if you fall out of the picture? No one does. And that's why most folks avoid planning their estates like they avoid root canal surgery. But if you're a business owner, your estate planning issues can get much more complicated, than say, an average Joe or Jane with a house, 401(k), savings account, and life insurance policy to distribute at the end of the road. You are building a business and a potentially valuable legacy for your children and their children. In addition, you may have business partners, fellow shareholders, and associates who count on you and your restaurant in their plans.

~ Restaurant Startup & Growth magazine/ RestaurantOwner.com

So, You're Thinking About Owning, Operating or Investing in a Restaurant...

157

Similarly, all property you own at the time of your death is valued to determine estate taxes. To the extent that the property you own is subject to valuation discounts, these taxes may be significantly reduced.

Ownership of your small business by an LLC, corporation or partnership can also allow you to retain voting control of your small business even as you make gifts of interests in the business.

For example, you may capitalize your small business so that it will have voting and nonvoting stock (or other equity interests). You may then start giving away the nonvoting stock to your children. You will still retain full voting control over the business. Your gifts of this nonvoting stock may qualify for an additional discount for lack of voting rights.

Eventually the plan is for you to give away your voting stock, too, or at least the majority of it, but not until you're ready to pass on control of the business. By doing this, you will be entitled to valuation discounts on the stock that you give away during your lifetime. You can retain voting control as long as you choose. In addition, if you give away enough of the stock during your lifetime so as to drop your ownership interest to below 50 percent, your estate also will be entitled to valuation discounts on the stock you own at the time of your death.

The Importance of 'Buy-Sell Agreements'

If you and others are the owners of a small business, a buy-sell agreement may be extremely important. Let's say you and another person own a small business, with no buy-sell agreement. If the other owner dies, that person's equity interest (e.g. shares) will pass to his or her beneficiaries. When that occurs, instead of running a business with someone you know and trust, you are likely to be stuck with someone you don't know well at all and maybe don't trust. And this other person may not want to continue in the business, and cash out instead. Can you come up with the cash? And how much to buy the other person out?

One of the best ways around this unpleasant set of circumstances is for you and your original co-owner to enter into a buy-sell agreement now. With it, you can agree that if one of you dies the other of you may (or must) buy the other out, at a set or ascertainable price.

For example, the two of you may determine that the business is worth $1 million, and if one of you dies the other may (or must) buy the deceased owner's share for $500,000. If the agreement for this is properly drawn, it will fix the value of the deceased owner's share of the business for all purposes (including estate tax purposes).

Why is this important? It can eliminate squabbling with the new owner over how much that share is worth. It can also eliminate the Internal Revenue Service (IRS) fighting with the deceased owner's estate over the value of this share, and thus how much estate tax the estate owes.

Since the value of a business tends to change over time, buy-sell agreements often call for the purchase price stated in the agreement to change from time to time, too. For example, it may call for the owners to redetermine the value of the business annually. Or, it may provide a formula to determine the value of the business, or for this value to be determined by appraisal.

In order to provide a source of funds for the survivor to buy the deceased owner's share, a buy-sell agreement may be "funded." This is frequently done with life insurance. For example, if the value of the business is $1 million and if the agreed purchase price to be paid upon the death of a co-owner is $500,000, each of the co-owners could take out a $500,000 life insurance policy on the other. This will provide a tax-free source of funds to the survivor with which to buy the interest of the one who dies first.

A buy-sell agreement will likely also restrict the ability of the owners to voluntarily transfer all or any part of their separate interests to an outsider. This is often done by giving the other owner a "first right of refusal," i.e. the option to first buy whatever interest the transferring owner wants to transfer.

Although a buy-sell agreement is probably most critical when the owners of a small business are not family members, it also may be used when the owners are all from the same family.

For estate tax purposes, any buy-sell agreement among family members must meet certain IRS requirements, one of which is that it cannot be a "device" to transfer property between family members at less than fair market value. Because of these requirements, property valuations involving family members are more likely to be accepted by the IRS if they're determined by appraisal, rather than some other method.

Who, What and When

Who will you name as your beneficiaries, what will they each receive, and when will each receive it? Married business owners, when asked what they want to do with their property upon their death, very typically will say that they want all their property to pass to their spouse, if living, and otherwise to their children equally. But, if the combined estates of the business owner and his/her spouse exceed a certain amount this could be a big mistake. Under current (2015) law, the federal estate tax exemption is $5.43 million. If a business owner leaves all property to the spouse, that person will then own all of their combined property. There will then be significant estate taxes to pay at the spouse/beneficiary's subsequent death, if this combined property exceeds $5.43 million.

For a lot of folks, a $5-plus million estate seems like a pipe dream. But many successful small-business owners, like you, can amass a net worth in excess of this amount. The tax is based on an accounting of everything you own or have certain interests in at the date of death The fair market value of these items is used, not necessarily what you paid for them or what their values were when you acquired them.

So, You're Thinking About Owning, Operating or Investing in a Restaurant...

159

Suffice to say, you should work with an attorney who has expertise in tax law to devise an estate plan that minimizes your tax liability and carries out your wishes. For example, your tax adviser might recommend that you set up a "credit shelter" trust. This trust is typically created so that all its income will be paid to the survivor for life, and that any portion of the principal needed for that person's health or support will be paid.

By doing this, up to $5.43 million of property may pass to this credit shelter trust tax-free (as of 2015). So, while the property in the trust is available to meet the needs of the survivor for life, it won't be subject to estate taxes when the survivor dies.

Another advantage of using a credit shelter trust is that it can enable the surviving spouse's estate to obtain valuation discounts for any interest the survivor owns in the business.

Other strategies you might consider (with the advice of your tax adviser) are gifting property to reduce your estates, and possibly using life insurance to replace dollars that will be lost to estate taxes.

If your spouse does not survive you, your first thought may be to simply leave all of your property (including the business) to your children equally. If all of your children are equally involved in the business, this may be fine. But this is usually not the case.

If some of your children are involved in the business and others are not, it may be best to leave the restaurant to the former and leave other property to the latter. Doing this avoids potential problems for the business — and family acrimony.

You also want to protect the children who aren't in the business from being "frozen out" of the benefits of being partial owners of the restaurant. It would be far better to give them other property instead.

Please note that no book should be considered a replacement for qualified legal and tax advice. Each transaction has specific circumstances and issues that need to be considered individually.

Point of Sale
System Primer

A modern POS system not only initiates the flow of orders, but records and helps collect revenue, keeps track of employee labor and much more. This system is at the heart of any restaurant because it touches every aspect of the business from the front to the back of the house.

Let your operation drive your technology, not vice-versa.
— *Joe Erickson, Restaurantowner.com.*

Choosing a point-of-sale (POS) system is a critically important decision. The right POS system can literally transform your operation by improving controls, efficiency, decision-making and even sales volume. If properly chosen, the system can pay for itself in a matter of months.

As with all technology, POS system capabilities and equipment has evolved in the past 10 years, and will continue to evolve. Wireless hand-held hardware, cloud-based software and backup and other advances have improved POS system functionality, flexibility and reliability. There are a number of new entrants in the market, as well as long-standing providers that pioneered cash register and other POS system technology.

The point is, we can't cover everything you might need to research to make the best choice of your new restaurant's POS system. In this chapter, we will cover some of the basics; however, if we can stress any point, it is do your homework. That includes talking to a number of vendors, asking other operators what they like and don't like about their systems, and involving your partners, managers and even prospective staff in the decision. Restaurant managers and staff who have worked at other restaurants can be a wealth of information on the good, bad and ugly of POS systems with which they have worked.

But Isn't a POS System
Just a Fancy Cash Register?

Many new operators get confused when it comes to defining cash registers and POS systems. All cash registers are point-of-sale systems — as are credit card terminals, kiosks and other devices that allow the operator to enter a sale and tender a payment.

So, You're Thinking About Owning, Operating or Investing in a Restaurant...

161

The term "POS" gathered prominence in the early 1970s when manufacturers began developing cash registers that went beyond simple guest check tracking. These POS registers featured remote kitchen and bar order printing, time and attendance tracking, and individual server tracking. In the late 1970s and early 1980s, other manufacturers joined in on the craze by enhancing the basic point-of-sale features and in some instances incorporating video order systems and back office functions such as reporting, polling and inventory control. Many of these first POS systems, advanced as they may have been for their time, might still be considered cash registers by today's standards since the POS systems being installed today are full-fledged, computer-controlled, in-house networks.

The Evolution of the POS System

The 1990s ushered in a new POS era with the introduction of the personal computer (PC). Software developers began creating POS programs that ran on standard PCs with operating systems such as MS-DOS, Concurrent DOS, UNIX and AIX. These software-based POS systems ran on "open architecture" (nonproprietary computer code) equipment such as IBM and Compaq PCs or even "white box" (a device dedicated to a particular function) computers assembled by local POS or computer dealers. Proprietary systems manufacturers also began developing software-based programs and the manufacturing of equipment, which used standard operating systems. It wasn't long before touch-screen technology was integrated, spurring a revolution in the POS industry.

Developers could now create intuitive programs designed to reduce training and simplify kitchen and bar order processing. Although touch-screen systems were used in both table-service (TS) and quick-service restaurants (QSR), it was the table-service demand that drove the features development for touch-screen POS. No longer was simplified order processing and remote printing the primary concerns for operators making POS decisions. Operators needed more advanced features in their POS devices. Separate checks, hold and fire, detailed reporting, table transfer, tip tracking, accounts receivable, integrated credit card processing and a host of other demands directed the growth of POS systems as we know them today.

So, what is the difference between advanced cash registers and POS systems? The answer requires a two-part explanation. We need to examine "functionality" and "hardware" as separate issues. Recognition of both is necessary to understand how these differences may affect your operation.

One of the major changes in recent years has been the move of having your POS system "in the cloud". The restaurant terminals communicate with cloud systems where programing changes are automatically updated and your restaurant data is processed off premises, as well as backed up on line and in your store.

Cash Register Functionality

A common view held by many operators is that a cash register is limited to ringing and reporting on items sold, tracking checks, and facilitating cash reconciliation. These are the basic requirements for any operation. Operators using a manual guest check or an order pad to record and submit orders to the kitchen (and this happens a great deal in smaller operations) might use a standard cash register to add the tickets, tabulate sales tax, and track the payment method for each sale. In addition, most cash registers provide usable reports, including item sales mix detail and hourly sales.

Preset keys help to ensure that the correct price is charged for the product being sold. Some cash registers only have open price keys that allow the cashier to enter the price for the item sold. Unfortunately, this method is not recommended because of the obvious reason that customers can be overcharged or undercharged. Since the vast majority of independent restaurants are owner-operated, it is common to see an owner or family member running the cash register. Theft, management data, table turns, labor cost control, ticket times, scheduling, and product ordering may not be primary concerns in conducting the day-to-day operations. As long as the owner is able to track sales tax and deposits, for purposes of tax reporting, their perceived needs from a cash register are satisfied.

POS Functionality

On the other hand, a POS system might be defined as a tool that is essential to conduct operations, not just track totals. For instance, when a POS system controls the order processing in the kitchen through requisition printing (automatic order printing on a remote device) or video, it becomes as valuable to the restaurant as a grill or fryer. Order processing can come to a complete halt when you lose a grill or fryer. So it is with the loss of your POS system if your operation relies on the server entering orders into the system before the kitchen can begin preparing them. Moreover, installing a POS system means installing controls. A POS system that incorporates requisition printing drastically reduces the opportunity for theft and helps to control food and beverage costs.

POS companies have documented proof that requisition printing can reduce food and beverage cost from 2 percent to 5 percent. Many smart operators using kitchen requisitions require that employees delay food preparation until the order is first entered into the POS system. This helps to prevent employee eating inventory and servers giving free food to friends or family. Employee meals, waste and guest comps are entered into the system and discounted accordingly, thereby preventing unaccounted sales.

Since operators are provided with menu costing for each item sold, they can calculate an estimated cost of goods sold from the item sales reports. This gives a theoretical cost based on sales that can be compared with actual costs from purchases and inventory depletion. In the event the variance is unacceptable, the focus on finding out why is directed to factors other than unrecorded sales. Operators that use a POS system, track purchases and conduct a physical inventory each week can calculate profit and loss on a weekly basis. Therefore, they are able to respond to cost increases before those become a drain on their bank account.

A POS System Can Improve Your Service

All customers have expectations when it comes to ordering, waiting, and paying for their meal. Consistent ticket turnaround times are essential to the success of any operation; therefore POS systems are necessary to achieve the operational consistency your restaurant needs.

Table-service restaurants find that a good POS system, with stations strategically located throughout the restaurant, can save valuable seconds or minutes from the time customers wait to be served their food. Servers can quickly enter orders into the POS system, and these are immediately printed at one or more stations in the kitchen or bar. This allows the server to spend more time in their station to attend to other customer needs such as clearing plates, refilling water, and presenting guest checks for payment. Likewise, fast-food restaurants rely on their POS systems to have the orders displayed on video screens placed at various points on the food production line. Many systems are programmed to display ordered items immediately upon the order taker entering it into the POS system so that the cook can begin preparation.

How to Choose the Right POS System

The first questions an operator should ask are, "What features do I need?" The next should be, "Which type of POS best fits my needs?" The service style of your restaurant defines your POS system requirements. Once you have gone through the process of defining the features your operation needs from a system, and you have qualified which POS systems will work for your operation, cost usually becomes the deciding factor.

Unfortunately, the vast majority of operators underestimate the budget for their POS system when planning a new restaurant concept. A sophisticated POS system with numerous touch-screen stations can run into tens of thousands of dollars. However, you must weigh the cost against the control it gives you over your operations. The reporting functions alone can spot operational and cash management problems that, over time, can cost a busy establishment many times the initial expense of the system.

The following steps are designed to help increase your odds of choosing the right and most appropriate POS system for YOUR restaurant.

Step One. Form a "POS Team". Assemble a few good people to help you evaluate and recommend a POS system. Even if you're opening a small restaurant, it's usually a good idea to get a few knowledgeable people involved in the process to share their ideas and insights and ultimately gain their buy-in. Remember, they will have to use and rely on the system too, so they want the right system installed. It may be smart to have a potential server, counter person, manager, line cook or accountant (bookkeeper) be part of the team.

> The eventual success or failure of your POS choice will be determined by the quality of programming that goes into it.
>
> ~ Joe Erickson

Step Two. Create a "POS Evaluation Worksheet". The POS Team should create a comprehensive list of features and functions the members need and want in a new POS system. Next, determine which ones qualify as MANDATORY, ones you can't live without, and features that are OPTIONAL, that is, nice to have, but not essential. This list of features and functions will become your POS Evaluation Worksheet.

The sample POS Evaluation Worksheet in Appendix D of this book is one way to organize and compare the features of the different POS systems you evaluate. Without an organized approach, it's very difficult to determine which system is best for your restaurant.

Step Three. Complete a "POS Requirements Checklist" for Each POS System You Evaluate. This can usually be done initially by phone with representatives of the POS system companies or dealers. Let them know that they're going to have to "show you" everything they claim in a live demo at some point. Also get a sense of the cost of the system at this point. You'll want to know upfront if a system is clearly not within your budget.

Step Four. Evaluate Vendor Responses. Eliminate the vendors whose systems don't meet your minimum requirements or are priced beyond your budget. Take into account years of experience, number of local installations and financial condition. Narrow the field to two or three vendors. This is a very important step as the local agent in most cases will also become your main contact for service and follow up.

Step Five. Observe Each System in Operation. Select 1 or 2 existing customers furnished by each vendor and observe the system operating during a busy meal period. Ask a few of their people such as the manager, servers, cashiers what they like and don't like about it. People are usually very candid, especially if they have had an exceptionally good experience or a really terrible one. Ask about how their installation went, how responsive the company has been to service calls and if they would buy this system again.

Step Six. Vendor Demonstration. A few days before the demo give the vendor a copy of your menu. Tell them you want to have the demo conducted with a few of your menu items. Have the demonstration take place in your restaurant, not in their office. Notice how easy or difficult it is for them to get it set up and running.

Have a prepared script of the transactions you want to see the system handle. 8 to 12 transactions might be sufficient in most cases. For example: a table of six comes in, they order drinks (you specify), appetizers, entrees', etc. Think of all the ways your customers modify those items. Like a steak can be ordered medium-rare with mushrooms on the side. Numerous condiments can be served with a baked potato, on the side or not. How easy will it be for the server to enter the modifications and will the POS accommodate all the kinds of modifications you have to deal with? What if the server presents one check to the table of six and they want separate checks? Test these types of situations and transactions that your people run into every day.

If the vendor conducts the demo, you will see what *they* want to show you, what they know works. So don't let the vendor conduct the demo. During the demo, if the system doesn't perform the way you want, listen closely for the vendor's response. Are they willing to make the necessary changes? Document what they say they will do and follow-up to see that it's done to your satisfaction before you sign a contract.

Step Seven. Negotiate Payment Terms. It is common to negotiate a payment schedule for the vendor to be paid at the following times:
* At execution of the purchase contract
* At installation
* When the system becomes operational
* At final acceptance

 For example you may negotiate the following payment schedule:
* 25% when the purchase contract is signed
* 25% at installation
* 25% when the system becomes operational
* 5% when you finally accept the system as complete

For obvious reasons, always negotiate hard to pay a large share of the contract amount at final acceptance. What constitutes final acceptance should be defined and understood by both parties and be part of the purchase agreement. Even if you purchase the system under a lease arrangement, you can instruct the leasing company to release portions of the proceeds contingent upon certain criteria being met. This will give the vendor plenty of incentive to get the system up and running quickly, your people trained and you happy.

Restaurant Failure Rates in Depth

The reasons restaurants fail are many and varied and, in some cases, not the least bit obvious. While a lack of working capital is most people's first guess, underlying factors can and often do include anything from a lack of proper planning for slow times or retirement to unrealistic expectations, quality of life issues and even the inevitable passage of time.

A man can fail many times, but he isn't a failure until he begins to blame somebody else.

~John Burroughs

Dr. H.G. Parsa decided to find out why. "People always said that 90% of restaurants fail in their first year," recounts Parsa, a professor at the Rosen College of Hospitality Management at the University of Central Florida in Orlando. "Then in the late '90s the NBC television network broadcast a program titled Restaurant: A Reality Show, sponsored by a credit card company and starring Chef Rocco DiSpirito. Every 15 minutes American Express put on a commercial saying that 90% of restaurants fail in their first year. That puzzled me. I'd been in the restaurant industry for 15 years and I'd never seen anything like that."

Parsa reached the company's vice president of media communications in New York. "I asked him, 'Look, you said this — 90% of restaurants fail in the first year — but where did you get the data from?' He said, 'I'll get back to you in a week.' Well, in a week I got a letter from him: they didn't have any data.

Parsa, an industry veteran who had worked his way up from the bottom to management positions with companies like Pizza Hut, Wendy's and Denny's, earned his Ph.D. in marketing at Virginia Tech, then taught at SUNY (State University of New York) Buffalo for seven years. While serving on the board of the Ohio Restaurant Association, he came across a fool-proof source for learning exactly how long restaurants remained in business: the health department.

"Every restaurant has to be inspected by the health department before it opens, and the license has to be renewed every single year. The only time they don't renew you is when you're closed. I thought, 'Wow, there we go — when a restaurant opens I know it because of the license, and when it closes I know because it's not renewed.' The research was done credibly, scientifically. That's

So, You're Thinking About Owning, Operating or Investing in a Restaurant...

167

Why Good, Hardworking People Lose Their Life Savings in the Restaurant Business

(and How to Keep It from Happening to You)

Would you be willing to put a large portion of your net worth into an investment that is highly illiquid and has a 50% or more chance of being worth zero, or less, at the end of five years?

No rational person would; however, thousands of individuals do it every year when they decide to open an independent restaurant and finance it completely with their own money.

It's tragic that decent, hardworking, well-intentioned people squander their nest egg when their restaurant dream turns into a financial nightmare — and it happens all the time.

If you want to open a restaurant, we have one rule that will help to keep you from making a really dumb mistake and reduce the odds of losing all your money in the restaurant business. The answer is to rely in part on smart investors. Involving them will require additional planning and legal work, and you will have to share of portion of the equity. The payoff is that you are required to prove the feasibility of your plan to others who will apply a critical eye, before opening their checkbook.

Some of the richest people in America purposely limit their personal investments in their own start-ups. Highly successful and self-made billionaires Stephen Spielberg, Jeffrey Katzenberg and David Geffen founded Dreamworks Pictures in 1994. They needed a half billion dollars to get it

Continued on page 169…

the point." Data was collected over four years from among 1,400 restaurants. The result: less than a third of restaurants — just 29.6% — went under.

While teaching at Ohio State University in 2005, Parsa published a research study two years in the making called Why Restaurants Fail, in the Cornell Hotel and Restaurant Administration Quarterly. Additional research was conducted later among restaurants in Columbus, OH, and Buffalo, NY. "With these qualitative interviews," he says, "we discovered that restaurants fail for reasons other than finance. That's a fascinating finding." Follow-up research among 5,000 restaurants in Cobb County, GA, in 2006 and 2007 helped to strengthen the findings.

Why Restaurants Fail

According to Dr. Parsa, the factors that can lead restaurants to ruin include the following:

Location. The number-one reason that restaurants fail, Parsa found, has to do with population density and location. The highest failure rate in restaurants comes about, "believe it or not — surprise, surprise, surprise — in downtown markets," he says. "As you and I know, the highest number of restaurants per capita is in downtown locations. High real estate costs, number one. Number two, labor — you can't get the labor. It's difficult to come to downtown to work, because no one lives there." But the single most important factor is simply that most downtown businesses operate Monday through Friday for breakfast and lunch. "Very little for dinner," he notes, "very little for the weekend."

Rainy days. Parsa's second most common reason is one, he reflects, that "you don't see in many books," and it's this: most entrepreneurs and restaurateurs "have enough capital to open the restaurant, but not enough capital to survive for three to six months of the slow days, the rainy days; so insufficient capital is the reason." Why so ill prepared? Entrepreneurs "believe that 'Once I open the restaurant the money will start coming in,'" says Parsa. "No, no: they need capital to survive for three to six months without a paycheck." How much they need depends on the concept.

Size. A third factor, Parsa found is that, as he puts it, "size matters. We found that the highest rate of restaurant failure happens in the smallest restaurants, the mom and pops." Why? Because such small operations tend to carry with them relatively low entry and exit barriers. In other words, it is easier for them to get into the business and easier to get out when fortunes wane.

"Say I've got $70,000," says Parsa. "I buy myself a grill, I can make my scrambled eggs — I'm a chef. Simple as that. Remember, restaurants have low fixed costs and high variable costs. Because of the low upfront investments everybody tries to get in, because it's easy. Nobody thinks about opening a book store or a movie theater because they have high fixed costs."

In the Cornell Quarterly article (co-authored by John T. Self, David Njite and Tiffany King), Parsa noted that, "In addition to the age of the firm, research has found a correlation between size and survival. In this regard, the larger firms are more likely to remain in business than small operations."

Quoting L. Richardson's article The Mechanics of Failure in the November 1991 issue of Asian Business, Parsa pointed out that "both suppliers and bankers are prejudiced against smaller firms. They tend to take longer to act against a slow-paying large enterprise than they do against a smaller firm, because they equate bigness with safety and security. That said, small firms tend to be positioned for growth, but if that growth occurs too rapidly, a restaurant's propensity to fail actually increases because of the ensuing financial stresses. These financial stresses include a high cost of goods sold, debt, and relatively small profit margins."

Quality of life. The fourth most common reason restaurants fail, Parsa maintains, has to do with quality of life. Of 50 operators questioned, he reports, "Many, many times restaurant owners quit because they can't take it anymore. They burn out." Dollars, of course, play a role even here.

High variable costs mean high maintenance, or more specifically "high management," he says. "That means somebody has to closely watch what's happening. Because of that they have to be in the business every day, seven days a week. They can be married to their wife or husband or their business, but not both. That's reality."

Retirement. Yet another factor is ill health — that of the owner or a family member — leading to retirement. "Because of this they find they can't stretch the time between the family and the business, so they leave." Retirement and the failure to adequately plan for it is a potential torpedo. "Restaurant owners don't live forever," Parsa reveals. "At some point they have to retire." Too many, though, have no "transitional plans. Most restaurant owners never, ever have transition plans. They think they're going to live forever."

The day inevitably comes when they have got to get out due to age or infirmity "but they don't know how," Parsa says. "They've never planned for it, so what do they do? They sell it, or the restaurant goes down because they can't commit — they're not that motivated anymore to be there, so they let it go. The employees may take advantage, so the restaurant loses money and he tries to get out by selling it." Parsa likens the scenario to war. "We get in, (but) we don't know how to get out. Same thing with restaurants: most restaurateurs never have a plan to get out. There is no exit strategy."

Taj Mahal syndrome. Another factor that contributes to restaurants going belly up is what Parsa, who was born in India, terms the Taj Mahal Syndrome. The famous landmark, he explains, was built "not for a living person, but for a dead person. Nobody lived in that building."

started. They could have funded the entire amount themselves but instead convinced Microsoft co-founder, Paul Allen to invest $400 million.

All startups are risky; successful, experienced investors understand this. They also recognize the difference between a reasonable gamble and throwing their money down the proverbial sink. And even if you have experience starting successful businesses in the past, you almost always lose objectivity when the ideas are your own.

Here's one more rule: don't include family members and close friends. They are likely to invest out of love, rather than objective business savvy. You don't want to lose your invitation to holiday parties along with your money if the business doesn't pan out.

If you're planning on opening a new restaurant, realize the odds are stacked against you. If your plan really has merit, you should be able to find one or more investors to finance the bulk of it.

You will need to do your homework. Develop your concept, thoroughly research your market and competition to determine if there's really a demand for what you intend to do. Then communicate your concept in a professional business plan that includes objective, realistic financial projections.

If you can't convince someone to invest in your restaurant dream, you probably shouldn't do it. Don't let what you think is a good idea, turn your life and future into a financial nightmare. We don't want to discourage you into giving up on your restaurant dream. Just be smart about it.

Restaurants are the same way, he explains. "People want to build but that's it; they don't know what to do with it once it's built. Restaurant owners most of the time have a dream of opening a restaurant, like the Taj Mahal, but they don't know how to do the next level, managing it and building it beyond. They thought that once they opened things would happen automatically. They don't. They never realized it's more about what happens after a restaurant is built. Before is easy. It's what I call entrepreneurial incompetence. They are competent enough to come up with the idea, but totally incompetent when it comes to taking it to the next level. That's why they fail." Another telling analogy: people who are dating. "They always think in terms of, 'I've got to marry this person,'" says Parsa. "They're thinking of the wedding, not the marriage. That's why most Americans spend so much money on weddings. No — we should spend more money on the marriage."

Time. The historical record shows indisputably that American food habits change every 10 to 15 years.

"I did research on this," says Parsa. "In the 19th century the number-one food item in America was steak. By the turn of the century, 1920, 1930, the number-one menu item was the hotdog." By 1947 to 1955, he continues, the hotdog was replaced by the hamburger. By 1980 it was pizza. "I told my students, 'Watch out — by 2020 or 2030 pizza will be replaced by something else, take-out salad or whatever it may be. We don't know.'" But the conclusion remains: with the passage of time American food habits change "dramatically. Our parents never taught us about eating a burrito for breakfast, but people do now."

Nor does the passing of time effect only taste trends. As decades go by, Parsa notes, "A restaurant's décor gets old. Diners experience the same ambiance forever so they want a change. If somebody down the street has a better ambiance, they go there."

People choose to dine in a given restaurant "basically for three things, and only for three things," Parsa maintains, "the food, the ambiance and the service." That said, he adds, "Every 10 years one of the three gets old. Service changes. Habits change. Technology changes. Guess what: people start looking for other things to do. By then you're too late."

Parsa calls updating product a "very, very touchy" affair. "I teach menu engineering, and there is a way to do it (see Chapter 3). Most restaurant owners don't know how to do it; that's why they fail. They've got to know how to do menu engineering and they must do it every three months. That tells you which items are selling and which aren't; which to keep and which to take out. And of course they must keep testing new products."

The Right Dream

Parsa admits that before he started his research he'd been "puzzled about what to expect. All the accounts, and Dun & Bradstreet, say that capital is

The combined total of your restaurant's 'prime cost,' is where the battle for restaurant profitability is truly waged.

~ John Nessel

the reason restaurants fail. No, it's not just capital. It's quality of life. It's lack of planning. It's the Taj Mahal Syndrome. It's entrepreneurial incompetence. It's more of a managerial issue than a financial matter." The key for anyone considering opening a restaurant, he says, is to realize that their dream should not be opening a restaurant, but having and operating one.

"Opening is the first step only," he emphasizes. "Do you have enough money to survive? Do you have the managerial skills to run it? Do you have plans for somebody to (care for) your family? Can you take time off and be involved in your kids' lives? Do you have a life plan so that the restaurant is a part of your life, not your life itself? Most restaurant owners don't think in these terms. But if you're reading this Chapter before you open your restaurant, really think it through — location, the concept, the finances." A restaurateur must remember, he concludes soberly, that "a restaurant is a living, breathing, real thing. Not a toy to play with."

So, You're Thinking About Owning, Operating or Investing in a Restaurant...

171

Real Restaurateurs, *Real People*
Stories about people who realized their restaurant dreams

Whenever You Think You Have it Tough

The Orrison Family was ready for a plague of locusts. Their business, The Shed Barbeque and Blues Joint in Ocean Springs, Miss, has already survived a hurricane and fire, so they figure they could handle whatever else Mother Nature might throw their way.

The Shed is exactly what the name implies — a chaotic consortium of junk and cast-offs bound together by duct tape and baling wire, flotsam and jetsam on a Mississippi bayou that is home to one of the most popular restaurants on the Gulf Coast.

Opened in 2001 by brother and sister team Brad and Brooke Orrison, just barely out of their teens, the family business survived its first natural disaster in August 2005 when Hurricane Katrina wreaked havoc throughout the region. The Shed received six feet of water inside and the refrigeration units imploded on themselves from the pressure, but otherwise, much of the structure itself remained intact.

Within three weeks, the Orrison family was operating again, feeding thousands of volunteers free of charge, and greeting guests who brought junk items to help redecorate The Shed.

The bigger challenge came on February 12, 2012 when a fire, possibly sparked by an outdoor bonfire, destroyed the entire business. Nothing survived except the meat in the fire pits, which was served to firefighters as soon as the embers cooled, and a food truck the Orrisons had used for festivals and other events. Within five days, The Shed was again feeding people and accepting donations of junk to rebuild.

After two catastrophic disasters, surely no one would think poorly of the Orrisons or anyone for just throwing in the towel and calling it quits. "We come from a long line of entrepreneurs in our family and if you are an entrepreneur, giving up is not an option," says Brad Orrison.

Instead, the Orrisons have done what all good restaurant operators should do — learn from the experience, make improvements and grow your business.

Lesson 1: The most important thing the Orrisons learned was to stop complaining about insurance premiums and make sure to have all the coverage you need. When the fire destroyed everything, the insurance they had left them short about $400,000.

Lesson 2: Make sure you have a healthy emergency fund and don't touch it except for emergencies.

Lesson 3: No matter how well you do things now, you can always do it better.

Within days of the fire, the Orrisons pulled the entire staff together and started asking how a new and improved back-of-the-house should operate. Everyone agreed that the slapped together, disheveled look of the front of the house was just perfect.

But preparing and serving more than a ton of meat a day, turning over a 750 seat dining room several times on Friday and Saturdays, and growing a business by about 30 percent a year for ten years takes its toll on employees. They had lots of ideas.

The best idea was to create a separate kitchen for prepping and smoking the meat. Raw meat never leaves that room. Health Department inspectors noted that the design went far above their requirements.

The meat kitchen also has its own air conditioning unit allowing better temperature control from the hottest work area in the restaurant to kitchens where less heat intensive labor is underway. A third HVAC unit controls the public areas of the restaurant.

The kitchen lay-out, three times bigger than it had been previously, is very long and narrow, allowing the moving of plates through the line in a manner that requires fewer handlers and less potential for mistakes.

Within 60 days of the fire, the new Shed in all of its rumpled, trashy glory was back in business.

From the beginning of the business, the Orrisons' marketing plan focused on appreciation to the community and to their customers. The natural disasters only increased that effort.

"For weeks after each crisis, we had a family member in the parking lot, personally shaking hands and saying thank you," says Linda Orrison. "After the fire, we had absolutely nothing, so I wrote old-fashioned thank you notes by hand."

Of course, social media is a major part of the plan, thanking customers in general and calling out individuals by name for stopping by or bringing more junk for the collection.

On Labor Day, The Shed gives away pulled pork sandwiches to "anyone who has a job, wants a job or has retired from a job" as a way of saying thank you to the hard working people along Mississippi's Gulf Coast.

And to top it off, after recovering from the fire, the Orrisons launched their own show "The Shed," on the Food Network.

So, You're Thinking About Owning, Operating or Investing in a Restaurant...

173

Common Mistakes Restaurateurs Make, and How to Avoid Them

Chapter 17

In any new business venture good decision-making is vital. Opening a new restaurant requires so many decisions that it's not hard to make some bloopers along the way. The trick is not to overlook the really important issues that can make or break your chances for success. Here are some of the more important common missteps new owners make in areas that play a big role in how well a new restaurant is likely to do.

Mistakes are always forgivable, if one has the courage to admit them.

~Bruce Lee

Underestimating capital needs. There are many good new restaurants with excellent prospects for success that simply run out of money. It's common for first time owners in particular, to leave out or inadequately project all the startup costs involved in opening the restaurant. Some of the reasons include construction overruns, change orders, delays, and additional costs mandated from local inspectors and building authorities.

Also, soft costs like permits, liquor licenses, insurance binders and pre-opening payroll are often missed completely or grossly under-budgeted. Unless you've done it before, it's usually advisable to seek some experienced, professional help in identifying and estimating, in detail, the startup capital you'll need. Even then, many pros still add a 10%-15% contingency for the host of things that can (and often do) happen to add more cost to the project than you plan on.

Believing you'll start making money on opening day. The odds are stacked against this happening. Even the best run chains, which open restaurants for a living, factor into their startup budgets an allowance for funding operating deficits for two to three months after the restaurant opens.

It usually takes time to build sales volume to an adequate level. Even if your sales are strong from day one, food and labor costs are usually sky high for the first several weeks as your managers and staff get acclimated, productive and have the time and energy to focus on anything other than just taking care of who's at the table. In time, most things can be fixed. Run out of money and you're done.

Lack of a clear vision and purpose. This may sound somewhat vague and intangible but a successful startup requires the coordinated effort of a dedicated staff pulling together in the same direction, united by a common goal. Getting this accomplished requires some leadership skills.

New operators who either don't have or can't communicate an underlying mission that the staff can rally around will find it difficult to create the kind of climate that supports teamwork, hard work and dedication to excellence that endures through the long hours and sometime chaotic conditions that take place during the startup phase of any new restaurant.

Lack of documented systems, procedures and training manuals. Restaurant operations involve the ongoing repetition of hundreds and even thousands of divergent tasks by many individuals and groups of individuals.

Organization and consistent execution is vital to creating a successful restaurant. Franchised restaurants start out with detailed recipes, checklists and procedures to do everything from prepping the lettuce, to cleaning the restrooms to closing out the cashier. In new independent restaurants, you often have to "make it up" as you go.

There may be nothing to go by other than what's in the owner's head. This makes it more challenging to train employees and execute consistently so customers get a consistent level of service and food quality regardless of who the server is or who's in the kitchen. The longer the restaurant operates without a documented way of doing business, the longer the restaurant stays stuck in the often unorganized and "do-what-it-takes" startup phase.

Failing to function like an owner. Instead, the owner functions like just another employee and ends up bussing tables, cooking in the kitchen and doing the books. Obviously this is often a necessity during the startup phase but eventually someone has to manage the business, not just run the restaurant.

Managing the business includes activities like monitoring cash flow, analyzing the P&L, deciding about next month's marketing activities, evaluating what's working on the menu and other "strategic" functions to position the restaurant for future success. If the owner is constantly training employees or working the line, guess who's managing the business? No one.

Having the grand opening on opening day. You only have to do this once and you learn to wait a month or two to declare your grand opening. There are few things worse than getting slammed with more business that you can possibly handle on day one. With so many restaurants, the public's first impression can easily be their last.

Blow it on opening day and chances are you won't see most of those people again, ever. And they'll tell their friends to stay away too. Soft, quiet openings are the way to go. Get your act together before you tell the world.

Focusing too much on what you like. What you like doesn't matter, because you are not the customer. What matters is what your customers like. Find out what people in your area want and the price they're willing to pay for it. Go to existing restaurants and find out what people are buying. Take formal or informal surveys, conduct focus groups, anything to get a sense of what people in your area are hungry for that they currently can't get in your market area and what they're willing to pay for it. Too many new restaurant concepts miss the mark by not analyzing what people want in their local market.

Deciding on a concept, and then finding a location. Restaurant industry legend Phil Romono, whose creations include national chains Fuddruckers and Macaroni Grill says that's a mistake. Don't marry yourself to a concept. Find a location in a good market with adequate parking, access, visibility and other positive traits, and then determine what the local market wants that it can't get and find a way to satisfy that unfilled desire.

Accepting a secondary location to save on rent. Don't be too sure that your restaurant is going to be so exceptional that customers will go out of their way to find you. With all the restaurants there are today, chances are they won't. High visibility and convenient access are more critical today than ever. Saving money on rent in a poor location often results in spending all that and more on advertising in an attempt to get noticed and bring in more business.

Trying to appeal to everyone. You can't and if you try you'll end up with too many items on the menu, an overly complicated kitchen, confused customers and no unique identity in the marketplace. The key to success for today's independents is identifying an unfilled niche in your local market and being laser-beam focused on filling that particular slice of the market. This will give you a much better chance to become really good at whatever it is you do.

If you have high turnover, generally unhappy employees or frequent arguments and meltdowns in your restaurant, take a long look at what you are doing to foster a healthy environment. If your investment in social events, employee meals, shift drinks or random acts of generosity to your staff is nonexistent or minimal, consider this as one of the first things to rectify if you want your crew to work efficiently side by side.

~ Restaurant Startup & Growth magazine/ RestaurantOwner.com

So, You're Thinking About Owning, Operating or Investing in a Restaurant...

177

Purchasing Basics

When you think about it the basics of providing even simple meal service are quite remarkable. In this county alone there are more than 300 million people who in general are able to consume three meals a day. Doing the math that means some 900 million plus meals a day making their way from farm to factory to table.

Purchasing power is a license to purchase power.

~Raoul Vaneigem

The key, of course, is that food has to be processed, packaged and delivered in the correct quantities and at just the right time. That's a job that falls to the distributor community and anyone considering opening and growing a restaurant operation needs to understand and develop relationships with those sources of supply.

The earlier you can make a connection with potential local and national distributors the better. You need suppliers for your inventory, equipment and services, and distributors need a steady source of new customers — which very often are startup independent restaurants. The distributors know what's going on in their markets and can be very instrumental in providing information, support and help establishing credit on all the things you're going to be purchasing. Restaurants are capital-intensive businesses and being able to set up good credit terms is a key to smooth operations. That's why picking the right distributors early on will make a big difference in reliable service, consistent supply lines, better delivery, access to the newest products and even the best values.

Good distributors have a knowledge and insight to the industry marketplaces that often go far beyond the buyer/seller relationship. They can become consultants and advisers that share ideas, concepts and provide feedback. According to a recent survey, they are the number one source for information on new products, an important ingredient in keeping your restaurant new and fresh.

Moreover, it is in their best interest to have you succeed and prosper as you open your doors. The better you do, the better they do. It's a simple formula that adds up to recurring business and profits for everyone.

So, You're Thinking About Owning, Operating or Investing in a Restaurant...

179

As you begin the restaurant development process, tell your distributors what you're planning and ask what services they offer. Have them help you identify and connect with resources that can help you develop and grow. Of course it is a two-way street in that you need to make sure you understand they also are in business to make a profit. Without them your restaurant is much more difficult, if not impossible to open. They are the doors to your success, just as you are the foundation of theirs.

Strategic Purchasing

There are few businesses in which strategic purchasing is as critical as a restaurant. You should realize early on that you'll need to fight for every penny on the bottom line. It is a reality of the restaurant business. Your inventory is often highly perishable, and guest demand for any item can fluctuate. In about any restaurant environment you're going to have a broad range of products that make your menus work.

Independent restaurants and small chains that stake their reputations on fresh, high-quality, and often specialty items, rely on vendors who can fill orders in a timely and consistent manner and at the best cost possible. At the heart of this issue is your relationship with distributors. But the questions don't stop there as you begin to investigate how you'll supply your new restaurant.

Are you better off working with one "broad-line" distributor to ensure the best cost and delivery? Is selecting a prime vendor for most items and cherry-picking specialty items the way to go? Or, will buying from multiple vendors for the best price and product in different categories reap the best results? The answer may depend on your concept and menu. As you might expect there's no simple answer and in the world of restaurateurs and distributors there are lots of opinions as to which is the best approach.

Most broad-liners handle two basic types of accounts. The first type is the national, chain or multiunit account, which are the accounts that many of the readers of this book will compete against. They use their buying power and product specification as leverage with distributors and manufacturers to get the lowest price possible. In most cases they don't have a distributor sales representative (DSR) calling on them. Their orders are placed electronically or over the phone with an inside service representative. Usually there is no real need for a sales rep as they can't deviate from the products their companies have specified. As a result they often don't have the luxury of some of the other services a DSR may provide, including the big one called "will call," 24-hour access to their DSR to fix any problem.

The second type of customer distributor's service is geared toward is the independent owner and operator. Usually they have no long-term contracts with their vendors (which allow them to lock in prices on products over several or more months), and it could be argued these accounts get quality and service but not necessarily the lowest price. It would seem to give a profitability advantage to the chains — no argument there. If you're going to fit in the second category you need to ask if you are getting the best quality and the best service. And more importantly are you making enough profit? To answer these questions we should examine each point separately.

The first component of the equation is quality. One would think this is fairly straightforward. Many people would agree the word quality means that something is the best and therefore the most expensive. One of the definitions of the word quality, according to Webster's, is an inherent or distinguishing characteristic; a property. In commercial foodservice, providing "quality" ingredients means using the products with the best characteristics and features for the specific item. As an example, if you were going to make a strawberry daiquiri, you would need strawberries. Using the best and most expensive theory, the choice would be fresh long-stem strawberries, these being the "best" strawberries available. Of course nobody would do this. Instead they would more likely opt for frozen sliced strawberries or some similar item.

While this example may seem a bit extreme it can play itself out over and over again on almost any menu item. Most distributors stock thousands of items, in some cases tens of thousands. The reason being they know that there are many variables to every application. A New York steak for example can come in the form of an entire strip loin to be further broken down into steaks, or as a precut steak either frozen or fresh. This doesn't take into account the other variables of portion size and grade. So the expectation of your DSR is not only to know what options they have as a distributor, but to know which product is the best for a given application. Good DSRs continually ask their customers questions. Good DSRs continually learn their product lines and new products being introduced to the market.

The second component in the mix is service. Service is easily the most subjective, and often the one least agreed on by both parties. One customer's definition of good service could be having "will call" regardless of the reason. Another customer's definition may be to see new menu ideas and have current market information as part of their weekly sales call, while a third customer may expect both. To have the most effective long-term relationship, it may be helpful to understand how the typical DSR earns a living. It is probably no secret that most DSRs work on some type of commission structure. It could be 100-percent commission based on gross profit, or a base salary plus commissions based on profit and or sales. Knowing this explains the sometimes-tenuous relationship that exists between customers and DSRs. The fact of the matter is they need to earn a living and put their kids through college just like their customers do. The real trick is finding the right balance between price paid for products and profitability of the item on your menu along with service provided. If the DSR isn't making any money on an account, it isn't realistic to expect them to drop everything to provide product in an emergency.

Pricing: The Big Issue

It is a commonly held belief that prices are the root of all food cost issues. You will hear restaurateurs advise "Shop around for a better price and your food cost will come down," or "Use multiple vendors and it keeps them all honest" or "The spreadsheet will be your salvation."

From the point of the distributor, it's all about profit. They have to mark up the cost of their product to cover overhead and show a profit. So what needs to happen for both the buyer and supplier to achieve their business and financial goals? First it should be said that food cost is not driven by price as much as one would think. Food cost is determined by menu mix first and everything else second. It should be noted that of all of the factors that influence food cost, price takes a backseat to a lot of other things that are much easier for an operator to control. Menu pricing, portion control, and spoilage can have a much greater effect on food cost than price.

This is not to downplay the importance of price. To the contrary many independent operators give up their single best pricing tool. This tool is the almighty lever. Let's say for the sake of illustration your business does a million dollars per year in food sales and you run a 30 percent food cost. That means that in food purchases alone you are spending $300,000 annually. I can tell you any distributor would see this as an excellent account. Let's take this a step further.

Let's say that $300,000 was being delivered to you by one supplier twice a week. That makes your account $2,400 per stop. Again, many distributors would view this as an excellent piece of business. It should be noted that the $300,000 account potential is for food purchases only and does not include chemicals, paper and disposable products or small wares and equipment. Which account has the most pricing leverage? The account that divides their purchases between five or more vendors making them a $60,000 a year account to each DSR, all trying to make a profit, or the account that is worth $300,000 to one vendor? It is through the power of buying leverage that independents can have all three: quality, service and price.

What other services you can expect from your DSR. The list is seemingly endless. For starters you may want to have your DSR give you feedback about your business. They can provide you with more objective observations about what's going on, whether it is the cleanliness of the restrooms or the level of service when they ate there last. You may see your restaurant like we sometimes see our own kids: Friends or family who don't see our kids as often as we do tend to notice their growth more readily. We see them every day so we miss the subtle changes. Sometimes operators don't notice what's going on in their business because it changes gradually.

Take advantage of a fresh set of eyes. Many distributors realize that like the accounts they service, it is more cost-effective to keep a good customer happy than to replace a dissatisfied one. Consequently many distributors have developed departments to provide their accounts with additional resources. This may include server training, customized shelf-to-sheet order guides, extensive sales reports, or the latest market and trend information. Some vendors and many trade associations have forged partnerships with companies that offer services at reduced rates for their customers or members. These partnerships could be with credit card processors, menu companies, etc. The purpose is to bridge the gap between the resources the large chains enjoy and what is available to the independent operator. Your best bet is to ask.

So how do you get the most out of your relationship? Talk to several distributors about your plans. Don't be afraid to have a frank conversation about your business and your expectations. Find out what they need from you to help you open your business. With all the challenges of opening a new restaurant, having a great relationship with vendors allows you to focus on getting the doors open and bringing in the customers.

The Benefits of "Cherry Picking"

The key benefits of cherry-picking and spot buying is obtaining the lowest prices on a weekly or monthly basis. There may be a strong belief among some operators that bidding out weekly to ensure that the lowest price is realized for their quality specifications is time well spent. There may also be a certain comfort level in seeing that reflected on paper, and that suppliers will be able to truly get them deeper discounts because those suppliers know that their prices are watched closely.

Is this truly the best way to get the lowest prices, or is it just an illusion of that? The facts of the matter are that cherry-picking or spot buying programs are usually handled by distributors as "street accounts," in which their representatives can adjust pricing up or down depending on the competitive market. The representatives are paid on commission and markups or margins will need to be higher with "no commitment" buying to accommodate that. Most of the time the distributor cannot guarantee your volume to their manufacturers, so they are unable to plan accordingly and take advantage of volume discounts, which would bring the price down further.

Another concern faced by weekly bid customers is that during product shortages, the product may be assigned to the "regular" customers instead to make sure that they are covered. This has occurred many times when natural disasters happen. One operator recalls a situation involving café tomatoes, which are highly coveted for their use in salsa, and are in high demand due to their unusually low cost. When a storm hit, the prices rose dramatically, but one produce company made sure that its contract customers had product on hand and the less frequent customers were forced to use higher-priced alternatives.

Conversely, in "sole and prime vendor relationships" the restaurant chooses to use a select supplier for all or most of their purchases. Typically, they are characterized by a good broad-line distribution partner and handled by

Got Lagniappe?

If asked, the majority of restaurant patrons would probably tell you that the ultimate guest experience for them is for a restaurant to simply meet their expectations. It's true; simply delivering basic service expectations goes a long way in building customer loyalty. However, to create a truly memorable experience, one that your customers will most certainly tell others about, a restaurant should go beyond the expectations by delivering something extra. The term "lagniappe" is often used in southern Louisiana and Southeast Texas when providing the guest with something unexpected — a bonus or indirect benefit. A restaurant that differentiates itself from its competition is more likely to develop positive word of mouth.

~ Restaurant Startup
& Growth magazine/
RestaurantOwner.com

So, You're Thinking About Owning, Operating or Investing in a Restaurant...

183

a great service representative. That component is usually an important factor in whether a supplier could be considered to handle all or most of your purchases. The determining factor really has to do with the dynamics of the concept. Are you really able to get all of your products (groceries, meat, produce, seafood, chemicals, soft drinks, etc.) through a single source to meet your quality and delivery frequency needs? If so, then the sole supplier relationship may be worth exploring. If quality and delivery needs are such that higher-end and specialty types of cuts are needed, then it may make sense to select meat, produce and/or seafood vendors who are able to better serve your needs, and explore the prime vendor relationship for all of the other purchases.

There is the opportunity to reach an agreement with a distributor on the level of markup/margin you will be charged going forward. You want it known that if you are going to give that distributor all of your business you agree to the markups they will be charging. Audits can then be conducted periodically to confirm that the contract terms are in compliance.

For the distributor, each delivery stop carries a minimum cost of operation (gas, driver, time spent). That equates to a minimum order size that they must meet to cover their costs. Since one of the ways distributors can earn profit is to "build the delivery truck" or add to the orders they deliver, they should be able to pass on those efficiencies of the higher-volume orders to the customer. This may very well enable them to lower prices and still operate profitably, making this a win-win situation for buyer and seller. Most restaurants are now faced with gas surcharges levied on each invoice to offset the high fuel costs. Many larger restaurant companies know that reducing those deliveries can greatly reduce the effect of those higher fuel costs.

Proper controls by the restaurateur are critical. While having a very good distributor most likely means that you have a great supplier's representative handling your account you still need the appropriate controls/checks and balances. Those responsibilities are best not placed on the shoulders of the supplier representative, who is ultimately paid by the distributor.

Before entering into a sole or prime vendor relationship:

• Benchmark some of your high-volume and some of your lower-volume items to make sure that as you plan your menu items you have a good idea of prices.

• Review your quality levels. Does the quality level of all or part of the distributor's inventory match well with your anticipated quality needs?

• Consider whether you will need a distributor's representative at your facility taking weekly orders. If you would be comfortable faxing orders or placing orders online you may be able to reduce your cost of goods further. Eliminating the order taker in your restaurant eliminates "cost" from your distributor's end that can be passed on to you with lower markups. Many, if not all, of the larger chains function in this manner. It would not eliminate the representative who visits on occasion to address concerns, or runs out needed products. But there is a downside in that you may miss out on feedback and advice you can use.

• Will your restaurant have the storage available to receive fewer deliveries? If so, reducing weekly deliveries on a prime or sole vendor program can reduce your distributor's cost and be reflected in your delivered price as well.

• Make sure that audit privileges are included into any sole or prime vendor agreement that you review. This will serve as the compliance check for you... whereas the distributor will be required to produce manufacturer invoices and freight documents on selected items periodically that can be traced to your actual invoice cost.

• Clearly understand how your distributor defines cost.

• Understand if there are additional charges incurred for splitting cases or for stocking proprietary products on your behalf.

• Lastly, either party should be able to walk away from the relationship whole if the relationship no longer fits your distribution needs with an appropriate "escape" clause with written notice, for any reason.

In the Long Run, Prime Vendors Can Save Money, but Specialty Vendors Can Be Especially Helpful to New Operators

Although the large houses (broad-line distributors) provide you with a one-stop shop, with the convenience of placing one order with one representative, and minimal deliveries, all of these positives can turn into negatives in certain cases. When you only have a relationship with one vendor, your choices of product and flexibility regarding delivery times and quantities purchased may be limited. Your representative may have a broad knowledge of many products, but lack depth of knowledge of product lines, such as beef, special produce, oils, vinegars and spices. The knowledgeable representative from a specialty vendor can be invaluable to a start-up operator, especially in the fine dining category. In all fairness, the big houses do have specialists in these fields, but rarely do you see them consistently. Even then, their knowledge may not compare favorably to many of the smaller specialized distributors who have had the business in their family for generations.

Broad-line vendors often do not break cases. You may need to order a whole case of something that it could take you a year to use. Many smaller vendors will break cases if only for a small upcharge. At times the large houses can only save you money if you order private label products and many times may not even carry name-brand product. Using many specialized vendors with some overlapping product lists can give you an alternative source if your usual vendor for an item is out of product, and it can also give you bargaining power on prices.

Sometimes it just boils down to philosophy and not just dollars. If you're an independent restaurant you may want to support your local independent vendors who may be the only ones who can provide you with the local product, meats and produce that are available in your area — especially organic and specialty products like pastas, raviolis, breads and tomatoes.

After time, however, you may get to a point at which you have the knowledge and adequate multiple vendor relationships to place at least 60 percent to 80 percent of your orders with a primary vendor. In this case, you can reap the main reward of this type of relationship — the cost savings can be enormous. This is especially true if you can join a buying group.

One Size Does Not Fit All

If there was one right way to open and manage every restaurant business life would be simple. We know it doesn't work that way. Purchasing is an art, and smart vendor relationships are critical to keeping food costs as low as possible, yet there is no single philosophy that works for every business.

The size of your new restaurant, the types of products you need for your menu and even your rapport with distributors all factor into the purchasing equation. Managing your future vendor relationships is an important ingredient in every type and style of restaurant. You certainly don't want to leave money on the table and working early with distributors as you go through the opening process is important.

Try to Negotiate Cost-Plus Programs Whenever Feasible

The vast majority of larger restaurant operators (with the midsize and smaller now following suit) set up a "cost-plus" program with their suppliers. Accomplishing this early is a great first step. This concept is an upfront agreement with the supplier of the markups or margins that the supplier will use to determine the prices charged on the products you buy. When negotiating cost-plus pricing, you should consider the following questions:

How is cost defined? New restaurateurs who look to enter into cost-plus agreements should request that this be defined as "true cost." True cost is simply the manufacturer cost of the product, plus the freight to get it to that distributor. The distributor then adds the agreed-upon markup or margin to the "true" or "landed cost," which results in the "delivered cost" on your restaurant invoice.

How do you know when you are big enough to have a cost-plus program? A good indicator that you are ready to effectively work with your supplier on a cost-plus program is when your volume is large enough for you to negotiate discounted allowances or contract pricing deals directly with manufacturers. How big is big enough? The "magic" number, if you will — for single- or multiple-unit operators to be eligible for cost-plus pricing seems to be around $5,000 per week in purchases according to many experts in the field.

Now, you would hope that the distributor representative would let the owner or chef know that they have the volume necessary for a cost-plus or other manufacturer deal, and work in their best interest. Being proactive and working in the best interest of their customers is a trait of the best representatives and suppliers, and the distributor typically will consider this a good opportunity to get a commitment from the operator and put more business on the truck. In practice, however, the distributor's representative may believe that he will lose some percentage of his commission if he switches a customer to a cost-plus contract, so, even though it would make sense for the distributor, the "street rep" may see this move as counter

Continued on page 187

Continued from page 186

to his interests. And that's why it is wise for the restaurateur to keep tabs on his weekly volume, and then, when average purchases begin to hover at that "magic" number, arrange a meeting with the right person at the distributor (e.g., a sales director or similar executive) who can help him achieve these savings and, in general, work in his best interest. Take the initiative and challenge the distributor to pursue deals on your behalf or at least encourage your representative to arrange meetings with the brokers or manufacturer representatives who might welcome the opportunity to deal directly with the restaurant.

How do you know if the markups or margins are fair? One way is to bid out all of your business to a number of suppliers to get a feel for the market; however, another valuable method to employ is to benchmark your top 10-15 items and bottom 10-15 items with some other distributors in the normal course of business. You should also request your supplier periodically run a weekly usage report by item with the unit costs and the number of units purchased, with the total estimated weekly savings under its cost-plus. If you extrapolate those savings over a year, you can project your annual savings under a program.

Can I audit my program? Here is where the checks and balances for the cost-plus program really come into play. Here is how an audit would work: By agreement, you would have the right to select a number of items periodically and require the distributor to produce manufacturer invoices and freight documents that contribute to the delivered price of the products. It is a great tool for compliance and is expected to be part of any transparent cost-plus program.

What are the supplier's assumptions? Your primary supplier will make some key assumptions about your business to be able to offer you a lower-cost program. These are the variables that they will drop into a formula to calculate your markups and margins. It would be important to make sure that you are familiar with these assumptions, because it is what that supplier will expect in return for lowering the markups. You should be aware of these before negotiating your pricing. Key assumptions include:

* Expected annual volume in sales from your location(s).
* Number of deliveries per week per location.
* Average delivery size (one of the most important variables).
* Number of proprietary items that they are willing to stock for you.
* Percentage commitment — usually between 80 percent and 100 percent in each agreed-upon category.

Cost-plus programs are now available from the vast majority of broadline distributors as well as many of the produce and meat companies. Again, anyone can walk in your back door with lower prices from time to time to gain business; however, they would not be able to sustain that level of pricing and make the profit they need to exist. Compliance by both parties is the key to success. In addition to the cost savings, you may see benefits in labor costs with streamlining the purchasing function.

So, You're Thinking About Owning, Operating or Investing in a Restaurant...

187

How to Build Successful Partnerships with Purveyors

Suppliers are an essential component of the turbine that runs any restaurant operation, but they particularly drive a startup or new location. Without them, the walk-in would be empty, the washrooms without soap, and the kitchen knives dull. To ensure a smooth-running system, the rapport between chefs and purveyors — like any efficient and successful relationship — needs continual care and maintenance. Unfortunately, it's not always easy.

There's no doubt that restaurateurs and their suppliers are critically dependent on each other. But sometimes the relationship can turn to a love-hate affair when each partner fails to look at the world through the other's eyes. Operators deal with a continuous stream of changing prices, quantity and quality, handling late deliveries, or worse, deliveries that show up during peak service times. Then, when salespeople finally understand your particular restaurant's wants and needs, they switch jobs and then start knocking at your door as an employee of another supplier.

On the flip side, some operators treat suppliers like grease traps. Some owners always take the position that suppliers are full of garbage and can't be trusted. They are rude to delivery drivers, abuse the salespeople and run them ragged. On top of it all, they think "net 30" means, "Whenever I get around to paying the invoice." That's one way to do business but for any startup it simply leads to a bad start and in just about every instance it's a bad approach.

Issues aside, the reality is that purveyors are the link to goods and services necessary for this business. They're an essential part of your business and you need them just as much as they need you. Period. Building a positive relationship with purveyors is more important now than ever.

As companies merge with larger suppliers, the selection of purveyors continues to shrink, making it tougher for a chef or kitchen manager to tell a supplier to take a hike. Consequently, it's important that operators view suppliers as partners in the restaurant business. They have a vested interest in a restaurant's success. As your business grows, so does theirs. If the supplier has extended a line of credit, your restaurant's financial future is closely tied to theirs.

Selecting the Right Purveyors

The first step in building a positive, trusting and lasting relationship with a purveyor is choosing not just the ones that best fit your needs but also the right ones, in general. The criteria should always include the "big three": quality, price and service.

What's the best way to get those "big three"? Always ask for references and then take the time to really make the calls and interview the restaurants or retailers that your potential suppliers do business with. You'll learn a lot early on and possibly save yourself thousands of dollars in both time and cash. Ask direct questions and inquire about their experience with the supplier, the length of the relationship and how long they've had the same salesperson. If they rave about the salesperson, get that person's name. Often a salesperson can be the deciding factor in choosing a supplier. Treat the supplier like a prospective employee; look for motivation, passion, conscientiousness and dedication.

After the references are checked and you find that fellow restaurateurs have given your prospective suppliers good marks, meet with the sales manager and the salesperson. If it's a small local company, don't be shy about asking for a meeting with the owner. If the owners and sales managers are too busy to meet with a new customer it might be a red flag that you could have service problems later. Conversely, a face-to-face meeting speaks volumes about the integrity of a company. It's unlikely that a restaurateur would hire an employee without an interview so apply the same attention to detail with a supplier.

Continued on page 189

Continued from page 188

Another important rule: Never buy any product without trying it first, whether it's mushrooms or floor cleaner. Ask for items that can be compared with currently purchased products as well as ones you would like to try. Sampling is an industry standard and is especially important with meat, fish and produce. Good distributors and brokers want you to compare because they are proud of the products they represent and know that in the end it's all about making sure your customers are satisfied. You should also inquire about the handling of items in delivery. Suppliers typically handle products differently. For example, Farmer A may grow the same tomato as Farmer B but the latter may refrigerate the product — the type of handling that cuts flavor.

It's essential to see, touch and sample the product before buying. A purveyor may send the highest quality, freshest product to you at first and then shortchange you later. Remember the quality that was sampled, and make sure that you receive the same quality level in future orders. The same goes for pricing. When bidding new pricing, beware of sellers who will low-ball prices to get your business. Once they have you on board, the numbers start to climb, hoping you won't notice the increases. These are not the types of companies you want to do business with and is another reason to spend the necessary time on the early interviewing process.

If possible, visit the operation of the prospective purveyor's business. Tour the warehouse. Look for an organized, clean storage space, free of debris and litter. If it's a seafood, meat or poultry vendor, check out the cutting and packing room. Walk through the coolers and freezers. Look for a sanitary working area, which is neat and tidy. The best suppliers will welcome your interest in what they are selling and how they are handling it. These companies take pride in their product and use high standards as a point of difference from competitors.

Establish Ground Rules From Day One

After you choose a new purveyor for your startup, it's important to establish some ground rules. For a relationship to work there needs to be an upfront understanding of what each party expects. The supplier may want you to know the company's delivery days in your area, and the cutoff times for ordering for the next day. You'd like them not to deliver during lunch, for example, and you may have some ordering specs for certain items. Whatever the information that needs to be shared, the key is it gets shared before the first order arrives at your backdoor.

Once both parties have agreed on terms, it's very important that you keep your end of the bargain. And that means pledging to pay on time. Keep your order sheets updated, making sure that you don't miss an order or forget to order items. This helps avoid miss-picks from your seller and limits the times you have to ask your salesperson for a favor to deliver an item you forgot to order. You'd like to save those calls for emergencies.

If the person checking in the product is different from the person who placed the order, use purchase order forms so the exact item information is at hand. This way mistakes can be handled when the driver is still at your door, making returns efficient, and limiting the number of trips your salesperson needs to make to your restaurant. Imagine yourself in the shoes of your salesperson; it should help to appreciate the benefits of working together.

Comparing products and prices takes a lot of time. But it is a necessary component of quality and cost control. Believe it or not it's the difference between staying in business and closing your doors. You need to know that you're always getting the best product at the best price. Make sure you let your salesperson know when you're shopping their prices. At least once each year compose a sheet of items you're using for grocery and produce. If you think you can get better pricing and quality, send out bids. Just make

So, You're Thinking About Owning, Operating or Investing in a Restaurant...

189

sure you're comparing apples to apples; the product list needs to be as specific as possible, and of course, without the prices of your current supplier. You may or may not be looking to change your purveyor, but you have to keep your purveyor's pencils sharp.

Keep yourself up-to-date on the current pricing of suppliers other than the ones you are using. Simply tell these companies that although you're happy with the supplier from which you're buying, you want to keep up with the market and not ignore opportunities to find better deals. You may have to take time for an occasional sales call or visit from these folks, but it's always good to have options. Take the time to compare the prices of these companies to what you're currently paying. This way you can stay on top of market prices for commodity items like dairy, meat and potatoes from your supplier's competitors. Purchasing is one of the most critical jobs in a manufacturing company, as it ensures that necessary unfinished goods will be available, of sufficient quality, and at a reasonable price. In many ways, the back of the house is a manufacturing operation, with raw goods coming in the door as inputs and the finished products being delivered to the customers' tables.

As your relationship builds with your supplier, items of their appreciation will start to come your way. These are lovely gestures; however, accepting tickets to a ballgame, free boxes of ribs for your company cookout, or an expensive round of golf, as inviting as it is, can be risky business. You need to know where to draw the line. Getting too close to suppliers can be dangerous. They start to take your business for granted and lose their competitive edge, as will you. You'll stop comparing prices, and the level of trust you worked so hard to build could become foolishness. You still need to keep business first with these working relationships. This doesn't mean that you treat your suppliers in an unfriendly manner; it just says that you realize the importance of keeping a business relationship first.

Don't Forget the Drivers

Another important player in the purveyor relationship is the driver. They are the final link in the restaurant supply chain. The delivery people are as important as the sales representatives. They do all the hard work, battle traffic and are responsible for getting product to your door in good shape and in a timely fashion.

Drivers who deliver produce; meat, poultry, and fish; and linen need to be treated like royalty. These guys represent the foodstuffs and products that cost the most, are critical to your menu, and can easily be mishandled. Get to know the delivery drivers' names and even a little bit about them. It's nice to be able to ask a guy how his kid is doing in little league. Offer drivers cold water or soda in to-go cups when they make their delivery. Let them know it's good to see them. Treating your deliverymen with respect and affability will lead to your product and delivery times getting the best consideration.

When I need product early on a Friday, I know my drivers will shuffle their route to hook me up first. When I'm busier than expected, my linen driver will leave us extra product, and often, off the invoice. A great driver can serve you serious savings by adjusting your pars with your business, keeping inventories low and saving you money. My linen driver gets fed lunch once a week, and during the holidays we send him off with a case of good beer. I know that when I'm stuck, he's going to help me out.

On the flip side, if you love the company you buy from, but your driver is not doing his job or is disrespectful to your crew, call his or her boss. Any solid supplier worth their weight in kitchen towels will want to know if they're not being positively represented. It's important that your hospitality becomes a two-way street.

Overall, though, I've found that most drivers and salespeople are good people, who on most days have to take some guff from their stops. Keeping your delivery from being a negative one will only make your job, and that of your deliverymen, easier and more profitable. Embrace them and watch your level of service rise, and your blood pressure fall.

Be the Talk of the Town in a Good Way

Restaurant people are the most gregarious lot you'll meet. They talk to each other, and create "the word on the street." They can tell you how the other restaurants are doing and what they are doing. They know who's doing well and who's not paying their bills, where the crowds are going and which trends are hot. Some might call it gossip but it's good gossip most of the time and it is amazing just how much your reputation and the reputation of your business is based on "the industry has it" commentaries of those calling on and delivering to you. If you're a son-of-a-gun, everyone is going to know it and likewise if you're tough, but respectful and fair, that word gets around to everyone. And that includes restaurant customers hunting for a dining recommendation from somebody in the business — whether that be a manufacturing operation supplier or another restaurateur

Restaurant
Rules of Thumb

I n this chapter we look at industry performance benchmarks with which you should be familiar. As you develop your business plans and projections, you will want to ask if you can hit these marks. If you want more information on these terms and their significance, you can familiarize yourself with them as a member of RestaurantOwner.com

Hammer rule of thumb: If your only tool is a hammer, every problem looks like a nail.

~Abraham H. Maslow

The first and most fundamental restaurant rule of thumb is "every independent restaurant is unique." However, rules of thumb regarding the financial and operational aspects of restaurants can provide a valuable starting point for evaluating and understanding the financial feasibility and performance of proposed and existing restaurants.

Restaurants generate a lot of numbers so particularly for those new to the industry, deciding what numbers to focus on first and knowing what they mean can be more than a little perplexing. Rules of thumb can help operators determine where to look first and what to expect.

We'll discuss several of the restaurant industry's basic rules of thumb. While there will always be exceptions, they have proven to be surprisingly reliable over the years that I have worked with operators who collectively manage thousands of diverse restaurant operations. Keep these numbers handy when planning your restaurant and assessing your performance after you open.

Investment Rules of Thumb

One of the primary indicators chain operators use for evaluating the feasibility of a new location is the sales-to-investment ratio. This ratio compares the projected annual sales of a proposed site with its estimated startup cost. The ratio looks like this:

Sales to Investment = Annual Sales /Startup Cost

Startup cost includes all the costs necessary to open the restaurant including leasehold improvements (or land and building), furniture and equip-

So, You're Thinking About Owning, Operating or Investing in a Restaurant...

193

ment, deposits, architectural and design, accounting and legal, preopening expenses, contingency and working capital reserve.

Sales to investment — leasehold. When evaluating the feasibility of a proposed restaurant in a leased space, a rule of thumb says that the sales-to-investment ratio should be at least 1.5 to 1, or a minimum of $1.50 in sales should be expected for every $1 of startup costs. This means that if the cost of opening a restaurant in a leasehold situation was estimated to be $500,000, the location should be given further consideration only if the annual sales volume of at least $750,000 could be a realistic expectation.

Sales to investment — own land and building. The rule of thumb for restaurant projects in which the operator owns the land and building calls for a sales-to-investment ratio of at least 1 to 1, or $1 in sales for every dollar of startup costs.

While there are many other considerations in deciding whether to open in a particular location, this is one ratio that many operators use as an early indicator of whether to move on to other factors in the go/no go decision process.

Profitability Rules of Thumb

Sales per square foot. While not all high-volume restaurants make lots of money, they do have the greatest opportunity to generate a sizable amount of profit. Sales volume is the most reliable indicator of a restaurant's potential for profit and a useful way to look at sales volume when evaluating profit potential is through the ratio of sales per square foot.

It's easy to calculate a restaurant's sales per square foot. Just take annual sales and divide by the total interior square footage including kitchen, dining, storage, restrooms, etc. This is usually equal to the net rentable square feet in a leased space. The ratio looks like this:

Sales Per Square Foot = Annual Sales / Square Footage

In most cases, full-service restaurants that don't generate at least $150 of sales per square foot have very little chance of generating a profit. For example, a 4,000-square-foot restaurant with annual sales of anything less than $600,000 would find it very difficult to avoid losing money. This works out to $50,000 in monthly and $12,000 in weekly sales.

Limited-service restaurants that generate any less than $200 of sales per square foot have little chance of averting an operating loss. Industry averages reveal that limited-service restaurants tend to have slightly different unit economics than their full-service counterparts. Higher occupancy costs (on a per-square-foot basis) and lower check averages are two of the primary reasons for this difference.

At sales levels of $150 to $250 per square foot (full-service) and $200 to $300 (limited-service), restaurants with effective cost controls may begin to approach break-even, with some well-managed operations able to achieve a net income of up to 5 percent of sales.

At sales levels of $250 to $325 per square foot (full-service) and $300 to $400 (limited-service), restaurants may see moderate profits, which are defined as 5 percent to 10 percent net income (before income taxes) as a percentage of total sales.

High profit can be defined as sales levels more than $350 per square foot (full-service) and more than $400 (limited-service). Generating sales at these levels affords the opportunity for some operators to generate a net income (before income taxes) in excess of 10 percent of sales.

There are many factors that influence a restaurant's profitability besides sales volume. Two of the biggest are prime cost and occupancy costs. Without competent management and effective systems and controls over food, beverage, labor and other operating expenses, no amount of sales will produce much more than mediocre operating results.

Likewise, occupancy costs, which are not controllable by restaurant management, will have a significant effect on profitability. The sales volume rules of thumb above assume an "industry average" occupancy cost from $15 to $22 per square foot. If your occupancy costs are higher than $22 per square foot, the sales numbers above will be low when using them to evaluate your restaurant's profitability.

Percentage of Sales Rules of Thumb

Food cost. Food cost as a percentage of food sales (costs/sales) is generally in the 28 percent to 32 percent range in many full-service and limited-service restaurants. More upscale full-service concepts, particularly those that specialize in steaks and/or fresh seafood can have food cost of 38 percent, 40 percent and even higher. Conversely, there are gourmet pizza restaurants in affluent markets that are able to consistently achieve a food cost of 20 percent and sometimes even less.

Alcoholic beverage costs. Alcohol costs vary with the types of drinks served. Among the reasons that bar service is so desirable are both the relative profitability of alcohol and the ability to control costs, as long as servers are trained to pour accurately, and theft is not a significant problem. Below are typical costs in percentages:

* Liquor — 18 percent to 20 percent.

* Bar consumables — 4 percent to 5 percent as a percent of liquor sales (includes mixes, olives, cherries and other food products that are used exclusively at the bar).

* Bottled beer — 24 percent to 28 percent (assumes mainstream domestic beer, cost percent of specialty and imported bottled beer will generally be higher).

* Draft beer — 15 percent to 18 percent (assumes mainstream domestic beer, cost percent of specialty and imported draft beer will generally be higher).

* Wine — 35 percent to 45 percent (the cost percentages of wine can vary dramatically from restaurant to restaurant depending primarily on the type of wines served. Generally, the higher the price per bottle, the higher the cost percentage).

So, You're Thinking About Owning, Operating or Investing in a Restaurant...

195

NOTE: All percentages above are the ratio of each item's cost divided by its sales, not total sales or total beverage sales. For example, liquor cost percentages above are based on liquor costs divided by liquor sales. This applies to the nonalcoholic beverage costs discussed below as well.

Nonalcoholic beverage costs. It is standard industry practice to record nonalcoholic beverage sales and costs in Food Sales and Food Cost accounts, respectively:

* Soft drinks (post-mix) — 10 percent to 15 percent (another rule of thumb for soft drinks is to expect post-mix soda to cost about a penny an ounce for the syrup and CO_2).

* Regular coffee — 15 percent to 20 percent (assumes 8-ounce cup, some cream, sugar and about one free refill).

* Specialty coffee — 12 percent to 18 percent (assumes no free refills) .

* Iced tea — 5 percent to 10 percent, iced tea is the low food cost champ of all time. Cost of the tea can be less than a penny per glass. Biggest cost component in iced tea is usually the lemon slice.

Paper cost. In limited-service restaurants paper cost should be classified as a separate line item in "cost of sales." Historically, paper cost has run from 3 percent to 4 percent of sales. However, the recent run-up in the cost of many paper goods has increased the paper cost percentage to more than 4 percent of sales in many restaurants. In full-service restaurants, paper cost is usually considered to be a direct operating expense and normally runs from 1 percent to 2 percent of total sales.

Payroll and Salaries. Payroll cost as a percentage of sales includes the cost of both salaried and hourly employees plus employee benefits, which includes payroll taxes, group, life and disability insurance premiums, workers' compensation insurance premiums, education expenses, employee meals, parties, transportation and other such benefits. Total payroll cost should not exceed 30 percent to 35 percent of total sales for full-service operations, and 25 percent to 30 percent of sales for limited-service restaurants.

Generally, you don't want management salaries to exceed 10 percent of sales in either a full- or limited-service restaurant. This would consist of all salaried personnel including general manager, assistant manager(s), chef or kitchen manager.

One caveat on this would be in a situation in which a working owner fulfills the role of the general manager and/or chef and takes a salary in excess of 3 percent to 4 percent of sales. When this occurs, management salaries can easily exceed 10 percent of sales and total payroll cost can appear excessive as well.

To compensate for a highly paid working owner when comparing costs and margins that contain management salaries, subtract the amount of the owner's salary that exceeds 4 percent of sales. This will make comparisons to industry averages and rules of thumb much more meaningful and useful.

Keep It Under Your Hat

When submitting a business plan for review by potential investors, bankers, and prospective partners, you should consider having reviewers sign a confidentiality agreement. In the critical planning and negotiating stage of a new operation you need to protect your trade secrets and confidential information. Chain restaurants use them in standard practice; however, independent restaurateurs should consider them as well, particularly if the concept is novel and involves significant proprietary market research.

~ Restaurant Startup & Growth magazine/ RestaurantOwner.com

Hourly Employee Gross Payroll.
* Full-service Restaurant — 18 percent to 20 percent
* Limited-service Restaurant — 15 percent to 18 percent

Limited-service restaurants generally have lower hourly payroll cost percentages than full-service restaurants. In limited-service restaurants, managers often perform the work of an hourly position in addition to being a manager. In some cases, however, hourly workers may also perform management roles on some shifts, which could lead to higher hourly payroll costs in these restaurants.

Employee Benefits.
* 5 percent to 6 percent of total sales
* 20 percent to 23 percent of gross payroll

Employee benefits can vary somewhat depending primarily on state unemployment tax rates and state workman's compensation insurance rates. California, for example, has had for the past several years very high workers' compensation premium rates as compared with rates in other states. Restaurants that are new or have had a large number of unemployment claims may have state unemployment tax rates that could cause their employee benefits to be higher than the rules of thumb above.

Prime Cost Rules of Thumb
* Table-service — 65 percent or less (total sales)
* Limited-service — 60 percent or less (total sales)

As prime cost exceeds the above levels it becomes increasingly difficult to achieve and maintain an adequate bottom-line profit in most restaurants. When looking at a restaurant's overall cost structure, prime cost can be very meaningful, particularly in cost of sales and payroll cost. Some restaurants may carry very high food cost and yet be extremely profitable. Again, this can be revealed by looking at prime cost.

Prime cost is arrived at by adding cost of sales and payroll costs as shown in the Prime Cost Calculation chart below:

Prime Cost		
Cost of Sales		
Food	$15,000	
Liquor	1,500	
Beer	1,000	
Wine	1,200	$18,700
Payroll Costs		
Management	5,000	
Hourly Staff	12,000	
Taxes and Benefits	3,400	$ 20,400
Prime Cost		$ 39,100

So, You're Thinking About Owning, Operating or Investing in a Restaurant...

Prime cost reflects those costs that are generally the most volatile and deserve the most attention from a control standpoint. It's very easy to lose money due to lax or nonexistent controls in the areas of food, beverage and payroll. Many successful restaurants calculate and evaluate their prime cost at the end of each week.

In the chart, if total sales were $60,000, then prime cost would be running $39,100 or 65 percent of sales.

Some people might be surprised to find out that some of the most profitable restaurants in our industry have a food cost in excess of 40 percent. Some very popular and successful restaurants that offer high-quality proteins, such as steaks and seafood, often have food costs of 45 percent or higher.

You might be thinking, how could any restaurant make money let alone be highly profitable when its food cost gets close to 50 percent of sales. Well this particular restaurant does more than $20 million in annual sales in about 20,000 square feet. This means that its sales are more than $1,000 per square foot, which is among the highest in the industry.

Even though their food cost is as high as say 45 percent, what do you think is their labor cost as a percentage of sales when they generate a sales level this high? I'm fairly certain it's much lower than the industry average, which is around 30 percent to 35 percent. In fact, their payroll, including management, hourly staff and taxes and benefits is probably around 15 percent to 18 percent of sales, but let's say it's 20 percent to be conservative.

Let's also assume a restaurant's sales mix is 85 percent food and 15 percent liquor, beer and wine. If their combined beverage cost is, 25 percent of beverage sales, here's an estimate of their prime cost percentage (by the way, these are numbers from an actual, highly successful restaurant in the Midwest. Very few independent single-unit operations reach these sales levels, but it shows what is possible):

Sales

Cost of Sales		
Food	$18,700,000	85%
Beverage	3,300,000	15%
Total Sales	22,000,000	100%
Cost of Sales		
Food	8,415,000	45%
Beverage	825,000	25%
Total Cost of Sales	9,240,000	42%
Payroll Costs	4,400,000	20%
Prime Cost %	13,640,000	62%

If our assumptions about beverage and payroll costs are fairly accurate, you can see that the prime cost is well below the 65 percent threshold. This means that even with a very high food cost, this particular restaurant should be very profitable, assuming its remaining costs and expenses are in line with restaurant industry averages.

Some restaurants, like many ethnic concepts, have relatively low food costs, with some well under 30 percent of sales. You might think that these restaurants would be extremely profitable. They might be, but often these restaurants have lower check averages and are more labor intensive, so their payroll costs are much higher as a percentage of sales than, a steak or sea-food restaurant.

Looking at cost of sales and payroll costs together as prime cost usually provides a much more meaningful and valid indication of a restaurant's cost structure and potential for profit.

Rent and Occupancy Cost Rules of Thumb

Rent (6 percent or less). Rent used here is the ongoing payments made by an operator to the lessor for the use of premises. Rent payments may be fixed or based on a percentage of sales. Generally, the goal is to limit rent expense to 6 percent of sales or less, exclusive of related costs such as common area maintenance (CAM) and other occupancy expenses.

Occupancy cost (10 percent or less). Occupancy cost includes rent, CAM, insurance on building and contents, real estate taxes, personal property taxes and other municipal taxes. Many operators want to keep occupancy cost at or below 8 percent of sales, however, 10 percent is generally viewed to be the point at which occupancy cost starts to become excessive and begins to seriously impair a restaurant's ability to generate an adequate profit.

Sales Value of Restaurant Business Rules of Thumb

Accurately determining the potential sales value in any restaurant requires the services of a professional business appraiser, preferably with experience appraising independent restaurants.

There are two rules of thumb that may be helpful to arrive at an initial, rough estimate of what your restaurant might be worth, assuming you operate in leased space:

Sales value of business (gross sales method) — 38 percent to 42 percent of gross sales. Sales value of business (cash flow method) — annual cash flow (basically net income before depreciation, debt service and owner compensation) times a multiple of three to four.

Following, we show how to estimate business value, based on the cash flow method:

So, You're Thinking About Owning, Operating or Investing in a Restaurant...

199

Business Value Estimation — Cash Flow Method	
Net Income – Annual	$50,000
Add back:	
Depreciation	15,000
Interest Expense	12,000
Owner's Salary and Other Compensation	75,000
Multiple	3.5
Estimated Value of Business	$532,000

When determining the value of a restaurant in leased space, one of the most important determinants is the terms, particularly the transferability and the amount of time, with options, remaining on the existing lease. Lease factors such as these and other terms can have a significant effect on the value of any business.

In restaurants where the operator owns the land and building, the inherent value of the business will be influenced significantly by the underlying value of the real estate. For this reason it is difficult to value the business in a meaningful way using rules of thumb.

Final Rule of Thumb: Not Every Rule of Thumb Fits Every Restaurant

Most restaurants will probably deviate from one or more of the rules of thumb discussed in this chapter. That's to be expected. Rules of thumb are merely guidelines, not an ironclad collection of industry mandates from which no successful restaurant can deviate.

Where your numbers do stray from these norms, it may be useful to determine "why." Determining the reasons for any differences may prove to be an insightful process in learning more about the financial and operating nuances of your restaurant.

Another rule of thumb says that the more you understand how your restaurant works, the better the manager you will become. Using these rules of thumb could go a long way in helping to better understand your restaurant and provide insights for building a more successful business.

At a Glance: Restaurant Rules of Thumb

Sales to Investment
(Annual Sales/Startup Cost)
• Leasehold — at least 1.5 to 1.
• Own land and building — at least 1 to 1.

Sales Per Square Foot
• Losing Money Full-service — $150 or less. Limited-service — $200 or less.
• Break-even Full-service — $150 to $250. Limited-service - $200 to $300.
• Moderate Profit Full-service — $250 to $350. Limited-service — $300 to $400.
• High Profit Full-service — More than $350. Limited-service — More than $400.

Food Cost
• Generally — 28% to 32% as a percentage of total food sales.

Alcoholic Beverage Costs
• Liquor — 18% to 20% as a percentage of liquor sales.
• Bar consumables — 4% to 5% as a percentage of liquor sales.
• Bottled beer — 24% to 28% as a percentage of bottled beer sales.
• Draft beer — 15% to 18% as a percentage of draft beer sales.
• Wine — 35% to 45% as a percentage of wine sales.

Nonalcoholic Beverages
• Soft drinks (post-mix) — 10% to 15% as a percentage of soft drink sales.
• Regular coffee — 15% to 20% as a percentage of regular coffee sales.
• Specialty coffee — 12% to 18% as a percentage of specialty coffee sales.
• Iced tea — 5% to 10% as a percentage of iced tea sales.

Paper Cost
• Full-service — 1% to 2% as a percentage of total sales.
• Limited-service — 3% to 4% as a percentage of total sales.

Payroll Cost
• Full-service — 30% to 35% as a percentage of total sales.
• Limited-service — 25% to 30% as a percentage of total sales.

Management Salaries
• 10% or less as a percentage of total sales.

Hourly Employee Gross Payroll
• Full-service - 18% to 20% as a percentage of total sales.
• Limited-service - 15% to 18% as a percentage of total sales.

So, You're Thinking About Owning, Operating or Investing in a Restaurant...

201

Employee Benefits
- 5% to 6% as a percentage of total sales.
- 20% to 23% as a percentage of gross payroll.

Prime Cost
- Full-service — 65% or less as a percentage of total sales.
- Limited-service — 60% or less as a percentage of total sales.

Occupancy and Rent
- Rent — 6% or less as a percentage of total sales.
- Occupancy — 10% or less as a percentage of total sales.

Real Restaurateurs, *Real People*
Stories about people who realized their restaurant dreams

A Fast and Furious Remodel

On New Year's Day, Patrick Guthrie had no plans to expand his popular restaurant, Black Sheep Burrito, in Huntington, West Virginia. However, by January 30, the doors to the second location of the popular Mexican-themed restaurant were open in nearby Charleston.

During that time, a chemical spill in the Elk River made life a living hell for residents of the community and particularly for restaurant owners whose business is directly related to clean water.

"We installed nine charcoal filters to the lines coming into the restaurant and that immediately added $5,000 to the cost of the remodel," says Guthrie. "But we spent thousands more on buying bottled water for our guests who were still hesitant to drink the water up to three months later."

The chemical spill was really the only hiccup in what Guthrie calls a "fast and furious" remodel that was complete in less than 30 days. And despite the economic impact on the community because of concerns about safe drinking water, the Charleston Black Sheep Burrito location quickly outpaced sales in the three year-old Huntington location.

The downtown Charleston location became available when the restaurant operation of the Charleston Brewing Company closed in December, just six months after it opened. Black Sheep Burrito carries the local brew, so the building's owner reached out first to Guthrie to fill the space. The brewery continues operation in the building.

The first thing Guthrie and his partners did was reconfigure the entry to the restaurant. Charleston Brewing Company had three entries to the restaurant that covers nearly a half block. Guthrie believed that left employees and guests confused and scrambling for seating and service.

The next step was to reduce the number of seats and expand the kitchen service area. The previous operators had seating for 160 in a cavernous space, which according to Guthrie, was too much for the poorly configured kitchen to handle. So Guthrie's team built walls and dividers to create more intimate spaces while contributing to noise reduction, in addition to adding acoustic tiles to the ceiling. The building is also a parking garage (all concrete makes for a noisy restaurant.)

Guthrie is a fan of reclaimed barn wood and the rustic image it creates. The various shades of wood that now cover the dividers and parts of the ceiling come from a farmstead in Tennessee, personally collected by Guthrie on a quick trip during the remodel.

The kitchen was a spacious 1,000 square feet, but did not have enough equipment to manage the crowd. Guthrie added a 24" char grill and a six foot flat top grill in addition to a ten foot hood. He also added more prep area in anticipation of opening up a back room, which will be used for catering and banquet services.

Black Sheep Burrito continues to rely on a chalk sandwich board as its only exterior advertising. Word of mouth and good social media has contributed to its success.

"We have a lot of people travel back and forth between Huntington and Charleston, so the word of mouth has been great," says Guthrie.

Local food bloggers and newspaper reporters picked up on the news of a new restaurant opening, which contributed to the buzz. The Black Sheep Burrito & Brews Facebook page has about 4,000 followers and that was all that Guthrie needed to do to get people walking in the door on Jan. 30.

The location at 7th and Quarrier Streets is also in a neighborhood where several other independent restaurants are finding success in a city that is otherwise dominated by chains. Guthrie believes Black Sheep Burrito fills a niche in the independent restaurant market.

Despite the chemical spill in the Elk River, the timing was just right and Guthrie is now looking forward to what another new year will bring.

Restaurant Business Terms You Should Know

86'd — Restaurant slang for a menu item that is no longer available or offered to guests for some reason.

ANSUL system — Shorthand for a popular restaurant kitchen fire suppression system manufactured by the Ansul corporation of Marinette, Wisconsin.

BOH (Back of the house) — Shorthand for kitchen operations.

Balance Sheet — An important financial statement that informs the reader of the ending balances of a business's asset, liability and equity accounts.

Bistro — A small restaurant with a modest and modestly priced menu.

Broadline distributor — A foodservice distributor that carries a broad range of restaurant food and other items.

Casual upscale — A restaurant that has a sophisticated ambience and cuisine and relatively high prices but a casual atmosphere as opposed to more formal "white table cloth" type dining.

CC&R — Abbreviation for Covenants, Conditions & Restrictions, which are the limits, rules and joint obligations placed on businesses in a development.

Center of the plate — The main item on the plate, for entrees typically some kind of protein (beef, fish, etc.) but not always, that is meant to have the diner's greatest interest and attention.

Check average — The average amount each guest spends in the restaurant.

Cherry-picking purchasing — Purchasing items from a variety of specialty distributors rather than one or two broadline distributors.

Combi oven — An oven with three functions: convection, steam and combi-

So, You're Thinking About Owning, Operating or Investing in a Restaurant...

nation cooking. The oven gives the chef significant control over the humidity level of the food, and allows chefs to cook at higher temperatures without burning or drying out the food.

Day part — One of the parts of the day that people typically dine out, e.g. breakfast, brunch, lunch, happy hour, dinner, late-night, etc.

Cover — A slang reference to an individual guest. Ex. "Table 6 has 5 covers."

DOL — Abbreviation for the federal or state Department of Labor, which regulates wage and hour laws.

DSR — Distributor service representative. A sales agent of a food or restaurant supply distributor.

EEOC — Abbreviation for Equal Employment Opportunity Commission, a federal agency that oversees laws related to workplace discrimination.

Employee manual (or handbook) — A handbook that states the rules employees much abide by when working in the business. Typically provided to and signed by new employees on the first day of work, and updated as necessary.

Employment agreement — A contract between employer and employee stating the terms of employment, including the "for-cause" conditions upon which the employee can be terminated. Not used very often except for managers and key staff as most employees are "at will", not subject to a formal agreement.

Farm-to-fork movement — A preference among diners and operators that food items are so be sourced from local growers to insure freshness and support regional agriculture.

Fast casual — A style of dining, often but not always seated, with relatively simple menus and where the food is prepared quickly for casual and fast consumption. Similar to quick-service restaurants (QSR), where food is typically prepared to be taken away.

Fine dining — A general term for upscale and sophisticated restaurant food and service.

FLSA — Abbreviation for the Fair Labor Standards Act, federal labor law that governs minimum wages and overtime pay in the United States.

FMLA — Abbreviation for the Family Medical Leave Act, federal labor law, requiring larger employers to provide employees unpaid leave for serious health conditions or to care for a sick family member or newborn or adopted child.

Franchise — An authorization granted by a company to another person or business entity enabling them to provide the company's products and services under the trade name of the company.

FOH (Front of the house) — Restaurant shorthand for the service operations of the restaurant, including the hostess, servers and bussers.

Host/Hostess — The restaurant staff member who greets guests as they arrive and often directs them to their tables.

ICE — Abbreviation for Immigration and Customs Enforcement, a federal law enforcement agency under the Department of Homeland Security, which enforces immigration laws in the U.S.

Impinger —An oven that uses hot, pressurized air to cook food, often as the food is transported through the device on a conveyer belt.

In the weeds — Restaurant slang for circumstances where the kitchen and service staff are struggling to keep up with the demand of guest traffic or problems during service.

Independent — Shorthand for a restaurant entrepreneurial business, as opposed to a chain unit or franchisee.

Kitchen manager — A manager who oversees all kitchen operations.

LLC — Abbreviation for Limited Liability Company, a business entity, that blends elements of partnerships and corporate structures.

Locavore movement — Similar to farm-to-fork, a philosophy that favors sourcing local ingredients.

Menu engineering — The art and science of placing and presenting items on a menu to maximize profitability and sales.

MSDS — Abbreviation for Material Safety Data Sheet, a document that contains information on the potential health effects of exposure to chemicals or other dangerous substances, and on safe working procedures when handling chemical products.

So, You're Thinking About Owning, Operating or Investing in a Restaurant...

207

No show — Slang for a guest who makes a reservation but never arrives.

NRA — Abbreviation for the National Restaurant Association, the leading national trade association representing the U.S. restaurant industry.

OSHA — Abbreviation for Occupational Safety and Health Administration, a government agency under the U.S. Department of Labor that helps employers reduce injury, illness and death in the workplace.

P&L — Abbreviation for Profit and Loss Statement (also known as an Income Statement), a major financial statement summarizing the business's performance as reflected its profitability.

POS system — Abbreviation for Point of Sale system, which is equipment used for retail and restaurant transactions. A cash register is a type of POS system, but modern systems have much greater functionality.

Premade — In the context of food service, a premade item is one that is mostly prepared for service to guests with minimum handling.

Prep — The process in a kitchen that prepares food for final mixing and cooking stages.

Prep cook — A kitchen staff member responsible for the preparatory stages of cooking, such as cutting and marinating.

Prime cost — The items on the profit and loss statement that reflect labor and food costs.

Protein — Shorthand for menu items that are typically animal flesh, such as fish, meat or poultry.

Purchase order — A formal offer to purchase products or services submitted to the seller by the buyer, indicating the types, quantities, and agreed prices.

QSR — Abbreviation for Quick Service Restaurant, a type of commercial foodservice concept that sells ready-to-eat foods quickly for casual dine-in or take-away service.

RecipeMapping — A proprietary name for a three-step process to help restaurateurs add new items to your menu consistently, methodically, and profitably.
Salamander — A metal utensil with a flat head which is heated and put over a dish to brown the top. In a professional kitchen a small broiler, used primarily for browning.

S-Corporation — corporation that elects to be treated as a pass-through entity (like a sole proprietorship or partnership) for tax purposes.

Scratch — In the context of foodservice, it means creating menu items from raw ingredients.

Server — A restaurant employee whose job is to provide tableside service to guests, including describing and suggesting menu items, recording and delivering orders to the kitchen, and insuring the guests' comfort and satisfaction while dining.

Sous chef — A culinary chef located just below the executive or head chef in a kitchen's chain of command, with a vital role in any commercial kitchen.

Smallwares — Any items in the restaurant used for eating food, including bowls, plates, glasses and utensils.

Speed scratch — A style of cooking that uses partially processed menu items in the recipe.

SRA — Abbreviation for State Restaurant Association, a state trade organization that represents and serve the interests of its restaurant members.

Statement of cash flow — a financial statement that shows how changes in balance sheet accounts and income affect cash and cash equivalents

Starch — Shorthand for food items most often used as sides to main menu items, such as potatoes and rice.

Startup — A new business that has been created from scratch and often financed by its original owners.

Takeout — Food prepared to be delivered to or picked up by a guest for off-premises consumption.

Tip credit — As explained by the U.S. Department of Labor, section 3(m) of the FLSA (see above) permits an employer to take a tip credit toward its minimum wage obligation for tipped employees equal to the difference between the required cash wage (which must be at least $2.13 – the federal tip credit as of January 1, 2016) and the federal minimum wage of $7.25 as of January 1, 2016). Thus, the maximum tip credit that an employer can currently claim under the FLSA is $5.12 per hour (the minimum wage of $7.25 minus the minimum required cash wage of $2.13). Please note that state laws may require higher required cash and minimum wages than required by federal law, and that both federal and state wages are subject to change.

So, You're Thinking About Owning, Operating or Investing in a Restaurant...

209

Triple-net lease — a lease agreement on a property where the tenant or lessee agrees to pay all real estate taxes, building insurance, and maintenance (the three "Nets") on the property in addition to any normal fees that are expected under the agreement (rent, utilities, etc.).

Two (four, six) top — Refers to the number of guests that can be seated at a given table. A two-top is a table for two guests.

Uniform System of Accounts for Restaurants — An accounting guide designed specifically to assist single-unit and small multiunit operators maximize the usefulness and value of their financial information as a tool to manage the ongoing operations of their restaurants.

Upsell — Encouraging a patron to order the next most profitable item on the menu or to purchase additional menu items.

User review site — A web site that allows restaurant guests to publish their impressions of a business they patronized.

Walk-in — Shorthand for a walk-in cooler or freezer (as opposed to a "reach-in"). Also refers to a guest who visits the restaurant to be seated without a reservation.

Workers' comp — Short for Workers Compensation, a form of insurance required by the laws of most U.S. states, which provides wage replacement and medical benefits to employees injured in the course of employment in exchange for mandatory relinquishment of the employee's right to sue his or her employer for the tort of negligence.

Systematic Restaurant Startup Timeline

A p p e n d i x **B**

Setting an opening date then working backwards with a solid opening checklist is a key to your opening success. The website restaurantowner.com has compiled a checklist of some 300 items that can guide you in the timing of a restaurant startup. On the website the checklist is given in both a time framework and a category listing.

A Year before Opening

CONCEPT:

☐ Examine successful concepts
- collect info on concepts that appeal to you

☐ Local market
- look for opportunities, including concept gaps in your chosen market

☐ Visit existing restaurants
- observe which concepts are busy; try to determine why

FINANCE/LEGAL:

☐ Investigate potential sources for startup capital
- savings, family, friends, banks, SBA, investors

SITE/PLANNING:

☐ Potential of local markets
- become familiar with local markets that show potential for new restaurants
- create shortlist of the most promising areas

Eleven Months before Opening

CONCEPT:

☐ Menu price range
- price points of the most successful restaurants in your area

☐ Preliminary food & bar menus
- begin collecting menu & recipe ideas

ADMINISTRATION:

☐ Start to interview/build team of professionals
- attorney, CPA, architect, designer, insurance agent, real estate broker

DESIGN/CONSTRUCTION:

☐ Graphic artist
- select graphic artist

FINANCE/LEGAL:

☐ Bank/SBA lending

    - find banks that have financed restaurant startups

☐ Business plan

    - begin drafting your business plan

☐ Capital/construction/opening budget

    - estimate total startup cost of project through opening day

    - incorporate this into business plan

    - refer to Capital Budget worksheet on "Startup & Feasibility"

☐ List of possible names for restaurant

    - solicit ideas from friend, relatives

Ten Months before Opening

CONCEPT:

☐ Further define concept

    - type of service, price range, menu

ADMINISTRATION:

☐ Collect info on permits/licenses

    - health, liquor, other

☐ Insurance

    - identify requirements; building, liability, workmen's comp, other

SITE PLANNING:

☐ Facility requirements

    - how much space, seats, parking will you need

☐ Site/location criteria

    - determine site/location criteria

    - demographics, traffic count

    - size, number of seats, rental rates

    - lease terms

Nine Months before Opening

CONCEPT:

☐ Points of difference

    - what will make your restaurant unique in terms of menu, service, ambance

DESIGN/CONSTRUCTION

☐ List of architects

    - check references, create shortlist of quality firms

☐ List of general contractors

    - check references, create shortlist of quality firms

☐ List of interior design firms

    - check references, create shortlist of quality firms

☐ Furniture, Fixtures & Equipment (FF&E)

☐ Preliminary equipment requirements

    - create a list of the equipment needed

FINANCE/LEGAL:

☐ Attorney & CPA
- find firms with restaurant experience
- get & check references

☐ Business entity
- consider corporation, LLC, partnership, limited partnership
- seek guidance from CPA/attorney

☐ Personal career accomplishments/work history
- prepare and include in business plan

☐ Review financial projections with your CPA
- have your CPA review for reasonableness, missing costs & expenses
- have experienced restaurant professionals review your financials

☐ Select attorney
- draft/file corporate documents
- review/negotiate lease agreement

☐ Select CPA
- determine corporate entity/review business plan financials

SITE PLANNING:

☐ Competitive analysis
- examine strengths & weaknesses of competitors in target areas
- evaluate relative success of restaurant in local market
- where is there potential?
- what dining segments are not being well-served?

☐ Square footage
- determine optimum square footage needed (range)
- including kitchen, dining room, storage
- rule of thumb is roughly 30 square feet per seat (total square footage)

☐ Tenant rep broker
- secure service of a tenant rep broker to assist you in site selection
- find a broker with a specialty or focus on restaurant sites

MARKETING:

☐ Competitive analysis
- create list of competitors
- obtain sample menus for research & reference

Eight Months before Opening

CONCEPT:

☐ Concept validation/testing
- interview potential customers on your concept plans

☐ Determine name of restaurant
- trade name search (attorney)

☐ Finalize concept
- menu, service, unique offerings, price range, ambiance, etc.
- draft concept statement fully describing concept

DESIGN/CONSTRUCTION:

☐ Ansul system (system use over cooking hoods to put out grease fires)
- what are local requirements
☐ Construction & development costs
- get estimates of buildout/construction costs from contractors
☐ Exits
- panic hardware requirements, emergency lighting
- fire code requirements
☐ Handicap access/requirements

FURNITURE, FIXTURES & EQUIPMENT:

☐ Equipment lists
- kitchen, bar, dining room, bar, office
☐ Lease or purchase kitchen equipment
- shop equipment leasing companies

FINANCE/LEGAL:

☐ Business plan
- complete business plan
☐ Capital/construction/opening budget
- update projections with actual bids/current estimates
☐ Personal financial statement
- prepare / update your personal financial statement

OPERATIONS:

☐ Visit restaurants with similar offerings
- take notes of good & bad items

SITE/PLANNING

☐ Bar seating
- estimate potential for bar revenue
- balance with space/seating needed for dining room
☐ Building/fire/safety codes
- obtain all applicable code requirements
☐ Electrical service
- evaluate adequacy of available power
☐ Floor plan (existing space)
- obtain floor plan of space
- include layout of load-bearing (permanent) walls
☐ Floor slope evaluation
- consider slope on handicap, OSHA requirements
- safety considerations for staff & guests
☐ Lighting fixtures
- inspect interior & exterior lighting including parking lot
☐ Liquor license
- know the process & cost of obtaining a liquor license
☐ List of existing kitchen equipment
- obtain detailed list

- verify & evaluate condition
☐ Number of tables/seats
  - estimate potential seating/revenue potential of dining room
☐ Parking
  - is there adequate parking
  - what is the ratio of seats to parking spaces, is there a local minimum
☐ Sales to investment analysis
  - estimate total capital costs & compare to projected annual sales
  - goal is to have minimum 1.5 to 1 sales to investment ratio in leasehold
  - goal is to have minimum 1 to 1 ratio when land & building is owned
  - go to RestaurantOwner.com for more information

SITE PLANNING:
☐ Traffic patterns
  - evaluate adequacy of traffic flow (foot traffic, if applicable)
☐ Zoning requirements
  - verify that there are no zoning problems with your concept/plans, such as inadequate ratio of parking places to seats, size of outdoor signs, and architectural standards.

ADMINISTRATION:
☐ Banking
  - open construction/development account
☐ Liquor license
  - investigate application process/availability of liquor license

DESIGN/CONSTRUCTION:
☐ Architectural/design
  - review & approve
☐ Builder's risk insurance
☐ Contractor
  - select contractor
☐ Demolition work
☐ Design-Exterior
  - siding, ramps, windows, awnings, lighting
☐ Design-Interior
  - kitchen, bar, dining room, bar, office, lighting
☐ General liability insurance
☐ Patio / outside seating
  - design, available seating, permits, w/w station, cost feasibility
☐ Select architect/designer

Seven Months before Opening

FURNITURE, FIXTURES & EQUIPMENT:
☐ Exterior signage
  - get local code/permit/approval requirements
FINANCE/LEGAL:

☐ Buy-sell agreement
- attorney prepares if you have partners/investors
- consider insurance to fund
☐ Landlord approvals
- determine what items require landlord approval
- plans, signage, other

DESIGN/ CONSTRUCTION:
☐ Utilities billing changes
- change name/party responsible for utility bills
- electrical, gas, water
☐ Utilities
- determine utility company options
- choose provider
☐ Operations

MENU & RECIPES:
☐ narrow menu offerings
- create & test recipes
- use distributor test kitchen if possible

SITE/PLANNING:
☐ Cleanup required
- determine cost of cleanup/demolition prior to construction activities
☐ Gas main / lines
- adequate size, capacity, age, condition
☐ Health department
- verify no health-related conditions present that could pose problems
☐ HVAC system
- inspect/evaluate condition
☐ Plans for location/site area
- inquire with local officials about proposed, planned projects in area
- road, water, sewer, drainage, commercial, residential, zoning changes
☐ Roof inspection
☐ Sewer lines
- evaluate adequacy; size, capacity, age, condition
☐ Termite report
- have property inspected for termite/pest problems
☐ Type of flooring
☐ Utility requirements
- verify no utility/capacity problems
☐ Water lines
- evaluate capacity, size, age, condition

ADMINISTRATION:
☐ Federal ID number
- apply for

Six Months before Opening

DESIGN/CONSTRUCTION:

☐ Acoustical ceilings

☐ Air conditioning/circulation

☐ Back door

    - peep hole, buzzer for deliveries, emergency bar

☐ Bathroom partitions & accessories

☐ Burglar alarm system

☐ Canopies & awnings

☐ Carpentry

☐ Carpet

☐ Concrete

☐ Construction timeline

    - time for each phase, completion date

☐ Design elements

    - logo, colors, type style

☐ Door locks

    - deadbolts, re-key locks prior to opening

☐ Door/exits hardware

    - alarms, push bars, emergency escape

☐ Doors & Windows

☐ Drywall

☐ Electrical/Lighting

☐ Exterior painting

☐ Hardwood flooring

☐ Interior painting

☐ Kitchen fire control

    - design & setup system

☐ List of inspectors

    - building, fire, electrical, plumbing, health

☐ Masonry

☐ Mechanical

☐ Parking lot

    - resurfacing, control access during construction

☐ Paving

☐ Plumbing

☐ Resilient flooring

☐ Roofing & waterproofing

☐ Select contractor

    - obtain bids

    - contractor prepares timeline/critical path for completion

☐ Smoke detectors

    - wire to alarm system

☐ Sound/music system

☐ Specialty items
☐ Sprinkler system
  - obtain requirements
  - have wired to alarm system
☐ Steel/railings
☐ Tile
  - kitchen, bathrooms, dining areas, wall and floor
SITE/PLANNING
☐ Site selection decision
  - finalize site selection

Five Months before Opening
ADMINISTRATION:
☐ Credit application sheet
  - create for setting up new accounts, include references
DESIGN/CONSTRUCTION:
☐ Electrical service
  - permits, procedures, plans, installation, inspection
☐ Gas service
  - permits, procedures, plans, installation, inspection
☐ Grease trap
  - permits, procedures, plans, installation, and inspection
☐ Landscaping
  - design & bid contract
☐ Lighting for parking lot
☐ Waste water
  - permits, procedures, plans, installation, inspection
☐ Water service
  - Permits, procedures, plans, installation, inspection
☐ Water quality
  - test for hard water, take bids for water softening, filtration, and trace elements considered harmful.
FINANCE/LEGAL:
☐ Tax ID numbers/accounts
  - apply for federal, state unemployment insurance, state sales tax
ONGOING SERVICES:
☐ Insurance agent
  - building, general liability, liquor liability, workman's comp, group medical
OPERATIONS:
☐ Table mix & arrangement
  - determine mix of 2 top, 4 top, round, booths
  - determine booth / table positions, table numbers
ADMINISTRATION:
☐ Liquor license

- apply for
- consider hiring firm to assist in processing application

Four Months before Opening

FURNITURE, FIXTURES & EQUIPMENT:

☐ Safe for office
- determine type, bid & order

FOOD & BEVERAGE:

☐ List of available suppliers
- create list of suppliers for food, beverages & supplies

MARKETING:

☐ Menu boards & pictures
- determine type, design, order
- pictures of key menu items bundled with side & beverage

☐ Banners
- NOW HIRING /COMING SOON / NOW OPEN

OPERATIONS:

☐ Hours of operation
- determine for each day/meal period

☐ Vending machines
- pay phones, video games, other

PERSONNEL:

☐ Employee benefits
- determine insurance coverage (medical, dental, life, disability) & eligibility
- vacation, meals, comps, tuition reimbursement, other

☐ Employee job descriptions
- create for all staff & management positions
- download templates on RestaurantOwner.com

☐ Management team
- start interviewing/selection process

☐ Organizational chart
- create organizational chart for restaurant

Three Months before Opening

SMALLWARES/SUPPLIES:

☐ Uniforms
- finalize design; kitchen, service, bar, host staffs, managers

ADMINISTRATION:

☐ Employee meal policy
- determine policy

☐ Employee timekeeping system
- decide on stand alone, time cards, manual, POS

DESIGN/CONSTRUCTION:

☐ Cleaning crew

- bid & select vendor for initial & final clean
☐ Exterior signage
- primary, handicap, reserved, valet, hours of operation, delivery times
☐ Supplier, contractor, sub-contractor contacts
- create master phone & contact list with emergency numbers

FURNITURE, FIXTURES & EQUIPMENT:
☐ Soda system installation
- select vendor & set up installation date

FINANCE/LEGAL:
☐ Line of credit
- set up working capital line of credit with bank

FOOD & BEVERAGE:
☐ Beer
- decide what bottled / draft beers to stock
☐ Food inventory
- create master inventory list of all ingredients/products to stock
☐ Liquor
- determine well/premium/super premium brands
☐ Liquor, beer & wine inventory
- create inventory worksheets for taking physical inventories
- download Inventory Worksheet template on RestaurantOwner.com
☐ Price menu
- determine final price points on all menu items
☐ Standard recipe files
- begin building recipe binder & laminated recipe card for menu items
- prepare recipe cards for all batch recipes
☐ Wine
- determine wines to stock
☐ Wine list
- design & print
- include in main menu?

MARKETING:
☐ Gift certificates
- design & print
- program gift certificate sales keys into POS (both sale & redemption)
☐ Local charities
- choose which charity(ies) to support
- consider a "charity night" pre-opening party
☐ Printing
- stationery, envelopes, labels, business cards
- invitations for opening parties; public relations for opening
- hire local PR firm
- send out press releases to local media outlets
☐ Establish website and social media plan

ONGOING SERVICES:

☐ Dining room cleaning
  - carpet, flooring, rest rooms
  - select outside vendor

☐ Hood/kitchen cleaning
  - select approved vendor

☐ Interior plant service
  - select approved vendor

☐ Landscaping/lawn services
  - select approved vendor

☐ Security guards
  - determine if needed on certain nights/hours

OPERATIONS:

☐ Checklists
  - prepare opening, closing, shift change checklists for all stations
  - download checklist templates on RestaurantOwner.com

☐ Guest (table ready) call system
  - determine system to use
  - pagers, sound system, other

☐ Happy hour
  - determine special, prices, food
  - check state/local laws regarding happy hour/discount programs

☐ Menu analysis
  - determine items for signature or high promotion status
  - base decision on gross profit margin, ease of preparation, quality

☐ Menu item cost
  - calculate raw food cost on all menu items
  - rank each category's items by gross profit margin
  - if prime distributor has food management software, ask for assistance

☐ Prep lists with pars
  - create prep lists with par levels

☐ Product specs
  - create detailed product specs for all food products
  - grade, size, packaging, brand, etc.
  - ask your distributor for assistance

OPERATIONS

☐ Reservation policy -
  - determine whether you will accept reservations
  - consider "call in" program to place names on wait list only

☐ Station setup sheets with pars
  - for kitchen & dining room(s)

☐ Customer comment cards
  - design & print
  - create procedures for receiving & responding

- download template on RestaurantOwner.com

PERSONNEL:

☐ Employee handbook -

   - create to document and communicate all employee & employment practices

   - download template on RestaurantOwner.com

☐ Employee training manuals

   - create for all positions

   - download templates on RestaurantOwner.com

☐ Management training materials

   - personnel hiring, training & management

   - operations

   - administrative

☐ Master training schedule

   - create schedule for staff training leading up to opening day

☐ Side work procedures & schedules

   - create server/front-of-house side work checklists

   - download template on RestaurantOwner.com

☐ Staff pay scales

   - determine starting pay scales for each position

   - determine employee review/raise policies

☐ Staffing needs

   - determine number of new hires needed by position

   - plan for turnover, hire 20% more than you think you'll need

TECHNOLOGY:

☐ POS phone line

   - dedicated line for charge approvals

   - tie into DSL/cable line

☐ POS system

   - list requirements

   - download POS Evaluation Worksheet on Restaurantowner.com

   - create list of brands/dealers used by other local operators

   - start evaluation/demonstration process

☐ Website

   - register domain name

   - contact web design firm

Two Months before Opening

ADMINISTRATION:

☐ Alcoholic beverage server certification

   - determine requirements

☐ Tax permits

   - apply for Sales Tax ID (state, local)

SMALLWARES/SUPPLIES:

☐ Dining room
- high chairs - infant cradles - booster seats
- water pitchers, wine carafes
- serving trays, tray stands

☐ Bar
- blender
- ice machine
- glass washer
- shakers, strainers, spoons, bottle openers, corkscrew
- jiggers
- scoops
- bar mats
- pitchers

FURNITURE, FIXTURES & EQUIPMENT:

☐ Communications/phone system
- phone lines for office, fax, kitchen, hostess station
- pagers, cell phones, fire & burglar alarms
- internet access, service provider

☐ Interior signs
- menu boards, restrooms, fire exit, hand wash, wait to be seated

☐ Office equipment
- copier, fax, computer, printer, calculators

☐ Office furniture
- desk, chairs, filing cabinet, shelving

☐ Receiving scale
- minimum 200lb capacity

FOOD & BEVERAGE:

☐ Determine local/state certification requirements
- arrange for manager/employee certification

ONGOING SERVICES:

☐ Payroll processing
- outsource to ADP, Paychex, other

SMALLWARES/SUPPLIES:

☐ Dishroom items
- bus carts, bus tubs, glass racks, tray racks
- chemicals, detergents

☐ Smallware & kitchen utensils
- source, specs, bid order

☐ Tabletop items
- tableware, flatware, glassware, sugar caddies, table tents, vases
- salt & pepper shakers

ADMINISTRATION:

☐ Banking
- open operating, payroll, reserve accounts

So, You're Thinking About Owning, Operating or Investing in a Restaurant...

223

- order checks, deposit slips
☐ Payroll processing
- in-house, outsource to ADP, Paychex, outside accountant

ONGOING SERVICES:
☐ Music
- Muzak, ASCAP, BMI (music licensing)
- satellite radio

OPERATIONS:
☐ Emergency exit procedures
- determine procedures, post maps
- discuss in safety meetings with staff

PERSONNEL:
☐ Employee recruiting
- Craigslist, Facebook, restaurant industry employment sites, etc.
- recruiting missions
- word of mouth campaigns
- bonus for referrals
- plan for turnover, hire 20% more than you think you'll need
☐ Pre-opening interview site
- trailer, temporary office
- equip with phone, furniture, hiring/selection forms

TECHNOLOGY:
☐ Computer software
- Microsoft office, scheduling, food management
☐ POS system
- make POS decision
- set up menu items & prices
- decide on comps & discount categories
- set up essential reports

ADMINISTRATION:
☐ Credit card merchant accounts
- set up for MC/Visa, Amex, Discover, Square, Others

DESIGN/CONSTRUCTION:
☐ Building & equipment plans
- retain full set of plans for operational files
☐ Walk-through with contractor
- create initial punch list

FURNITURE, FIXTURES & EQUIPMENT:
☐ Restrooms
- hand towel/dryer dispensers, soap dispensers, hand soap, baby changing tables

FOOD & BEVERAGE:
☐ Menus
- covers & inserts, to-go, catering, children's

ONGOING SERVICES:

☐ Chemicals
- select approved vendor

☐ Grease trap
- select approved vendor

☐ Knife & blade sharpening
- perform in-house
- use outside service

☐ Monthly accounting
- determine monthly or 4-week cycle
- use industry standard chart of accounts
- outside accounting service or in-house bookkeeper/accountant

☐ Pest control
- select approved vendor

☐ Trash disposal
- select approved vendor

☐ Window washing
- do in-house or outsource
- select approved vendor

OPERATIONS:

☐ Bulletin board
- for employee schedule, mandatory postings
- choking poster
- emergency hospital & doctor numbers & instructions

☐ Children's amenities
- menu, crayons, coloring book, high chairs, booster seats, balloons

☐ Cleaning & maintenance schedules
- set up schedules & procedures
- download Cleaning Checklists on RestaurantOwner.com

☐ Emergency numbers
- map, directions to hospital
- make arrangements with local doctor, clinic

☐ Entertainment
- obtain permits if required
- create list of potential entertainers

☐ Floor maintenance
- get ongoing floor maintenance procedures
- purchase cleaning / polishing supplies

☐ Valet parking
- valet stand
- key control system
- valet only parking area signs, cones

PERSONNEL:

☐ Food safety training

- purchase food safety training materials/videos
- contact state or National Restaurant Association

SMALLWARES/SUPPLIES:

☐ Employee name tags

TECHNOLOGY:

☐ Phone on hold message
- select service provider
- message/music

ADMINISTRATION:

☐ Accounting software
- if accounting done in-house; Quickbooks, Peachtree, other
- format P&L consistent with NRA Uniform System of Accounts

☐ Petty cash
- setup petty cash fund for cash payments
- create petty cash reimbursement form

DESIGN/CONSTRUCTION:

☐ Compressors & valves
- label and check for accessibility

☐ Electrical labeling
- label switches, breakers and check for accessibility

FURNITURE, FIXTURES & EQUIPMENT:

☐ Janitorial equipment
- wet floor signs, mops, buckets, vacuum
- trash cans, cordless dust pan

ONGOING SERVICES:

☐ Armored car service
- select approved vendor

☐ Building & HVAC repairs
- select approved vendors

☐ Dishwasher service
- select approved vendor

☐ Laundry & linen
- select approved vendor

OPERATIONS:

☐ Approved vendor list
- create Master Approved Vendor List
- include primary & backup vendors

☐ Birthday specials
- determine policy, special desserts, b-day song, other

☐ Seating chart & wait staff sections
- create seating chart diagram with wait staff sections

PERSONNEL:

☐ Assemble new employee materials
- application forms

- uniforms
- W-4, I-9 forms
- employee handbook, job descriptions
- orientation & training checklists
- check RestaurantOwner.com for forms & templates

☐ Employee files
- set up for employment application, status changes, and other personnel records

SMALLWARES/SUPPLIES:

☐ First aid kit
- emergency burn kit, automated external defibrillator

☐ Tip trays, check presentation folders
- may be free from AMEX/MC or VISA

ADMINISTRATION:

☐ Deposit procedures
- armored car service or other

DESIGN/CONSTRUCTION:

☐ Inspections
- schedule for fire, health departments

OPERATIONS:

☐ Initial food, beverage & supplies orders
- determine quantities for training, mock shifts, pre-opening activities

One Month before Opening

ADMINISTRATION:

☐ Insurance
- verify with your agent that all policies are in force

DESIGN/CONSTRUCTION:

☐ Parking lot striping
- handicap space requirements

FURNITURE, FIXTURES & EQUIPMENT:

☐ Emergency equipment procedures
- determine emergency shut-off steps
- label equipment

☐ Equipment tests
- test each piece with supplier prior to training

Kitchen clock
- purchase & install

☐ Kitchen tools/toolkit
- purchase & designate location for storing

FOOD & BEVERAGE:

☐ Initial food order
- prepare & place initial order
- request free samples from suppliers to test

- have sufficient quantities for testing & training
☐ Photographs of menu items
  - for display in kitchen area
☐ Initial alcoholic beverage order
  - prepare & place initial order

MARKETING:

☐ Opening party(ies)
  - press event, VIPs, contractors & suppliers
  - create guest lists, send invitations

PERSONNEL:

OSHA
  - review OSHA standards with managers

SMALLWARES/SUPPLIES:

☐ Initial chemicals order
  - degreasers, drain treatment
  - disinfectants, sanitizers
  - floor care solutions
  - hand care
  - cleaners for dish room/restroom/dining room

Linen
☐ Tablecloths, napkins, bar & kitchen towels
☐ Initial paper good order
  - napkins, take-out, delivery, coasters, doggie bags
  - straws, cups, lids
  - filters, butcher pager
  - patty paper, food wrap film, aluminum foil
☐ Janitorial supplies
  - carpet, tile, floor cleaner, spot remover
  - gum solvent, liquid hand soap, paper towels, toilet paper

TECHNOLOGY:

☐ Internet service provider
  - DSL or cable
☐ POS/register
  - set up installation & training

ADMINISTRATION:

☐ Bank supplies
  - deposit stamp & pad, deposit bags, deposit slips
☐ Accounting/bookkeeping system
  - have CPA review sales, deposit, payroll and accounts payable system
☐ Permits, licenses, inspections, approvals
  - verify that licenses, etc. have been secured
☐ Initial change order
  - get change & small bills from bank
☐ Music licensing fee applications to Performing Rights Organizations, if

you will be offering recorded and or live music for guests.

☐ POS/merchant accounts

    - test credit card approval/processing

☐ Receive certificate of occupancy

DESIGN/CONSTRUCTION:

☐ Alarm system

    - install & inspect

☐ Beverage service

    - set up installation of post mix system, coffee, iced tea

☐ Fire extinguishers

    - install with visible operating instructions

☐ Exterior signage light timer

    - set light timer

☐ Update construction punch list

FURNITURE, FIXTURES & EQUIPMENT:

☐ Ansul system

    - inspect

☐ R&M binder for all equipment

    - prepare repair & maintenance binder for operating instructions, manuals

    - mail in warranty cards

☐ Storage shelves

    - clean, organize & label; walk-in, freezer, dry storage

☐ Calibrate temperatures on equipment

    - fryers, griddle, oven, stove, other

☐ Check walk-in & refrigeration temperatures

☐ Clean & sanitize walk-in, freezer

☐ Receive furniture

    - tables, chairs, desk tops, benches, patio furniture

☐ Test all equipment

OPERATIONS:

☐ Order & delivery schedule

    - prepare weekly schedule with each vendor's order & deliver dates

    - download "Ordering & Receiving Schedule" template on RestaurantOwner.com

☐ Padlocks for cooler doors

    - create control system for access & keys

    - limit access to storage rooms to deliveries & requisition into production

☐ Deposit bags

    - obtain from bank

☐ Hostess stand supplies

    - reservation book, call clock, pencils, notebooks, kid's stuff

☐ Light levels

    - determine for each meal period

    - lable light switches

So, You're Thinking About Owning, Operating or Investing in a Restaurant...

229

☐ Music sound levels
PERSONNEL:
☐ Alcoholic beverage server certification
    - determine state/local requirements
    - assign employee(s) for certification course
☐ Hazard Analysis & Critical Control Points (HACCP) training / certification (HACCP is a management system in which food safety is addressed through the analysis and control of biological, chemical, and physical hazards from raw material production, procurement and handling, to manufacturing, distribution and consumption of the finished product.)
☐ Safety checklist & audit
    - create safety checklist & perform safety audit
    - download Safety Checklist template on RestaurantOwner.com
☐ Wine training program
    - arrange for wine supplier to provide
☐ Begin staff training
☐ Safety & first aid training
    - conduct training program for all employees

Two Weeks before Opening
DESIGN/CONSTRUCTION:
☐ Continue construction punch list
☐ Exterior cleanup
    - parking lot, landscaping, building, windows
☐ Final clean
    - interior & exterior of building
FURNITURE, FIXTURES & EQUIPMENT:
☐ Complete equipment warranty cards
☐ Final clean all equipment
☐ Hang pictures, wall dÈcor
☐ Install interior plants
☐ Run ice machine
    - empty/sanitize/refill
    - find ice company for backup
OPERATIONS:
☐ Change order
    - prepare initial change order; change & small bills
☐ Check inventory levels
    - on all food, beverage, paper & supplies
    - prepare orders for opening week
☐ Opening inventory
    - take full physical inventory on all food & beverage items night before opening

- necessary to calculate accurate food & beverage costs after opening

PERSONNEL:

☐ Conduct practice runs/mock service
- full dress with uniforms

☐ Finalize opening week employee schedules
- staff heavy
- plan for turnover, no-shows

ONGOING SERVICES:

☐ Equipment repairs
- select approved vendors

As this checklist or "to do" indicates there's a lot that must be accomplished to open the doors of any restaurant. As the old saying goes "The devil is in the details," and the restaurant business is full of details.

The Case for Restaurant
Association Membership   Appendix C

At the end of this chapter you'll find a list of addresses and telephone numbers of the State Restaurant Associations. One of your first moves as you investigate the idea of opening or buying a restaurant should be to pick up the telephone and call the one in your State. They can help you through the process from licensing to vendors to all the other information you're going to need to get your doors open.

These organizations are the unsung heroes in the world of restaurant operations with their legislative successes and efforts, including averting unreasonable and costly laws that often arrive on the desks of unknowledgeable State legislators and government bureaucrats. They help battle onerous state controls on liquor and offer a litany of association member benefits, including group purchase discounts on liability and workers' compensation insurance, payroll processing, music licensing, health insurance programs and other economic benefits that conform to their State's regulations and laws.

The value and benefits of state restaurant association membership and the challenges facing the state associations in their efforts to serve the industry and muster adequate resources to perform their jobs is an important part of the information gathering process any one opening or buying a restaurant needs to be aware of.

In every industry, it is easy to take national and regional trade associations as much for granted as we do government agencies. In fact, state and national restaurant associations are private, nonprofit organizations that must work for membership with as much vigor as they fight to influence unrealistic legislation and provide valuable benefits to their members. What do they do that can help you? At lot!

Every restaurateur should belong to a State Restaurant Association!

Unlike restaurants that sell tangible products and services to a well-defined market, state restaurant associations' most important stock in trade is an intangible — the ability to get face time with state legislators, in an effort to influence laws and regulation in favor of the industry. The fact is that lobbying is the top priority for most state restaurant associations and those efforts can mean a lot to anyone contemplating entering the restaurant

So, You're Thinking About Owning, Operating or Investing in a Restaurant...

233

business. At the same time state associations offer their members discounts and other benefits. But many state associations have limited resources for marketing and membership development. The word doesn't reach everybody and that's why it is important for those entering the business to be supportive. State associations do have a "social" aspect to them but they are not merely "social clubs".

While association membership expense is not insignificant; most states offer a sliding scale that makes it a bargain for the smaller and startup restaurateur. In a number of states, a restaurant with less than $500,000 estimated gross annual sales can join for several hundred dollars. At the top of the dues scale are large chains, which can pay as much as $10,000 in annual dues; however, association membership tends to be sparser among the smaller independents.

A Diverse and Demanding Membership Base

Like your restaurant, associations are striving to meet the needs of their "customer"; in this case, they are restaurant owners who are current or prospective members. State restaurant associations are under constant pressure to remain valuable and relevant to their members. The associations are making an ever-increasing commitment to training and education. For example, in today's highly regulated restaurant industry sanitation is a key issue with one mistake causing not only bad PR but the possibility of even shutting down a business location. Another vital area of education is alcohol service and control of alcoholic beverages, where the liability issues for restaurants are tremendous. The state associations have become experts at making sure restaurant owners understand all of the issues and how to solve problems that may arise from them. Associations guide restaurateurs as to what training is required and often provide that training.

Additional Benefits

One long time state restaurant association president says the greatest disappointment he finds among his members is that they do not understand all of the opportunities and benefits offered by his association. "They say, 'if you only had a group workers' compensation insurance program.' Unfortunately, they did not have time to read that we offer that," he says.

Many of the state associations hold an annual trade show for members and vendors to get together. These are excellent forums for those entering the business to find information and suppliers along with learning more about "the lay of the land". Another benefit of these meetings is the "peer to peer" networking opportunities. The value of networking is not lost on active members who meet monthly for a business presentation and a social hour. It is here that there is an exchange of ideas and members say they always learn ways to save money in their operations. They not only learn from fellow restaurateurs but also from suppliers who belong to the association.

One restaurateur mentions "We have a relationship with purveyors and allied members, and they're on our board and they help us run our businesses better". A recent monthly meeting included a presentation on fire safety equipment and this owner was able to learn how new regulations would soon affect his operation.

"Without question, it pays for itself" says one association member. "When I first got in the business, I was having the typical employee problems and thought I didn't know how to buy food. I went to a meeting, and people were talking about the same problems I have. I realized it wasn't just me, and that alone was worth the charge of joining. So many things can go wrong and so many decisions have to be made," he says. "You have questions you can't answer 10 times a day." The state associations can help.

"They are more than willing to answer your questions," this owner goes on, "Pick up the phone and the odds are you'll get an answer." Another member says that the benefits of his state association are its labor law hotline. "If an employee says, 'I'm quitting and you must give me my paycheck now,' you can consult with the lawyer and find out what the law requires," the member point out.

State Associations Form a Vital Grassroots Network

There are state restaurant associations in all 50 states, plus the District of Columbia, Puerto Rico and the Virgin Islands. The National Restaurant Association in Washington, D.C., leverages this widespread local presence to gain grassroots support for national issues of importance to the restaurant industry. While the NRA and state associations are independent organizations, they are highly networked. NRA keeps in constant communication with the state association leaders and lobbyists at least daily with many states, and weekly with other states. In many cases, the NRA provides automatic membership for state association members.

The restaurant industry is the largest private-sector employer and no other industry is more regulated. The health department can close your doors before dinner. That's why the importance of joining a state restaurant early on can be so critical for your new restaurant business.

State Restaurant Associations

Alabama Restaurant and Hospitality Alliance
61 B Market Place
Montgomery, AL 36117
334-244-1320
http://www.alabamarestaurants.com

So, You're Thinking About Owning, Operating or Investing in a Restaurant...

235

Alaska Cabaret, Hotel, Restaurant and Retailers Association
1503 W. 31st. Ave. Suite 202
Anchorage, AK 99503
907-274-8133
http://alaskacharr.com/alaska-charr

Arizona Restaurant Association
4250 N. Drinkwater Boulevard, Suite. 350
Scottsdale, AZ 85251
602.307.9134
http://azrestaurant.org

Arkansas Hospitality Association
603 South Pulaski St.
Little Rock, AR 72201
501-376-2323
http://www.arhospitality.org

California Restaurant Association
621 Capitol Mall, Suite 2000
Sacramento, CA 95814
916.447.5793
http://www.calrest.org

Colorado Restaurant Association
430 E 7th Ave.
Denver, CO 80203
303-830-2972
http://www.coloradorestaurant.com

Connecticut Restaurant Association
38 Hungerford St.
Hartford, CT 06106
860-278-8008
http://www.ctrestaurant.org

Delaware Restaurant Association
 500 Creek View Rd., Suite 103
Newark, DE 19711
302-738-2545
http://www.delawarerestaurant.org

Empire State Restaurant and Tavern Association
12 Sheridan Ave.
Albany, NY 12207
518- 436-8121
http://www.esrta.org

Florida Restaurant and Lodging Association
230 South Adams St.
Tallahassee, FL 32301
850-224-2250
https://www.frla.org

Georgia Restaurant Association
3520 Piedmont Rd., Suite 360
Atlanta, GA, 30305
404- 467-9000
http://www.garestaurants.org

Golden Gate Restaurant Association
220 Montgomery St., Suite 990
San Francisco, CA 94104
415-781-5348
http://ggra.org

Hawaii Restaurant Association
2909 Waialae Ave. #22
Honolulu, HI 96826
808-944-9105
http://hawaiirestaurant.org

Idaho Lodging & Restaurant Association
P.O. Box 1822
Boise, ID 83701
208-342-0010
http://idaho-lodging-restaurants.com

Illinois Restaurant Association
33 W. Monroe, Suite 250
Chicago, IL 60603
312-787-4000
http://www.illinoisrestaurants.org

Indiana Restaurant & Lodging Association
200 S. Meridian St., Suite 350
Indianapolis, IN 46225
317-673-4211
http://www.indianarestaurants.org

Iowa Restaurant Association
1501 42nd St., Suite 294
West Des Moines, IA 50266
515-276-1454
https://www.restaurantiowa.com

So, You're Thinking About Owning, Operating or Investing in a Restaurant...

237

Kansas Restaurant and Hospitality Association
3500 N Rock Rd., Building 1300
Wichita, KS 67226
316-267-8383
http://www.krha.org

The Kentucky Restaurant Association
133 Evergreen Rd., Suite 201
Louisville, KY 40243
502-896-0464
https://www.kyra.org

Louisiana Restaurant Association
2700 N. Arnoult Rd.
Metairie, LA 70002
504-454-2277
http://www.lra.org

Maine Restaurant Association
45 Melville St. Suite 2
Augusta ME 04330
207-623-2178
http://www.mainerestaurant.com

Restaurant Association of Maryland
6301 Hillside Ct.
Columbia, MD 21046
410-290-6800
http://www.marylandrestaurants.com

Massachusetts Restaurant Association
333 Turnpike Rd., Suite 102
Southborough, MA, 01772
508-303-9905
http://www.themassrest.org

Restaurant Association Metropolitan Washington
1625 K St., NW, Suite 210
Washington, DC 20006
202.331.5990
http://www.ramw.org

Michigan Restaurant Association
225 West Washtenaw
Lansing, MI 48933
517-482-5244
http://www.michiganrestaurant.org

Minnesota Restaurant Association
1959 Sloan Place, Suite 120
St Paul, MN 55117
651-778-2400
http://www.mnrestaurant.org

Mississippi Hospitality & Restaurant Association
130 Riverview Drive, Suite C
Flowood, MS 39232-8908
601-420-4210
http://www.msra.org

The Missouri Restaurant Association
1810 Craig Rd., Suite 225
St. Louis, MO 63146
314-576-2777
http://morestaurants.org

Montana Retail Association
1645 Parkhill Drive, Suite 6
Billings, MT 59102
406-256-1005
http://www.mtretail.com/montana-restaurant-association

Nebraska Restaurant Association
1610 S 70th St., Suite 101
Lincoln NE 68506
402-488-3999
http://www.nebraska-dining.org

Nevada Restaurant Association
1500 East Tropicana Ave., Suite 114-A
Las Vegas, NV 89119
702-878-2313
http://www.nvrestaurants.com

New Hampshire Lodging & Restaurant Association
16 Centre St.
Concord, NH 03301
603-228-9585
http://www.nhlra.com

New Jersey Restaurant Association
126 W. State St.
Trenton, NJ 08608
800-848-6368
http://njra.org

So, You're Thinking About Owning, Operating or Investing in a Restaurant...

New Mexico Restaurant Association
9201 Montgomery NE, Suite 602
Albuquerque, NM 87111
505-343-9848
https://www.nmrestaurants.org

NYS Restaurant Association
409 New Karner Rd., Suite. 202
Albany, NY 12205
800-452-5212
http://www.nysra.org

North Carolina Restaurant & Lodging Association
222 North Person Street, Suite 210
Raleigh, NC 27601
919-844-0098
http://www.ncrla.org

North Dakota Hospitality Association
1025 N 3rd St., Suite 3
Bismarck, ND 58501
701-223-3313
http://www.ndhospitality.com/homepage.htm

Ohio Restaurant Association
1525 Bethel Rd. Suite 301
Columbus, OH 43220-2054
614-442-3535
http://www.ohiorestaurant.org/aws/ORA/pt/sp/home_page

Oklahoma Restaurant Association
3800 N. Portland Ave., Suite 101
Oklahoma City, OK 73112
405-942-8181
http://www.okrestaurants.com

Oregon Restaurant & Lodging Association
8565 SW Salish Lane, Suite 120
Wilsonville, OR 97070-9633
503-682-4422
http://www.oregonrla.org

Pennsylvania Restaurant & Lodging Association
100 State St.
Harrisburg, PA 17101
717-232-4433
http://www.prla.org

Rhode Island Hospitality Association
94 Sabra St.
Cranston, RI 02910
401-223-1120
http://www.rihospitality.org/riha

South Carolina Restaurant and Lodging Association
1122 Lady St., Suite 1210
Columbia, SC 29201
803-765-9000
http://www.scrla.org

South Dakota Retailers Association
320 E. Capitol Ave.
Pierre, SD 57501
605-224-5050
https://www.sdra.org/about/hospitalitydivision

Tennessee Hospitality & Tourism Association
475 Craighead St.
Nashville, TN 37204
615-385-9970
http://www.tnhta.net

Texas Restaurant Association
1400 Lavaca St.
Austin TX 78701
800-395-2872
http://www.restaurantville.com

Utah Restaurant Association
5645 Waterbury Way Suite D203
Salt Lake City, UT 84121
801-274-7309
http://www.utahdineout.com

Vermont Chamber of Commerce
751 Granger Rd.
Barre, VT 05641
802-223-3443
http://www.rihospitality.org/backup/rest42.html

US Virgin Islands Hotel and Tourism Association
P.O. Box 2300
St. Thomas, VI 00803
340-774-6835
http://virgin-islands-hotels.com

So, You're Thinking About Owning, Operating or Investing in a Restaurant...

241

Virginia Hospitality and Travel Association
2101 Libbie Ave.
Richmond, VA 23230
804-288-3065
www.vhta.org

Washington Restaurant Association
510 Plum St. S.E., Suite 200
Olympia, WA 98501
360-956-7279
http://warestaurant.org

West Virginia Hospitality and Tourism
2306 1/2 Kanawha Blvd. East
Charleston, WV 25311
304-342-6511
http://www.wvhta.com

Wisconsin Restaurant Association
2801 Fish Hatchery Rd.
Madison, WI 53713
608-270-9950
http://www.wiscrest.org/

Wyoming Lodging & Restaurant Association
1825 Carey Ave.
Cheyenne, WY 82001
307-634-8816
http://www.wlra.org

POS Evaluation Sheets A p p e n d i x **D**

Point-of-Sale (POS) System Evaluation Worksheet

Use this POS Evaluation Worksheet to identify and document what features you must have in a new POS system. You can indicate on the worksheet whether an individual feature is MANDATORY (M) or OPTIONAL (O) for your operation. Check Yes/No to indicate whether the system you are evaluating offers the features. Copyright © 2015 by RestaurantOwner.com

Brand: **Dealer:**

Salesperson: **Phone:**

GENERAL / SECURITY	M	O	Yes	No	COMMENTS
Windows operating system?					
Operating system version?					
Is the vendor a Microsoft Certified Solution Provider?					
Date of last upgrade to software?					
Cost of upgrades?					
Off the shelf, non-propriety hardware?					
System requirements -					
Server (processor/memory/storage)					
Workstations (processor/memory/storage)					
Graphical user interface?					
Customizable screens & screen flow?					
Built in data redundancy?					
Fingerprint ID to clock in?					
Fingerprint ID for manager/server log in functions?					
Integrated with all other software (i.e. deliver, frequent diner, etc.)					

Point-of-Sale (POS) System Evaluation Worksheet

Use this POS Evaluation Worksheet to identify and document what features you must have in a new POS system. You can indicate on the worksheet whether an individual feature is MANDATORY (M) or OPTIONAL (O) for your operation. Check Yes/No to indicate whether the system you are evaluating offers the features. Copyright © 2015 by RestaurantOwner.com

Brand: **Dealer:**

Salesperson: **Phone:**

ORDERING	M	O	Yes	No	COMMENTS
Can tables be access by graphical table layout, station or table #?					
Can orders be easily split after the fact?					
Can a menu item be split between 2 or more customers?					
Speed windows for most popular items by day or time?					
Is menu items/check voids issued by management only?					
Can special instructions be easily sent to prep stations "on the fly"?					
"One touch" drinks reorder function?					
Flexible hold & fire by time, time of day or server controlled?					
Can voids & over-rings be tracked & reported by employee?					
Can menu items be transferred to another guest check?					
Can checks be easily transferred among servers & bartenders?					
Product count down/out of stock messaging?					
Can customer comment/survey forms be printed on receipt?					
UPC scanning for retail items?					
Flexible & detailed server reporting?					
Can server reports be easily customized?					

Point-of-Sale (POS) System Evaluation Worksheet

Use this POS Evaluation Worksheet to identify and document what features you must have in a new POS system. You can indicate on the worksheet whether an individual feature is MANDATORY (M) or OPTIONAL (O) for your operation. Check Yes/No to indicate whether the system you are evaluating offers the features. Copyright © 2015 by RestaurantOwner.com

Brand: **Dealer:**

Salesperson: **Phone:**

FULFILLMENT/ORDER DISPLAY	M	O	Yes	No	COMMENTS
Flexible order routing to kitchen station/bar?					
Kitchen chit printing options by station?					
Menu item routing by kitchen video monitors?					
Flag orders for expedited preparation?					
Orders recall verification?					
Print/display drink recipe?					

SETTLEMENT	M	O	Yes	No	COMMENTS
Unlimited number and type of discount & comp categories?					
Are comps issued by managers only?					
Can guest checks be customized to include "coupons" or other messages					
Can "smart coupon" be issued based on items ordered or not ordered?					
Can coupons be easily customized?					
Is credit card processing integrated with POS?					
Can credit cards be pre-authorized for bar tabs?					
Either server or cashier banking?					
Can guest checks be combined for single payment?					
Is there complete reporting for tips in compliance with IRS requirements?					
Are magnetic strip gift certificate cards supported?					
Can closed checks be re-opened for adjustments?					

Point-of-Sale (POS) System Evaluation Worksheet

Use this POS Evaluation Worksheet to identify and document what features you must have in a new POS system. You can indicate on the worksheet whether an individual feature is MANDATORY (M) or OPTIONAL (O) for your operation. Check Yes/No to indicate whether the system you are evaluating offers the features. Copyright © 2015 by RestaurantOwner.com

Brand: **Dealer:**

Salesperson: **Phone:**

MENU MANAGEMENT	M	O	Yes	No	COMMENTS
Can multiple menus be maintained?					
Unlimited number of menu items & menu modifiers?					
Menu changes can be made easily?					
Can discounts be assigned to specific menu items?					
Can menu items be bundled to create new menu items?					
INVENTORY/RECIPE MANAGEMENT	**M**	**O**	**Yes**	**No**	**COMMENTS**
Fully integrated?					
Unlimited inventory items?					
Analyze actual/ideal usage of key items?					
Recipe costing?					
Create and maintain batch and sub recipes?					
Easy conversion of purchase units to recipe units					
Calculate ideal food cost based on sales mix, recipe, and ingredient costs?					
Print inventory count sheets by storage room/shelf order?					
Enter physical inventory item counts?					
Update ingredient and menu costs automatically when purchases are entered					

Point-of-Sale (POS) System Evaluation Worksheet

Use this POS Evaluation Worksheet to identify and document what features you must have in a new POS system. You can indicate on the worksheet whether an individual feature is MANDATORY (M) or OPTIONAL (O) for your operation. Check Yes/No to indicate whether the system you are evaluating offers the features.
Copyright © 2015 by RestaurantOwner.com

Brand: **Dealer:**

Salesperson: **Phone:**

SALES HISTORY/REPORTING	M	O	Yes	No	COMMENTS
How long can transaction detail be maintained?					
Can all reports be sent to printer or viewed on screen?					
Is there a customer report writer?					
Can certain reports be viewed graphically?					
TABLE MANAGEMENT	**M**	**O**	**Yes**	**No**	**COMMENTS**
Customizable graphic table floor plan?					
Supports multiple table floor plans?					
View status of all tables in graphic display					
Easily move table and change stations?					
Create timers & alarms to remind employees of certain conditions?					
Create priority levels on alarms?					
Recommend table based upon guest preferences?					
CUSTOMER MANAGEMENT	**M**	**O**	**Yes**	**No**	**COMMENTS**
Support unlimited number of customers?					
Create multiple customer reward/frequency programs?					
Can customer coupons be printed on POS based on points/purchase history?					
Capture customer purchasing habits in sales volume, frequency of visits, days of week, menu items?					
Capture customer interests, preferences & special dates?					
Server access to customer interests & preferences?					
Generate mailing labels from the customer database based on specific criteria?					

So, You're Thinking About Owning, Operating or Investing in a Restaurant...

Point-of-Sale (POS) System Evaluation Worksheet

Use this POS Evaluation Worksheet to identify and document what features you must have in a new POS system. You can indicate on the worksheet whether an individual feature is MANDATORY (M) or OPTIONAL (O) for your operation. Check Yes/No to indicate whether the system you are evaluating offers the features. Copyright © 2015 by RestaurantOwner.com

Brand: **Dealer:**

Salesperson: **Phone:**

TIMEKEEPING/SCHEDULING	M	O	Yes	No	COMMENTS
Can function as timekeeping system?					
Create schedules based on employee availability?					
Create labor budgets based on hours & pay rates?					
Clock in/out control based on employee schedule?					
Print labor schedules by employee, department, and restaurant?					
Export employee information/hours electronically?					
DELIVERY/TAKE-OUT	**M**	**O**	**Yes**	**No**	**COMMENTS**
Can functions be added to any station?					
Can be used for delivery & take-out orders?					
Maximum size of customer database?					
Both caller ID and telephone # driven?					
Can delivery zones be assigned to drivers?					
Can delivery instructions be printed for each order?					
View customer preferences & delivery instructions on screen?					
Customizable prep tickets and guest checks?					
Targeted mailings based on customer purchase history?					
Driver settlement per run or shift?					
Print "food contains" labels?					
OTHER FEATURES/FUNCTIONS	**M**	**O**	**Yes**	**No**	**COMMENTS**
Can cash paid outs/ins be recorded by type?					
Can a receipt be printed for cash paid outs/ins?					
Integrated house accounts with AR functions?					
Handheld interface?					

About *Restaurant Startup & Growth* and RestaurantOwner.com

In the restaurant business, it is one thing to provide good food and service, and quite another to do so profitably and with a minimum of risk. Via print and electronic publishing, video, webinars, templates and online utilities, *Restaurant Startup & Growth* and RestaurantOwner.com are a combined educational resource for owners and operators in the independent commercial foodservice sector.

Restaurant Startup & Growth's primary demographic is independent and emerging chain restaurant owners and managers. Its circulation model introduces the magazine to these operators as they are in the process of launching or expanding their concepts. The magazine was launched in February 2004 as the print complement to RestaurantOwner.com, its official website. Its editorial mission is to fulfill the need for ongoing in-depth education on management best practices for restaurant entrepreneurs.

Restaurant Startup & Growth and RestaurantOwner.com books include the National Restaurant Association's Uniform System of Accounts, 8th edition, the managerial accounting benchmark guide for the U.S. restaurant industry.

For more information, visit RestaurantOwner.com

What Our Members and Readers Have Said About RestaurantOwner.com and *Restaurant Startup & Growth*...

"I am a small business owner. I must say this is the best tool I've ever subscribed to. I was suspicious at first, I did not expect much but this is awesome. Thank you so much."

~ Gesine Franchetti – The Topaz – Santa Rosa, CA

"Your website and magazine have been extremely helpful to our growing business. We are just about finished with the construction of our new location. I have learned so much from your articles, the online seminars, the discussion forum and the spreadsheets are an invaluable asset. I continue to learn something new every day."

~ Belinda Self – Ginza Japanese Restaurants, Inc. – Winston Salem, NC

So, You're Thinking About Owning, Operating or Investing in a Restaurant...

249

"You are giving me a great education. I can't soak it up fast enough. The articles, templates and especially the online training are heading me in the right direction to having a great business."

~ Martin Hardy – City Bagel Café – Siloam Springs, Arkansas

"I've found everything on the site to be a big help. From the financial side to the menu, the amount of information has been a bargain for the price of a subscription!"

~ Eddie Scoggins – Tavern At The Village Green – Cleveland, TN

"I am now in my second year of being a member. My only regret being that I did not find you in my prior 8 years as I would have saved a lot of money and grey hairs from your tips and formats. Thank you for indirectly saving my restaurant & for the growth I now see."

~ Marc Cedron – Printer's Alley Bar & Grill – Memphis, TN

"Your web-site and magazine have helped our independent restaurant grow from 1 restaurant with revenue of $350,000 to 3 restaurants bringing in $3.5 million in only 4 years."

~ Donald Spahr – Spahr's Seafood – Thibodaux, LA

"So far, we've revised our accounting system and introduced the prime cost concept. My prime costs are dropping because of focusing on both inventory and labor together. This will improve my contribution margin by $120,000!"

~ Brian Fitzgerald – Paddy's Brewpub & Rosie's Restaurant – Kentville, Nova Scotia

"Thank you for this site. Little guys like me need all the help we can get and it is wonderful to be able to get answers to questions here."

~ Margaret Williamson – Hizzoner's Uptown Deli – Bellingham, WA

"I have sung the praises of your site to many of my friends, associates, and suppliers. There is a wealth of information and material available from your site that is of tremendous benefit to all independent restaurateurs. We have used virtually everything you offer in some form or another, from the restaurant by the numbers material to all of the articles on service, management, training, etc. The templates for training manuals and various forms have saved us a lot of time which would have been spent compiling and organizing this vital information."

~ Robert Hodgson – Lefty's Restaurant – Parksville, B.C.

Index

So, You're Thinking About Owning, Operating or Investing in a Restaurant...

251

So, You're Thinking About Owning, Operating or Investing in a Restaurant...

253

N

national restaurant associations 233

P

parking 22, 58, 96, 149, 173, 177, 203, 212, 214, 215, 218, 225, 227

partnership 54, 81, 109, 110, 113, 114, 115, 156, 157, 183, 188, 207, 209, 213

payroll 89, 96, 98, 175, 196, 197, 198, 199, 201, 202, 223, 224, 228, 233

POS (point-of-sale) 39, 86, 88, 89, 161, 162, 163, 164, 165, 220, 222, 229, 243, 248

pre-made 35, 36, 37

prep cook 63, 66, 67

prime cost 89, 170, 195, 197, 198, 199, 202, 208, 250

profitable 11, 13, 14, 15, 20, 28, 29, 34, 39, 42, 47, 50, 94, 96, 102, 103, 107, 191, 197, 198, 199, 210

Profit and Loss Statement (P&L) 89, 100, 103, 140, 147, 176, 208, 226

purchasing 8, 12, 15, 16, 28, 39, 64, 77, 89, 113, 116, 117, 118, 119, 120, 124, 179, 180, 186, 187, 190, 205

R

recipe 17, 19, 20, 27, 34, 35, 37, 49, 63, 64, 65, 67, 69, 107, 139, 176, 208, 209, 211, 216, 220

rent 56, 100, 103, 139, 146, 149, 177

RestaurantOwner.com 9, 12, 56, 62, 63, 69, 105, 106, 161, 193, 211, 215, 219, 220, 221, 222, 225, 227, 229

Restaurant Startup & Growth 9, 10, 11, 249

S

sales per square foot 194, 201

sales to investment 56, 193, 194, 215

scratch 12, 14, 15, 35, 36, 42, 47, 136, 209

seating 25, 26, 68, 82, 135, 136, 203, 214, 215, 226

SEC regulations 107

server 14, 36, 42, 49, 63, 65, 66, 67, 68, 69, 88, 140, 153, 162, 163, 164, 165, 166, 183, 195, 207, 209, 222, 230

signage 25, 58, 71, 73, 87, 138, 149, 215, 216, 220, 229

smallwares 209, 219, 222, 223, 226, 227, 228

sole proprietorship 81, 113, 114, 115, 117, 119, 156, 209

staff 11, 14, 15, 20, 21, 23, 24, 25, 27, 33, 35, 36, 39, 45, 55, 62, 64, 66, 87, 94, 96, 97, 127, 128, 131, 132, 138, 139, 140, 142, 150, 153, 161, 175, 176, 177, 197, 198, 206, 207, 214, 219, 222, 226, 231, 235

startup 175, 176, 188, 189, 193, 194, 201, 209, 211, 212, 234

So, You're Thinking About Owning, Operating or Investing in a Restaurant...

255

CPSIA information can be obtained
at www.ICGtesting.com
Printed in the USA
LVOW09s2255080317

526617LV00005B/68/P

9 780692 549551